The Literature Reader

Key Thinkers on Key Topics

EMC Publications

The Literature Reader

Edited by Lucy Webster

Editorial assistance: Andrew McCallum

Cover design: © Rebecca Scambler, 2019

Published by English and Media Centre, 18 Compton Terrace, London, N1 2UN

© English and Media Centre, 2019

978-1-906101657

Acknowledgements

Thanks to the following publishers for permissions to reproduce the following copyrighted material:

Chapter 1 'What is English Literature' is adapted from Robert Eaglestone's book *Literature: Why it Matters* published by Polity Press, 2019

Lavinia Greenlaw and Faber & Faber Ltd for 'Mephisto' from *Minsk*.

'Lene Gammelgaard' from *No Map Could Show Them* by Helen Mort. Published by Chatto & Windus, 2016. Copyright © Helen Mort. Reproduced by permission of the author c/o Rogers, Coleridge & White Ltd., 20 Powis Mews, London W111JN

With thanks also to Emma Barker for comments on the text and to Andrew for his advice on editing.

A note on capitalisation

With the exception of the chapters on Modernism and Romanticism, we have attempted throughout the book to follow the convention of capitalising nouns denoting movements (such as Naturalism) and using lower case first letters for the adjectives derived from these nouns. We recognise there are alternative conventions and that we've probably not managed to be entirely consistent.

Contents

FOREWORD

If you earn your living teaching English Literature or writing literary criticism, you sometimes get asked an unsettling question: 'Do you still read for pleasure?' As if being a critic meant forgetting what it was to enjoy a book. As if there were a chasm between that wonderful experience of being completely taken over by what you read, so that you hardly notice what is going on around you, and the hard-headed business of studying a literary work.

I would answer that there is no such chasm – or that there shouldn't be. The great novelist Vladimir Nabokov declared, 'the beauty of a book is more enjoyable if one understands its machinery, if one can take it apart'. (He said it in a lecture on Jane Austen's *Mansfield Park*, whose concealed ingenuity he had recently discovered with surprise and delight.) All of the contributors to this collection try to do justice to that claim. Leading academic specialists, they know that teachers have lessons to give and students have essays to write and they try to serve those purposes. But they have also written their essays to show how enjoyable it is to re-read a good poem or play or novel. For this is one definition of good literature: books that become better when you re-read them. This is, therefore, the point of good criticism: to take the reader back to what he or she has already read in order to see it afresh, relish it more.

Robert Eaglestone's opening chapter notes that, before you get to any critical approach to literature, 'you study literature by reading a lot'. Good writers have also been good readers, and we should follow in their tracks. Books are made of other books. Kazuo Ishiguro's *Never Let Me Go* re-imagines Mary Shelley's *Frankenstein*; *Frankenstein* begins with a memory of Adam's creation in Milton's *Paradise Lost*; Adam in *Paradise Lost* sees his reflection in water like Narcissus in Ovid's *Metamorphoses*. So, the echoes spread backwards – then forwards again. The essays in this book group literary works first by period, hearing them question and answer each other – and then by genre, where they often influence each other across time. Our critics listen for those echoes.

For most of all, the various and variously exciting essays in this collection all show that we should read with the ear as well as the eye – that literary works are different from other kinds of books because their language is not a means to an end, but a pleasure in itself. It is a pleasure that the essays in this book hope to sharpen.

John Mullan, Lord Northcliffe Chair of Modern English Literature,
University College London

LITERATURE – A CONVERSATION ACROSS TIME

In the opening chapter 'What is English?' Robert Eaglestone wrestles with what exactly is this subject we are all doing. What does it mean to do English Literature? He suggests that to do English is to be part of a long and ongoing conversation between people who read, think, talk and write about literature. This collection of essays invites you to join this conversation – not to stand on the edge of the group but to take part: to listen and reflect on what you read, of course, but also to engage actively with the ideas and interpretations in writing and in discussion.

Conversation is a word that crops up across the different essays – and not only in relation to the act of 'doing' English. As Michael Rosen explains, poetry is a conversation: texts speak to each other across time. Read Tim Turnbull's 'Ode on a Grayson Perry Urn' and behind it echoes Keats's 'Ode on a Grecian Urn'. Not only that but (and this is an idea to blow your mind), having read the Turnbull, you will never again read Keats's ode in quite the same way. Doing English we become time-travellers, the texts of the present re-writing the texts of the past.

The conversations between key texts and authors are woven throughout this book. So as well as being part of the conversation in Stephen Donovan's discussion of Modernism, Virginia Woolf also features in Andrew McCallum's exploration of experimental literature, Pamela Bickley's discussion of the twentieth-century novel and Judy Simon's reflections on the critical essay. Such reappearances, each of which shows the individual novel, play or poem in a different light, will both enrich your appreciation of English Literature and challenge your thinking.

So what conversations can you take part in? The first essays in the collection look at some of the broader aspects of doing English, beginning with Robert Eaglestone's questioning of what this means. Judy Simons looks at writing (and reading) essays – the form in which poems, plays and novels have been discussed for centuries. Peter Barry discusses – and problematises – the relationship between a text and its context, while Emma Smith's essay looks at Shakespeare in the light of context, arguing for a complex and sceptical approach.

Then there are conversations on the novel, poetry and drama. Jenny Stevens explores the novel's rise in the eighteenth and nineteenth centuries, while Pamela Bickley looks at the diverse ways in which it developed through the twentieth century and up to the present day. Critic and short story writer Chris Power looks at the development of the short story form from the nineteenth century to the present day. Poets from Anglo Saxon times to the twenty-first century join the conversation in Michael Rosen's celebration of English poetry and ways of reading it. The Romantic poets take centre stage in Malcolm Hebron's discussion of this revolutionary and influential movement. Sean McEvoy discusses the influence of

European theatre in reinvigorating and shaping British and Irish drama in the twentieth and twenty-first centuries.

Nicolas Tredell faces the *isms* head on, discussing the importance of key critical movements (Romanticism, Modernism, Leavisism, Structuralism and Poststructuralism) and how each changed the way we approach both reading and writing. The significance of Modernism is explored by Stephen Donovan who begins by outlining this seismic shift in art, sculpture and architecture, before moving on to look at modernist literature.

Two chapters broaden our horizons beyond (mainly) British literature: Leila Kamali explores postcolonial literature and questions what it means for older texts to be read from the perspective of Postcolonialism, while Nicolas Tredell provides a sweeping overview of American literature from the mid-nineteenth century onwards.

For a long time considered too disreputable, too popular and too exciting to merit study, genre fiction – Gothic, dystopian and crime – is now a central feature of university and A Level courses. Novelist Andrew Hurley explores the Gothic through the lens of his own novels *The Loney* and *Devil's Day*, while Nathan Waddell focuses his discussion of key dystopian texts through the concept of freedom. Christopher Pittard traces our fascination with crime in literature from the nineteenth-century 'Newgate Novels' onwards, revealing the ways in which even the most subversive postmodern novels are in conversation with the classic texts of the past.

While many of the essays explore the ways in which writers have sought to challenge, subvert and develop the form in which they write, Andrew McCallum revels in texts with experiment at their heart: from eighteenth century classics to computer-generated poetry.

On the whole the essays take a broadly chronological approach, some providing a broad sweep and others taking a slice through the topic, exploring it from a particular angle. Each essay provides you with a taste of the subject – a conversation starter to grab your interest, to give you a way into thinking, reading, writing and talking about it. All the writers provide a short list of further reading suggestions and questions or prompts to help you take further the ideas raised in relation to the texts you are studying and those you are reading for pleasure.

Who are our contributors? There are many academics and teachers, a poet, a short story writer and a novelist – all are experts in their field. Find out more about who they are and what else they have written in their biographies on pages 175.

There's no set order to the essays – dip into whichever conversation takes your fancy. And remember, you too are part of this conversation, not only as a listener and reader but as a thinker, talker and writer. Don't hold back – plunge in!

Lucy Webster, Editor

WHAT IS ENGLISH LITERATURE?

Robert Eaglestone

What is English Literature?

Anyone can read and think about a work of literature: that openness to everyone is part of what makes literature so significant and exciting. But studying English means you get even better at reading, thinking and analysing literature – more creative, more interesting, more responsive. First, you study literature by reading a lot: after all, the more you do any activity the better you get at it. Second, you will learn some really useful conceptual tools which will improve how you read and understand texts: even obvious ideas like 'plot' and 'character' are tools (but perhaps ones you are so familiar with that you hardly notice them anymore). But (and here's the first problem) none of these tools are as straightforward as they seem. They all come from somewhere and have wider implications. So if you find yourself interested in 'gender representation', say, or 'character type' or 'ethical questions', these come from different conceptual frameworks or theories. So, third, in studying literature, you will be learning about these different conceptual frameworks, because they provide the tools, often unknowingly, which shape what people have thought and argued about literature and the world. Perhaps the most obvious issue for a conceptual framework should be the concept of 'literature' itself, a definition of what is being studied. But (and here's the second problem), it's impossible to define what 'literature' actually is, and this has consequences for how we study it.

The impossibility of defining literature

People have been trying to define literature for (at least) two and a half thousand years. To define means (originally) to 'set limits' (the Latin word *fines* means limits). But literature always seems to slip these limits – to escape definition. Consider some of the ways we might try to set limits – to define – what literature is. If you define literature as fiction – something we understand to be made up, invented – then what about all the novels and plays based on history or on current political issues, that is on 'true' events? Or writing that's autobiographical? Interestingly, the root of the word fiction doesn't mean 'untrue': it comes from the Latin word *fingere*, meaning 'to shape, fashion, form' and every writer – from a politician composing a speech to the person writing the instructions for using a kettle – shapes and chooses their words. In any case, if literature tells us truths about the most important aspects of ourselves, about how we really are, or what, say, being in love is like, do these things become untrue if in a poem or novel? Of course not! So using ideas of truth and untruths as a way of limiting our subject doesn't really work.

Or take the idea that literature tells stories – it is a narrative form. On the one hand, there are countless texts we think of as literary that don't tell a story: these range from lyric poems written centuries ago to contemporary experimental novels (such as David Markson's *This is not a Novel* (2001), a text composed of a series of 'found' statements harvested from other writer's work). On the other, there are lots of things we don't think of as literature which do use narrative: an account of scientific research is a narrative.

What about writing? Can we limit our subject to the written word? Not necessarily: 'graphic novels' like the moving *Fun Home* (2006) by Alison Bechdel combine text and pictures and some computer games are often so like novels – *Red Dead Redemption II,* for example – they are called 'ludo-fiction'.

There's a further more philosophical problem. When you read, you never encounter 'literature' in the abstract: you encounter a particular text, a novel by Jacqueline Wilson or James Joyce, or a poem by Rupi Kaur or Carol Ann Duffy. It's easier to explain why a particular work of literature matters to you (you identify with the main character or their situation, maybe, or perhaps your mum read it to you when you were a kid); it's harder to explain what 'literature in general' is. You might even be tempted to say that literature (meaning, 'literature in general') doesn't exist.

You can play this game of 'exceptions' with any definition of 'literature', and you will find holes in every one. And yet the study of literature is an accepted subject to study, delimited, like all the other subjects in their boxes. The backstory of how it got there is really the story of different attempts to define and then study literature.

English: the backstory

Of course, people have been reading books and watching plays for hundreds of years but the word 'literature' used to mean, roughly, just 'knowing about letters and books' or 'what is written down in books', and included what we now call science, history, philosophy, news and so on. But English Literature as an academic subject is only around a hundred years old, recent compared to music or philosophy or physics. From Shakespeare's time to, roughly, the end of Queen Victoria's reign, what marked one out as an educated gentleman was the study of 'the classics', ancient Greek and Roman plays, poems, historical and philosophical texts. Notice it is gentleman – women generally weren't allowed to study them. In *A Vindication of the Rights of Woman* (1792), the early British feminist Mary Wollstonecraft (1759-1797) argued that the right to study the classics was vital for women's equality. This was a long way from the English we have today: oddly, the source of our English didn't begin in England, or even in the UK.

At the beginning of the nineteenth century, the British ruled India through the East India Company, a company which had a complex contract or 'charter' concerning trade and the exploitation of territory. (A fictionalised, but equally rapacious, version of the East India Company is also the villain in the *Pirates of the Caribbean* films.) In 1813, Parliament changed their charter, making it harder for the Company to support the work of Christian missionaries and preachers, perhaps because it was worried that attempts at religious conversion were unsettling the people. In response the East India Company devised another way of making sure that the native population would be eager to follow an 'English way of life', closely enough, at least, to be good Company servants. Studying English literature was seen as a way of shaping or 'civilising' the native population which aimed, in the words of the British politician and administrator Thomas Babington Macaulay (1800-59) to create a 'class of persons, Indian in blood and colour, but English in taste, in opinions, in morals, and in intellect'. So the idea of a school subject called English which involved reading and writing about novels, plays and poems written in English, was formed in India. This is one reason why the subject is called 'English': the idea that the study of English literature was a 'civilising force' remained very strong and was brought back to Britain.

However, this is not the only source of the subject. The most exciting new subject in the nineteenth century was philology (etymologically, it means 'love of words'): the study of language, and the historical origin and evolution of languages. More, in tracing the 'family tree' of languages, you studied the origins of nations (English told you about the English) and of our whole species. Some of today's study of English language stems from philology, and the idea that literature is an expression of 'national character' or identity, too, comes from this (the clue is in the name of the discipline: English).

At the same time, schools and universities also taught rhetoric, the art of speaking and writing well. Being taught how to write an essay or deliver a speech today is a version of this subject: how to speak and write clearly and persuasively. Literature clearly played a role in this, not least as a source of good (and bad!) examples.

And finally, the nineteenth century saw a huge growth in the amount of literature published: especially novels, but also magazines and journals about literature. Just as people today watch discussions of films and games on YouTube, so people read not only stories but also discussions of – and arguments about – literature. Just like today, these writers were interested in what literature told us about ourselves, about how to live, and in thinking about which stories were more valuable and more important. Because this seemed less rigorous than either philology or rhetoric, it was often dismissed as 'pretty writing' (*belles lettres*) rather than a demanding study.

English, then, grew from these four ideas: from the colonisation of India, that studying English writing was a 'civilising force'; from philology, that the study of language told you about identity; from rhetoric, that you could learn to write and speak effectively; and from *belles-lettres* that literature was about 'how to live', and that literature could be judged. Not all these ideas agreed with each other and each one clearly had a different sense of what 'literature' was.

By the end of the nineteenth century, the subject of English as we know it still didn't exist but there was a huge public interest in literature in English. There were very many 'literary societies' (a bit like today's book groups) and courses taught in the University Extension Movement (a bit like 'adult education' today). Many universities set up 'extra-mural' (literally, 'outside the walls') courses to attract working and middle-class people keen to improve themselves. These courses began to pioneer new ways of teaching and new ideas about learning. After World War One, many of these ideas were formalised in the government-commissioned *Newbolt Report* of 1921 and English began to grow as a discipline in schools and universities.

As a more formal subject, English still maintained diversity. However, from the 1930s to the 1960s, one version became very strong: that the key issue in studying literature was understanding its value. Led and inspired by controversial University of Cambridge academics F.R. and Q.D. Leavis, the study of literature became literary criticism. For them, the definition of literature became strict: it was Literature with a capital L. Only those novels, poems and plays that were the most valuable, the greatest, as decided by (capital L) Literary (capital C) Critics counted as Literature.

This Leavisite way of studying literature lost its influence in the 1970s and 1980s. In its place came a whole range of new ideas from politics, philosophy, sociology, Feminism, history and many other subjects. These ideas were called 'literary theory' (though they should perhaps be called 'literary *theories*'). These proved very controversial: people (rather melodramatically) talked about 'theory wars' for example. Each brought a different view of what literature was: for some, who took their critical tools from politics, literature was a form of political propaganda or resistance (or sometimes both); for others, literature was a less rigorous but more interesting version of philosophy; for still others, literature was like an archive which gave us a way to understand the past.

In the last twenty years or so, this last approach, seeing literature in its historical context, has come to be seen as the most important. However, it may be that this version is now being challenged. A sense of the importance of literature for our lives, for how we understand ourselves and not simply the past, is re-emerging.

Government policy in schools since 2010 has also revived the idea that English is a kind of nationalist project, and that by studying English texts we learn to be a certain sort of 'English'.

Neither 'ology' nor 'ography' nor 'ics'

We're still faced, of course, with the problem of how to define what our subject is. Other academic subjects announce their discipline in their name: geography is literally the 'writing of' ('graphy') the 'earth' ('geo'), physics is that which 'pertains to' ('-ics') nature ('phusis'). If literature eludes definition, English Literature could never be 'literography' or 'litics'. I want to use a different, more sympathetic and literary approach to describing both literature itself and the subject we are engaged in. To do this I'm going to propose a metaphor: literature is a living conversation.

As conversation, literature is a communication. We often think of communication as simply the transfer of data from one point to another, but much more is implied in it. Communication needs at least two people, a language and a medium (books, signs, lights, vibrations of sound in air, even looks). Just as even a tiny piece of data can tell us a great deal about the people, society and the world it comes from, so even the smallest piece of literature can rely on and somehow manifest a whole world.

Just as a conversation you hold with your friends can be about anything, so too literature can be about anything. It can shock or provoke or amaze or bore or amuse or reform or corrupt you. Literature can be about the things that matter: beginning and birth, lies and truth, good and bad, ending and death. But it's also things that don't matter or don't even exist: mythical people, unicorns, mermaids.

Indeed, one of literature's mysteries is that it makes things matter. Prince Hamlet looks in wonder at the actor who is crying over the death of the mythical Queen Hecuba and the ruin of the city of Troy: 'What is Hecuba to him, or he to Hecuba, that he should weep for her?' Similarly, a discussion of Dobby the House Elf makes a generation of readers tear up. Thinking of literature as a conversation helps us explore this. In a conversation we 'bring a subject up' or 'bring to light issues' that concern us or mean something to us, and in doing this we show our own selves. Sometimes, in conversation with others (or even, silently, with ourselves) we discover what we didn't know before, or reframe what we already somehow knew, in order to talk about it. Literature does the same: like conversation, it reveals, brings things up, puts events, experiences and thoughts into language, so giving them meaning.

But this process of revealing isn't shapeless. We talk about 'making conversation' because we make, we shape what we say. (Think back to that definition of 'fiction' – 'to shape, fashion, form'.) We do this not just in the content of words we choose but also, for example, in the tone we take: the form. We can say 'hello' angrily, kindly, lovingly, sarcastically and so on. In conversation, how we say something is as important as what we say. This is even more powerfully true for literature: the form is as important – or even more important – than the content. Form has meaning: learning about literature is learning about form. Simple examples: an epic, whether it's *Paradise Lost* or *Game of Thrones* or the superhero films that culminate in *Avengers: Endgame*, shows its importance by being very (very) long: in contrast, a sonnet shows its sophistication, its control and style in its brevity. The leading British critic Terry Eagleton makes these two points – about how literature makes meaning and the nature of form – when he writes luminously that poetry is 'concerned not just with the meaning of experience, but with the experience of meaning'.

Talking with someone is a creative act: conversation is a kind of improvisation between people, after all. So using the metaphor of literature as a living conversation means that creativity exists not just in the work of literature, or in the head of a famous author, but also in us, the reader. The creativity of literature is shared precisely because literature is an activity. This means that literature isn't just about the books on the shelf: it's about you thinking, responding, writing about, talking with the books too: and that dialogue can involve many speakers, arguing, discussing, thinking, a shared conversation. This creativity is not confined to lessons or libraries: everyone uses and responds to 'literary techniques' – figures of speech, metaphors, suspense, stories – all the time in our everyday life. As the philosopher Aristotle (4th century BCE) suggests, imitation comes naturally to us – and so just as we are experts in conversation, we are experts in creating, responding to, listening to and judging literature. Whatever people say, 'doing literature' shouldn't be cut off from everyday life or exist on a pedestal.

Just like a conversation, your creative response to literature draws on your mind, heart, feelings, your past and your hopes for the future. But, of course, you change over time, and as you change so the literature which speaks to you changes. The preface to the wonderful novel *The Golden Notebook* by the Nobel laureate Doris Lessing is one of the best things written about literature and reading: in it she says 'Remember that the book which bores you when you are twenty or thirty will open doors for you when you are forty or fifty – and vice-versa. Don't read a book out of its right time for you'. As a living conversation, our relationship to a book changes: reading is a process. We respond to a book and a book also responds to us: we become attuned, just as an instrument shapes a piece of music and a piece of music shapes the instrument. Reading and learning about literature is a sort of 'becoming attuned'. This means, of course, that knowing about literature is something different from just knowing facts about say, the dates of an author, what happens in chapter three or reading the Wikipedia summary. Knowing about a work of literature is about experiencing it as a process, not – although it can sometimes feel like this – as a collection of answers for a quiz or exam: literature is the walk not the map. Knowing the chemical makeup of water is not the same as knowing what it's like to get soaked in a sudden summer storm.

Studying literature – joining the conversation

If literature is like a conversation, it means that reading it is an active process, something you do. It can seem passive – you often read sitting or lying down, after all – but it doesn't just happen. Reading is a dynamic act of interpretation. And knowledge is made through the experience of reading and can't simply be 'poured into you', as if it were water and you were a bucket. This means that 'reading' and 'interpreting' are almost the same. When you interpret, it means that you find some things important and not others or that you focus on some ideas and questions and so disregard others. Your interpretation is shaped by a number of presuppositions. These are the 'taken for granted' ideas, tendencies and preferences you carry with you (and which you might not even realise you have). Like glasses that you can't take off, you always read 'through' these conceptual frameworks. People from different backgrounds, sexes, sexualities, religions, classes, ages and so on will be struck by different things in any text. Being aware of how these aspects of your identity and personal context shape your interpretation of a text is an important part of doing English.

Your interpretation will also be affected by the context in which you read and the expectations you have of the text. For example, if you read a novel about women in the Victorian period for a history project, you'll think about it in one way (perhaps, to find out facts about how women were treated or represented); if you read the same novel for fun, you'll read it in another way (perhaps, to find out what happens next).

As the idea of literature as conversation implies, everything you have read and experienced previously will also affect how you interpret the novel, poem, play, critical essay you are reading now. All this means that, in the study of literature, no interpretation is neutral or objective but has to be argued for and explained. And it means that how we read is as important as what we read because our conceptual frameworks and the tools we take from them, to a great degree, shape our reading.

Again, if English the subject is a conversation, it is a continually developing subject. Ideas about literature change and shift with each generation. What people thought about, say, *Macbeth*, thirty years ago is not what they think now. As I suggested, in the last forty years, the subject has been transformed by ideas about, for example, Feminism and gender, sexuality, the mind and the body, politics, race, globalisation, the environment and the contemporary world, about the use of digital technology and about other art forms, as well as ideas drawn from all sorts of other disciplines. These new ways of thinking about literature have stimulated new ways of studying literature and even helped rediscover books, trends and authors that were previously passed over or ignored. These newer ideas are like new phrases in the conversation. You'll want to know what people have said, why, what they want to do next, and you'll also want to join in, because, for sure, your views will vary and contrast with theirs. Learning the subject is really coming to join that conversation, which, like ripples in a pool, begins with reading a book and talking about it with friends or family and then spreads wider and wider until, just for a moment, it seems to touch everything.

Questions to take your thinking further

- How would you define literature? Where are the holes, the exceptions, in your definition?
- What do you think of the suggestion that literature is like a conversation? How might this idea shape your own engagement with the subject?
- In what ways do you think studying literature is active and creative?
- Is your reading always constrained by your presuppositions? How can you read in a way which acknowledges these?
- How might you join this ongoing conversation of 'doing English'?

Reading list

Barry, P. 2017. *Beginning Theory: An Introduction to Literary and Cultural Theory.* Manchester: Manchester University Press.

Eaglestone, R. 2017. *Doing English: A Guide for Literature Students.* London: Routledge.

Eaglestone, R. 2019. *Literature: Why it Matters.* Cambridge: Polity.

Eagleton, T. 2013. *How to Read Literature.* New Haven: Yale University Press.

North, J. 2017. *Literary Criticism: A Concise Political History.* Cambridge Mass.: Harvard University Press.

THE CRITICAL ESSAY

Judy Simons

Introduction

This chapter briefly surveys some key moments in the history of essay writing and considers how modern approaches to texts have helped to shape and establish a new tradition of literary criticism. How far is the essay a reflection of its time and how viable are recent, cutting-edge interpretations of classic texts?

The essay is a formidable weapon in the critical armoury, whether it takes the form of an academic journal article, a book review, or a chapter in an edited collection such as this one. It is also a fundamental part of the student toolkit, a mandatory task set for examinations and coursework. So the chapter also explores what a critical essay means for today's students and what are its essential components. It closes with a glance at the evolution of the essay in the digital age.

What is a critical essay?

An essay is a compact and self-contained thesis on a specific topic. That definition, however, does not even come close to capturing the vitality of the form nor the challenges that confront an essayist. Whether you are a student or professional critic, the challenge remains the same: how can your analysis help to elucidate or re-vision a work of literature? Not only that but how can it do so in 1500, 2000 or 5000 words? For a central feature of the essay is that it is short. It requires discipline to marshal relevant points into a compelling argument and to do it within a strict word limit that allows little space for digression. At the same time, the essay offers real opportunities to the enquiring mind: the opportunity to reflect on what literature means, to engage in active discussion with other similarly curious readers, to understand and sift received critical opinion, and to probe in depth a literary text to formulate a personal view.

But why should anyone attempt a defence of Macbeth's motivation or try to dissect Virginia Woolf's technique in *Mrs Dalloway*? If, as the counter argument goes, a novel, play or poem is a form of entertainment, then why cannot it be enjoyed on its own terms? The excitement that good literature engenders comes from an instinctive response to the power of language. Reading constitutes an intellectual, spiritual or emotional adventure, which can take many different forms. At its most straightforward, this can be discovering who committed the murder in an Agatha Christie novel or re-living the anguish of the Great War alongside Wilfred Owen's unsung heroes. Readers are moved to tears, horror-struck or determine on life-changes as a result of books. A critical essay, which requires meticulous scrutiny of an author's ideas and technique, intervenes in this process and destroys the pleasure and spontaneity of the text. Or so the opposition might claim.

For it is obvious to any theatre-goer that Macbeth is a monster, a murderer who becomes trapped in a spiral of wickedness once he has been tempted by a vision of power. The dramatic impact of the play partly rests on its insights into the psychology of evil, which create an intense, nightmare vision of a distorted society where inhumanity reigns supreme. Similarly, the opening passage of *Mrs Dalloway* plunges the reader directly into the interior consciousness of the central character. Its mellifluous prose instantly captures Clarissa's world-view, pinpointing her social position, her mood and the London milieu she inhabits. The long, snaking sentences propel us through different time frames to mimic the elusive thought processes that lurk beneath the veneer of an apparently confident individual.

If this sort of textual immediacy is the hallmark of good literature, and most readers would agree that it is, then why should we bother to look further? Can a critical essay really improve on that primary experience?

The critical essay is far more than just an adjunct to the main meal. It is a respected literary genre in its own right with discrete internal conventions and an impressive heritage. It is no accident that some of the best essayists are also novelists, poets and dramatists. Furthermore, the composition of a critical essay is an active learning process, which enables both writers and readers to become more alert and self-aware in their literary practice. For writing, as much as reading, is an intellectual journey. The more a book or poem absorbs the reader, the more that reader engages with the imaginative world it fashions. The critical essay provides one of the best ways of appreciating and conveying that experience. It has also proved to be one of the most influential.

Looking to the past

In his essay on *King Lear*, the eighteenth-century critic Samuel Johnson wrote that, 'I was many years ago so shocked by Cordelia's death that I know not whether I ever endured to read the last scenes of the play until I undertook to revise them as an editor'. This one sentence sums up the conflicting impulses that beset many literary critics – the tension between a powerful emotional reaction and the intensive focus required for serious scholarly inquiry. Johnson's series of essays, collected in his *Preface to Shakespeare* (1765), remain a model of how a relatively brief treatise can penetrate to the heart of a subject. Its outstanding features are the authority with which Johnson writes, his command of his subject and his break with the critical assumptions of his time. Basically then, conviction, knowledge and originality: the three foundation stones of great essay writing.

Johnson departed from the widely held view that the Greek and Roman literary classics were the blueprint against which all subsequent works should be measured (and found deficient). Instead he judged Shakespeare's plays in terms of their 'credibility', their ability to capture a common humanity that could transcend historical barriers. For Johnson, Shakespeare is a genius because of his universality, for 'Nothing can please many, and please long, but just representations of a general nature'. This approach to literary evaluation was to dominate critical thinking for the next two centuries.

But it is the nineteenth-century poet and critic Matthew Arnold who is often considered to be the father of the modern critical essay as a professional activity. Arnold saw criticism as an art form, and the critic as an artist, sensitive, expert in analysis and therefore qualified to make judgements about literary value. Criticism for Arnold was 'a disinterested endeavour to learn and propagate the best that is thought and known in the world, and by in its turn making this known to create a current of fresh and true ideas'. In other words, by discussing works of literature, the essay keeps alive intelligent debate.

Arnold's essays determined future approaches to the study of English in universities and his is a view still cherished by some scholars today. Importantly, he shifts attention from the emotional appeal of literature to its moral dimension. No longer is reading poetry purely a private enjoyment, justified by the lyric beauty of its language or the power of imagery to evoke feeling. Literature has a serious educative purpose, and the critic a collective, social responsibility. Arnold's essay established the focus on ethics, on message and on judgement as central components of a critic's duty.

In his defining essay, 'Tradition and the Individual Talent' (1919), T.S. Eliot argued that every author is part of a literary continuum, and that 'dead poets, his ancestors, assert their immortality' through their impact on a writer's consciousness. Eliot used the term 'impersonality' to suggest the removal of a writer's subjective autonomy and to acknowledge his or her debt to the past. This revolutionary way of looking at creativity became ingrained in modernist and postmodern literature and its self-reflexive character.

Equally influential was the school of essay-writing that developed in the 1930s, known as the New Criticism. Based on 'practical criticism', this involved in-depth scrutiny of the multivalent properties of language. In highlighting the formal characteristics of a poem or prose work, these essays made judgements about literary value that deliberately divorced a work from the time when it was written. Its legacy is seen in today's A Level syllabus where students are encouraged to examine sections of a text or to deconstruct a poem on the basis of its technical merits, irrespective of knowing anything about the contexts or conditions in which it was produced.

It is of course perfectly possible to produce a good critical essay on works that do not necessarily constitute 'great' literature. George Orwell's essay on

'Boys' Weeklies' (1940) marked a turning point in the history of critical practice, widening its scope and its cultural parameters. It signals a transition in thinking about literature as both reflecting and shaping its cultural moment. Its audacious analysis of comics with their school-stories featuring Billy Bunter, their stereotyped foreigners and their super-heroes based on 'bully worship and the cult of violence' exposed the hidden ideologies that infuse literature and perpetuate prevailing assumptions about class and society. The essay drew attention to a swathe of material, disregarded by the elite, which had a huge impact on a general reading public. It is probably because of Orwell that popular media, such as film, TV, song lyrics or graphic novels, are now respectable subjects for study. Pre-Orwell, it would have been unthinkable that a writer such as Bob Dylan could win the Nobel Prize for Literature.

Modern approaches

The essay remains one of the most energetic and influential forms of literary writing. The best essays are immersed in current debates, and offer informed readings of texts, often from sophisticated theoretical perspectives. There seems to be a constant supply of different interpretations of the same work from eminent scholars, all of which can be robustly defended. Even a conservative novelist like Jane Austen can be transformed into a radical when her books are put under the microscope of feminist, psychoanalytic, historicist or post-colonial theory. Today's readers are alert to issues of gender identity, fluidity of personality, child abuse or underage sexuality in ways that were just not part of the mind-set of earlier reviewers.

Lydia Bennett's seduction by Wickham, for instance, which in 1811, the year *Pride and Prejudice* was published, was scandalous because it tarnishes a young woman's reputation, can be reinterpreted as an example of underage grooming and exploitation. Austen, whose own appetite for sensational fiction was voracious, effectively relocates Gothic villainy to a domestic everyday world. Similarly, the focus on Darcy rather than Elizabeth, in the BBC TV adaptation of the novel by Andrew Davies, spawned a whole raft of essays about troubled masculinity. Historicist critics equally point to the uncertain, nomadic existence of many of Austen's characters as evidence of the social upheavals of the period or the impact of the Napoleonic wars on the English way of life so that readers recognise the historical inflections and the novel's portrait of contemporary political and economic disruption.

The critical essay does not conform to a single format which has to be rigidly adhered to. Like other literary genres, it is a flexible medium, a creative space in which academics, students, authors and general readers can share opinions. Literary experience is not constant but changes over time, and modern essays are generous in acknowledging the diversity of readers and their backgrounds. In her brilliant collection of critical essays, *Written With Intent* (2005), the Canadian author, Margaret Atwood, uses Virginia Woolf's *To The Lighthouse* as an example of how her own reading has matured so that only in middle-age can she fully appreciate the subtleties and the wisdom of a work to which she was immune when she first read it as a nineteen-year old.

The poet, Michael Rosen, has explained not just how all writers draw on their own history of reading when they write but how the literary canon constitutes an ongoing dialogue between writers, who are also importantly readers.

> My argument [...] is that when we write, we write with what the French critic and theorist, Roland Barthes, called the 'already' – in other words, what has already been written and spoken. I have a further argument which says that we read with our own 'already' or what another critic, Wolfgang Iser, called our own 'repertoire' of texts. This way of looking at writing and reading has been called 'intertextuality' because it sees texts as interlocked, in conversation with each other, influencing and affecting each other, whether we are readers or writers or both. (2018)

Rosen's essay is interesting partly because his own persona and poetic style are unashamedly relaxed, direct and unpretentious. As a children's writer, he represents the antithesis of the arcane, theoretical ground occupied by many critics. Yet this essay reveals the deep erudition that underpins Rosen's poetry and his insight into his own practice. It makes important points about literary history and textual production and engages seriously with the dynamics of reading. It is a perfect example of how a short essay can set out a logical argument, offer searching insights into a text, cover poetic technique and stimulate thinking. Rosen even manages to include a dig at the current educational climate that he believes is undermining the true purpose of university teaching.

Many of the best critical essays take the form of book reviews, and it is no accident that press reviewers are frequently from academic backgrounds, bringing a trained eye to the evaluation of new work. Others are themselves creative practitioners. Margaret Atwood's review of Toni Morrison's *Beloved* remains one of the finest essays on that novel despite the huge range of critical commentary that has succeeded it. In advising potential purchasers, reviewers have enormous sway over sales and markets. Their task is to give readers a flavour of what lies in store for them balanced by judicious appraisal. Atwood's essay begins:

> *Beloved* is Toni Morrison's fifth novel, and another triumph. Indeed, Ms Morrison's versatility and technical and emotional range appear to know no bounds. If there were any doubts about her stature as a pre-eminent American novelist, of her own or any other generation, *Beloved* will put them to rest. In three words or less, it's a hair-raiser.

Atwood opens with an unqualified verdict on the novel's achievement, identifies three features – 'versatility and technical and emotional range' – to justify her assessment and positions the author within a national literary tradition. Her final short sentence suggests the chilling theatricality of the story that would make any reader want to rush out and buy it. It is a terrific introduction to an essay that goes on to describe the stylistic inventiveness of *Beloved* through more granular analysis of its ambitious subject. As Atwood says, 'reviewing the work of others forces you to examine your own ethical and aesthetic tastes. What do we mean by 'good' in a book? What do we mean by 'bad' and why?'. These are key questions for any student of literature.

The student essay

'The great enemy of clear language is insincerity,' wrote George Orwell. 'When there is a gap between one's real and one's declared aims, one turns as it were instinctively to long words and exhausted idioms, like a cuttlefish squirting ink'. Orwell's *Inside the Whale* (1940) is both a classic example and a clear-sighted assessment of the art of writing critical essays. Wide-ranging in scope, beautifully structured, eschewing jargon or complicated terminology, it addresses its central subject head on. Its insistence on clarity and honesty is sound advice. Believe in what you are saying and do not try to dress up your ideas in highbrow language or rely on clichés.

There are many student guides on the market which provide a template for essay-writing. Websites such as *essaydragon.com* advise on the different stages of planning, structure and style while a number of university English departments publish online handbooks, which contain excellent practical pointers. There are also helpful YouTube videos, which take you through the composition process step by step. Yet because an essay should always be personal, there can be no absolute prototype. It is helpful to remember that the verb 'to essay' also means 'to try'. Your essay is a means of testing out ideas and polishing the techniques used to structure them.

My own top five tips are:

1. **Know your subject.** This relies on reading the text for yourself. At A Level you may feel that you have done this exhaustively. Yet, understanding is also about engaging with that text, the story it tells, and whether or not it has the power to speak directly to you as a reader, not just via your teacher. Literature that is set for A Level has usually been selected for its complexity and its potential to enlighten or affect your thinking. So, read and read again!

2. **Conduct research.** This does not necessarily involve seeking out obscure primary sources, although reading Keats's letters or Mary Shelley's 1831 introduction to *Frankenstein* will offer considerable insights into their works. Rather it means reading around the text, understanding

the contexts, including its literary history, and knowing what other commentators have said. Writing an essay is not an isolated activity. When you embark on it, you are entering an ongoing debate about literature, including with other students and with academic critics, whose ideas will help inspire your own. Remember that there is no 'correct' interpretation of a text and that it is perfectly acceptable to disagree with others' opinions. This is an important step in articulating your own position.

3. **Answer the question.** Most essay topics offer a deceptively simple proposition that demands a more subtle answer; for example, 'How far do you agree with the view that in *King Lear*, Goneril and Regan are victims rather than villains?'. Your essay should of course sustain a focus on these two characters and the scenes in which they appear. But the phrasing also invites a review of the primary value system embedded in the action, such as the human and social values of family, respect for order, filial obedience, love, charity and kingship. How do Shakespeare's dramatic methods, the juxtaposition with Gloucester's family or the positioning of Lear's speeches excoriating his daughters fit into the play's exploration of power? Is there really scope for ambiguity here? Don't forget that the best essays show evidence of an enquiring mind so you should not be shy about using question marks.

4. **Structure your argument.** Where an author can be equivocal or abstruse, the critic should be aiming to be clear and to untangle. Planning what you are going to say is essential. You may find that as you make notes on your reading, your proposition evolves in unexpected ways. The key is to organise your points into a logical format that supports your main case. This avoids your ideas spilling out onto the page in a random sequence that results in a disjointed or rambling piece of work. In a comparison piece, for example, you should aim to keep your paragraphs balanced alternately between the texts. Remember too to keep to the prescribed word count. Do not make the mistake of thinking that the more you write the more compelling your thesis will be.

5. **Provide the evidence.** Every claim you make must be underpinned by reference to the text or to relevant contexts. This is what makes your line of reasoning convincing. You need to be selective about the material you use, but if you have followed points 1-4 above, this should come naturally. Quotations from the text underpin and strengthen your interpretation. They can be used alongside any background information you have, for example about the cultural climate in which a writer's work was produced and the literary conventions of the day.

Do not make the mistake of expecting characters in a Victorian novel to behave according to twenty-first century codes. It is the judicious use of reference to characters, scenes, authorial voice and imagery that will ensure your essay comes alive.

The critical essay in the digital age

Digital technology has opened up a massive literary resource. It provides access for researchers to a range of materials which were once available only in a specialist library, such as copies of original manuscripts, out of print books and articles and biographical or historical information. It allows for new scholarship and literary discoveries that contribute to the essay's intervention in an evolving live debate.

Wikipedia, Google and other search engines can, however, tempt a reader towards simplistic analysis. A work of literature amounts to more than its surface narrative or plot synopsis. The internet is seductive because it appears to be comprehensive but its information is only as reliable as the person who posted it, and not all online views are equally valid. A critical perspective located via Google can range from incisive analysis by a learned scholar to a barely literate high school essay on *Jane Eyre,* such as some of those on the Bartleby website. Surfing the internet requires scrupulous discrimination on the part of the consumer, and it should never, ever be used as a sales outlet from which to purchase ready-made, supposedly bespoke coursework essays.

On the plus side, digital media have created a new approach to essay writing, with online magazines such as *Electric Lit* offering alternative publishing outlets. A whole blogosphere has emerged, populated by enthusiastic litbloggers, who exchange views, reviews and mini-essays. Blogging, where typical posts are between 800 and 1500 words, affords a spirited, democratic space for literary discussion. As one commentator has noted, 'it does more than an essay because of its playfulness'. Yet its explosive growth has sparked controversy, with some, such as one chair of the Man Booker judges, claiming that blogging will only result in the 'detriment of literature'. Check out the regularly updated Literature Blogs UK Top 10 and make up your own mind.

Rarely do blogs follow the accepted conventions of critical essay writing. They are more casual, allowing for impromptu, open-ended observations that reaffirm a collective passion for literature. They can be quirky, playful or angry. They challenge the specialised rhetoric of the literati and what some see as an ivory tower complacency. Yet many academics, authors and teachers are themselves active bloggers, who find in the blog release from academic conventions and who know they can reach new audiences with a speed and directness that gives their views both currency and significance.

Readers live in the contemporary moment, and the power of present-day media shapes both textual meaning and production. Technology has opened up a world in which literary experience is not confined to the traditional print format. This is why the essay remains such a dynamic form, constantly renewing itself with each external stimulus. Do not give up on its rewards.

Questions to take your thinking further

- What is the purpose of writing or reading a literary critical essay?
- How can reading or writing a critical essay enhance the primary experience of literature?
- To what extent is the critical essay a literary genre in its own right?
- Is there a place for the student voice in ongoing critical debate?
- Can the critical essay survive in a world dominated by social media?

Reading list

Atwood, M. 2005. *Writing With Intent: Essays, Reviews, Personal Prose 1983-2005*. New York: Carroll & Graf.

Eliot, T.S. 1920. *The Sacred Wood, Essays on Poetry and Criticism*. London: Faber & Faber.

Orwell, G. 1940. *Inside The Whale*. London: Victor Gollancz Ltd.

Pirie, D. 1991. *How to Write Critical Essays: A Guide for Students of Literature*. London: Routledge.

London Review of Books Blog (ongoing since 2009) https://www.lrb.co.uk/blog/

READING IN CONTEXT

Peter Barry

Content and context – some starter questions

Let's start with a cliché. In literature, the content is inside the work (it's in 'the words *on* the page'), and the context is outside it (it's in 'the words *off* the page'). This means that the potential amount of available context is infinite, so the problem is always that of narrowing potential context down to relevant context. We might feel (for instance) that any work written and/or published between 1914 and 1918 must be either foreshadowed, overshadowed, or backshadowed by World War One, but you will still need to narrow down that gigantic macro-event to something micro-focused if you hope to write convincingly about the war as a context for a specific work. This article suggests ways of doing just that.

No advice can make practical sense without a worked example, so let's use this poem by Helen Mort.

Lene Gammelgaard[1]

Now you're a woman and that's all
they'll know, no matter
what you carry or how far
you go, alone, in rationed light.
Behind you, there must be
a mother, wringing her slim hands.
A husband who understands.
A house, two children held
in the imagined door. You are
less after than before. You'll never be
what you are now, a silence, framed
by sun. You are what's said.
You'll never be what's done.

Here are ten numbered statements related to the poem. Your starter discussion task is to decide whether each of them is about the content of the poem, the context of the poem, a hybrid of these, or neither of these. (1) Helen Mort was born in Sheffield in 1985. (2) The poems of Helen Mort's second collection offer an unforgettable perspective on the heights we scale and the distances we run, the routes we follow and the paths we make for ourselves. (3) These are poems of passion and precipices, of edges and extremes. (4) Helen Mort is a climber as well

---

[1] *No Map Could Show Them*, Chatto & Windus, 2016, p.62.

as a poet. (5) Lene Gammelgaard was involved in the 1996 Everest disaster [in which eight climbers died]. (6) Gammelgaard was the first Scandinavian woman to summit Everest. (7) She has written about the fateful expedition in her book, *Climbing High*. (8) To date, 548 different women have reached that summit, some more than once. (9) 'Mountains are not fair or unfair, they are just dangerous' (Reinhold Messner). (10) 'A poem is a speaking picture, and a picture is a silent poem.'[2]

I will come back to these starter questions at the end.

Context in a Jane Austen novel

Perhaps we can arrive at some notion of a sustainable balance between text and context in our literary discussions by considering a well-known example of a critic 'importing' a new context into the study of a major literary work. The literary work is Jane Austen's novel *Mansfield Park* (published in 1814), and the critic is Edward Said (1935-2003), whose book *Culture and Imperialism* (1995) discusses this novel in the part-chapter 'Jane Austen and Empire'. The English estate of Mansfield Park in the novel is owned by Sir Thomas Bertram, whose income is partly derived from another property he owns, which is overseas. At a crucial stage in the book he has to absent himself for some months to attend to business affairs in Antigua, and Said's view is that at the time, 'Sir Thomas's property in the Caribbean would have had to be a sugar plantation maintained by slave labour (not abolished till the 1830s)'. So the handsome country house in the English shires, with its surrounding park, is maintained by a far less gracious estate on the other side of the world.

My own experience is that the issues of personal conduct and morality which are central to this novel are significantly expanded by Said's reading. Austen does not say a lot about Antigua, but she does mention it a number of times, and in such a way as to justify our further enquiry into it. Said's treatment of the issue is actually quite broadbrush. Only one passage from the novel is read 'closely' in his book: it follows Sir Thomas's sudden arrival home, and his putting matters there to rights like an absolute monarch, a Robinson Crusoe in total charge of his island, as Said puts it. The passage he dwells upon is the moment in chapter twenty-one when Fanny mentions how she raised the topic of slavery with Sir Thomas, finding that he is not generally averse to talking about the West Indies. She tells her cousin Edmund 'I love to hear my uncle talk of the West Indies. I

---

[2] In the above list of statements: (1), (2), and (3) are from the back cover of *No Map Could Show Them*, (4) is from the poet's website (5), (6), and (7) are from her own note to the poem, with my addition in square brackets, (8) is from Wikipedia, (9) is the overall epigraph to the 'Everest' sequence of five short poems, of which 'Lene Gammelgaard' is the fourth, and Messner is the Italian mountaineer who made the first solo ascent of Everest, and (with Peter Habeler) the first without supplemental oxygen, (10) is an influential remark about the difference between poems and pictures: the Ancient Greek historian and philosopher Plutarch attributes it to the poet Simonides of Keos.

could listen to him for an hour together'. Edmund replies, 'I only wish you would talk to him more. You are one of those who are too silent in the evening circle'. Fanny denies this with, for her, considerable warmth: 'But I do talk to him more than I used [to]. I am sure I do. Did not you hear me ask him about the slave-trade last night?' Edmund acknowledges this: 'I did – and was in hopes the question would be followed up by others. It would have pleased your uncle to be inquired of farther'. Fanny's response is to turn the accusation of silence onto her cousins: 'And I longed to do it – but there was such a dead silence!' So the whole topic of silence and its interpretation is crucial here, as it so often is in matters concerning literary context.

William Wilberforce's bill for the abolition of slavery was passed in Parliament in 1807, but slavery continued in the West Indies until 1838, as the Parliamentary Act abolished the slave trade, not slavery. Hence, slavery was an issue of moral and legal ambiguity for a period of thirty years in the early part of the nineteenth century. Assuming that we see the Antigua issue as an important factor in how we read the novel, perhaps an interesting question is which side Jane Austen and her heroine Fanny Price are on – are they abolitionists or not? The general view is that Fanny 'is unmistakably a "friend of the abolition"', and Austen herself probably was too. But her own family had some involvement in the trade, as in 1760 Jane's father, the Reverend George Austen, 'was appointed principal trustee of a plantation in Antigua', so that 'the Austens too had a dependence, however slight, upon the prosperity of a plantation in Antigua'.

So what is needed in the literary text to validate the importation of a specific context like this? Well, firstly, the book should not be totally silent about the context you want to say is relevant. There should be an explicit 'textual trigger' in your literary work which 'cues' or 'activates' that context. In the case of *Mansfield Park* the general silence about Antigua and slavery isn't total – they are mentioned in the novel, and not just once, so it meets that vital criterion. Secondly, the relevance of Antigua is pervasive, affecting not just a single incident, but the whole foregrounded moral and thematic core of the novel, which concerns issues of conduct, and questions of how we can aspire to live the morally good life at the same time as living the materially good life. So the fact that the claimed context pervades or is embedded in the through-running themes and concerns of the novel is vital too. After all, it might have been put in simply to give an air of topicality or authenticity of a superficial kind. And thirdly, Said's reading of the novel adds a dimension to the work which expands its central moral concerns, showing that personal good behaviour is not enough, and that we need to show political and ethical good behaviour as well. So these are our three basic criteria for deciding when a context is relevant – *explicitness*, *embeddedness*, and *expansiveness*.

'To Autumn', Peterloo, and gleaning

Let's now look at another well-known example using these same three criteria: explicitness, embeddedness, and expansiveness. When Andrew Motion's biography of Keats was first published (*Keats*, 1997), reviewers seemed shocked to find the poet viewed so much in terms of the politics of his day, especially the ode 'To Autumn', Keats's most celebrated poem.

1

Season of mists and mellow fruitfulness,
    Close bosom-friend of the maturing sun;
Conspiring with him how to load and bless
    With fruit the vines that round the thatch-eves run;
To bend with apples the moss'd cottage-trees,
    And fill all fruit with ripeness to the core;
        To swell the gourd, and plump the hazel shells
    With a sweet kernel; to set budding more,
And still more, later flowers for the bees,
Until they think warm days will never cease,
        For Summer has o'er-brimm'd their clammy cells.

2

Who hath not seen thee oft amid thy store?
    Sometimes whoever seeks abroad may find
Thee sitting careless on a granary floor,
    Thy hair soft-lifted by the winnowing wind;
Or on a half-reap'd furrow sound asleep,
    Drows'd with the fume of poppies, while thy hook
        Spares the next swath and all its twined flowers:
And sometimes like a gleaner thou dost keep
    Steady thy laden head across a brook;
    Or by a cyder-press, with patient look,
        Thou watchest the last oozings hours by hours.

3

Where are the songs of Spring? Ay, where are they?
    Think not of them, thou hast thy music too, –
While barred clouds bloom the soft-dying day,
    And touch the stubble-plains with rosy hue;
Then in a wailful choir the small gnats mourn
    Among the river sallows, borne aloft
        Or sinking as the light wind lives or dies;
And full-grown lambs loud bleat from hilly bourn;
    Hedge-crickets sing; and now with treble soft
    The red-breast whistles from a garden-croft;
        And gathering swallows twitter in the skies.

Motion linked it closely to an event that happened in Manchester the month before it was written, on 16 August 1819, when soldiers killed eleven people during a political demonstration at St Peter's Fields, Manchester. This was immediately dubbed the 'Peterloo Massacre' in mocking contrast to the heroic behaviour of soldiers in the Battle of Waterloo four years earlier. While walking by the Water Meadows in Winchester on Sunday 19 September, Keats saw the just-harvested fields in the evening light, and these appear in the poem as 'stubble-plains', roughly meaning 'recently harvested fields', touched with the 'rosy hue' of the setting sun. That, at least, is how the lines were read until the late 1980s, when the American scholar Jerome McGann first linked the 'stubble-plains' and the 'rosy hue' to the blood-stained ground of the previous month at St Peter's Fields in Manchester. Further, says Motion, 'the word 'conspiring', in the third line, both embraces and deflects the plotting that Keats knew surrounded Henry Hunt's recent activities.'[3] The reference to the gleaner is more certainly charged with contemporary references. Gleaning, the practice of allowing locals to gather stray ears of corn left by the reapers, had been made illegal in 1818, and 'the figure [of the gleaner] ... also refers to his sympathy for the denied and the dispossessed. So does his description of the bees.'[4] The whole poem, then, is turned into a kind of encrypted political statement, and all its favourite features – the 'conspiring' mists, the bees, the gleaner, and so on – acquired hidden political meanings. Other critics developed the McGann approach in the 1980s and 1990s, the period when the study of Romanticism was being 'historicised' by an influential and talented group of British and American critics. These included Andrew Bennett, who examined the manuscripts of the poem and is suspicious of the line 'barred clouds bloom the soft-dying day' because, in an earlier draft, the wording had been 'a gold cloud gilds the soft-dying day' (*Keats, Narrative and Audience: the Posthumous Life of Writing*, 1994). He sees this as part of a psychic melodrama of concealment, maintaining that the poet makes this change because of his 'silent barring of money from 'To Autumn''. This follows the lead of McGann in seeing Romanticism as 'a bankrupt ideology of evasion' of the material facts of social injustice, materialism, and the encroaching forces of capitalist industrialisation.

So these critics claim a context for 'To Autumn', but does it satisfy our three criteria of *explicitness*, *embeddedness*, and *expansiveness*? On the first; many contextual 'triggers' are identified within the literary text, but the problem is that they are all disguised or 'encrypted', so that, for instance, we have to decrypt the red of the evening sun and see it as emblematic of the spilt blood of Peterloo. Likewise, the 'gold cloud' of the manuscript draft is decoded as the financial imperatives

---

[3] Henry Hunt (1773-1835), known as 'Orator Hunt', was a radical speaker and agitator who was a pioneer of working-class radicalism. It was the soldiers' attempts to prevent him speaking at the rally in St Peter's Field which led to the Peterloo Massacre. A fortnight later, Keats was one of 30,000 people who gathered to watch Hunt's triumphal arrival in London.

[4] As 'worker bees'. Bees were incorporated into Manchester's coat of arms in 1841, and seem to have already become an emblem of the city before then, so the bees too may be a covert reference to Manchester.

of proto-capitalism, and the humming bees as a reference to Manchester, and so on. There is no explanation of why the poet wanted to disguise these meanings – other poets of the day wrote open and savage, left-wing poems against the much-hated government of the day. On the second criterion, embeddedness, the claimed context doesn't seem to sit convincingly with the rest of the content or tone of the piece. It is sad and subdued in tone, but not angry or indignant, which would surely be the only way to address the matter of Peterloo. Thirdly, on the last criterion, expansiveness, the claimed context seems to lock the poem into a single track of meaning, rather than opening up its range, and the view it presents of Romanticism (as being evasive and self-deceived) seems to disempower and belittle the writers concerned. The best I could say for it would be that this is a contextual reading which is unproven.

Broad context and deep context

Context is usually understood as something very broad, and especially as large-scale social and historical forces exerting a pervasive effect on all literature. Hence the 'time-lines', listing major world events, inventions, discoveries and so on, which are now often printed in (for instance) modern academic editions of nineteenth-century novels. I have never really understood what time-lines are for, or found much in them which has been useful in literary interpretation or appreciation. That is because context is never just waiting ready-made, to be snipped out of a time-line and pinned onto our reading of a literary work. Rather, every context has to be identified and assembled by the reader – every con*text* is a con*struct*. Context can be literary, cultural, generic, and biographical as well as historical and social. We should look for 'deep context', which is the opposite of the broad social-historical kind. Deep context is rooted in elements which are tailored to fit one text alone, and it is, in the end, scarcely distinguishable from content.

As an example of deep context, consider the poem 'Mephisto' by Lavinia Greenlaw (1962-), quoted on page 30. The relevant context is mainly a literary one, and it is 'triggered' by the title, 'Mephisto' being another version of the name Mephistopheles, the Satanic figure of Christopher Marlowe's play *Dr Faustus* (first performed in 1592, and based upon German legends), which tells the story of a scholar who sells his soul to the devil. The much later version of the same tale is the play *Faust* (first version 1808) by the German writer Johann Wolfgang Goethe (1749-1832). *Faust* is set in the German city of Leipzig, and it contains a famous scene of student drunkenness at an inn called 'Auerbach's Keller', now a 'must' for tourists visiting the city. The speaker in the poem has visited Leipzig while on a reading tour, and the following morning she is 'up in the air again' – that is, both literally, for she is flying off to her next stop on the tour, and, metaphorically, for she is in a state of confusion or uncertainty. The flying recalls how Faust in the play flies over the icy wastes with Mephistopheles, one of the perks of his 'Faustian pact' with the devil, before the passing of time brings him to his inevitable end. As she looks down from the aircraft at the ice-bound river, now beginning to thaw after three months of winter, she seems to be asking herself what residue is left from an unsatisfactory experience there (whether romantic or professional, or both, we are not told) with a 'Mephisto' character who, like Mephistopheles, fails, in the end to deliver on his promises:

Mephisto[5]

After a night in the cellar
Goethe returned to with Faust,
I am up in the air again,
cumulo-cirrus, thin ice, a voice
that is crushing and reasonable:
Your little life...
We fly over a river,
part frozen, part cracking up
at the end of a beautiful winter:
a three-month blinding heaven
that will leave its smallprint
and otherwise nothing on earth.

The Leipzig context, as outlined above is explicitly 'cued' by the title of the poem and the mention of Goethe's *Faust* in the first two lines of the poem. It is all 'deep context', or 'micro-context', which would not fit any other poem. Much of the poem features idiomatic English phrases commonly used with reference to inter-personal situations – 'up in the air', 'thin ice', 'frozen', 'cracking up' and so on. One could say that similar terms are used about relations between nations, including, for instance, the period of distrust and hostility, known as the Cold War, between the Capitalist 'West' and the Communist 'Eastern Bloc', from 1945 to 1990. A broader approach to context might mention the fact that events in the city of Leipzig in 1989 were crucial in the build-up to the re-unification of Germany and the fall of the Berlin Wall. But I can't really see anything in the poem which would 'trigger' that wider, non-literary Leipzig context here.

Retro-context: Byron's 'Darkness'

I had a dream, which was not all a dream.
The bright sun was extinguish'd, and the stars
Did wander darkling in the eternal space,
Rayless, and pathless, and the icy earth
Swung blind and blackening in the moonless air;

---

[5] This is the complete poem, from Greenlaw's *Minsk*, Faber & Faber, 2003, p.32

These are the opening lines of Byron's vivid narrative poem 'Darkness', which is about the end of the world. He wrote it in Geneva in July of 1816, a year known as 'the year without a summer', because ash clouds filled the atmosphere for months and darkened the sky all over the world. They were caused by the eruption in April of the previous year of the volcanic Mount Tambora on the island of Sumbawa, in what was then the Dutch East Indies, and is now part of Indonesia. This was the largest volcanic eruption in recorded history, and ten thousand people died on the island, in the explosion or as a result of the tsunamis that followed. In 1816, as the dust and debris of the huge explosion was dispersed around the globe, frost and heavy snow persisted in Europe into June, July, and August. Byron was in Geneva that summer, and (according to one possibly unreliable source), said that on the day he wrote it, people were lighting candles at midday, and the birds thought the darkness meant it was night-time, and that was what gave him the idea for the poem. There is no explicit mention of Tambora in the poem, because the cause of these widely-prevalent weather conditions was not yet known, making them all the more fearsome. Instead the discernible references (including that of the poem's very title) are to apocalyptic writing from the Bible, such as the lines 'The sun shall be turned into darkness, and the moon into blood, before the great and terrible day of the Lord' (Joel 2:31). He also evokes the visionary writing of his own day, such as Coleridge's epic poem 'The Rime of the Ancient Mariner' in which 'slimy things did crawl with legs / Upon the slimy sea', and 'Ships sailorless lay rotting on the sea'. Such end-of-the world fears were provoked by the post-Tambora conditions of light, temperature, and atmosphere because over the four years of failed crops all over the world following the eruption, it seemed not so much a change in the weather as a permanent change in climate

We can make use here of a distinction between meaning and significance, put forward by the American critic E.D. Hirsch (b. 1928) in his book *Validity in Interpretation* (1967): 'meaning' is something inherent in the work, whereas 'significance' is something we perceive in the work, which is necessarily shifting. Significance, then, is like the sea, which seems a different colour when seen in different light conditions. Hence, reading Byron's 'Darkness' today we inevitably see it in the light of our fears about global warming and the unsustainable use of the earth's resources. We now see it, in other words, in *that* context, even though that context was not available then, when the poem was written. When we see the hazy polluted light of major cities today, we see, not a change of weather, but what we know is a change of climate. The atmosphere is the same hazy, orangey-reddish light in the pictures of J.W. Turner and Caspar David Friedrich which were made in the post-Tambora Romantic period, when the atmosphere was still suffused with volcanic ash. We see it now and shudder with grounded fear, like the benighted beings in Byron's 'Darkness'. So here is a context without a verbal trigger in the text (for reasons just mentioned) which we nevertheless have to recognise. This kind of 'retro-context' comes into the category which Adrian

Barlow (see further reading) simply calls 'unusual contexts'. The existence of the category means, among other things, that there is no neat and tidy overall solution to the problem of context, and that, in the end, allowances must be made for the seepage of extraordinary events into every facet of our cultures.

Back to context and content

The main thrust of my ten pieces of contextual information in the opening section is to encourage you to re-think your ideas of context. Items (2) and (3) remind us, in effect, that books have themes. In a collection of poetry, themes may run across the separate poems. This can also be true across the different novels or plays of an individual writer's work, so that a major aspect of context is inter-textual. Items (2) and (3) also make the mountains into metaphors – they are 'encrypted' and become more than 'just' literal mountains, so that the 'edges', 'cliffs', 'pathways', 'precipices', and so on, turn the mountains in the poem into what Robert Macfarlane called (it's the title of one of his best books) 'mountains of the mind'. Items (1) and (4) also point to the human and the personal aspects of writing – not just to what we write, but to where our gendered paths begin, and where the edges might be that will daunt us. Items (5), (6) and (7) are the context explicitly identified by the poet, which we should not always trust without question, but which we must always note and ponder. Are these authorial notes and other 'peripherals' (such as titles or glosses) part of the poem or novel? Are they words on the page or off it? Where exactly are the lines that separate texts from their own verbal contexts? Items (9) and (10) bring in 'far-horizon' considerations: on (9), we might call a slope or precipice 'treacherous' as if it were trying to betray us by giving way at the wrong time, or going in the wrong direction, like a scheming opponent seeking to mislead us, but Messner reminds us that mountains are only dangerous when mountaineers forget that they are. On (10), Simonides reminds us that another major aspect of context is genre: genres shift about and change all the time, but there are things that novels, poems, and plays (respectively) can do, and things that they can't, and the 'play' and negotiation between a given specimen of one of these and its generic frame is an important aspect of its context.

Questions to take your thinking further

When using this approach to context, ask yourself the following questions:

- What types of context might be relevant to this text? Which of the following would I shortlist as being particularly relevant?[6]

  - The period or era, including social, historical, political and cultural factors
  - The writer's biography or milieu
  - The whole work
  - Other works, including those by the same author
  - The literary context, including generic factors and period-specific styles
  - The language context
  - The reception context.

- What general aspects of the text might 'trigger' or validate the relevance of my shortlisted types?
- Of the three specific textual 'triggers' for context (explicitness, embeddedness, expansiveness), how many are identifiable for the types on my shortlist?
- Are any of these textual triggers 'encrypted' or disguised? If so, how convincing are my arguments for them, and how could I strengthen them further?
- Are there some aspects of the context I am constructing for this text 'tailored' and specific to it? Have I given these enough prominence?

Reading list

Allen, G. 2011. *Intertextuality* (New Critical Idiom series). London: Routledge.

Barlow, A. 2009. *World and Time: Teaching Literature in Context.* Cambridge: Cambridge University Press.

Barry, P. 2007. *Literature in Contexts.* Manchester: Manchester University Press.

Orr, M. 2003. *Intertextuality: Debates and Contexts.* Cambridge: Polity Press.

Rylance, R. and J. Simons, eds. 2001. *Literature in Context.* London: Palgrave Macmillan.

---

[6] The above list of contexts, developed by Rick Rylance for the Qualifications and Curriculum Authority in 1998, is reproduced in Rylance and Simons (2001).

POETRY – A CONVERSATION ACROSS TIME

Michael Rosen

Any poem we may be reading or listening to is not 'alone'. It exists in many traditions or cultures:

i.   Those of its making
ii. Those belonging to those reading or hearing the poem
iii. Those that the maker of the poem has adopted and adapted to make the poem.

Three terms are useful here. At the time of the poem's making, the poem exists *synchronically* in a culture of other poems being produced along with the broader cultures and society where this writing and performing is taking place. It exists *diachronically*, as the poet has drawn on historical traditions of poetry and attitudes to poetry. We might also say that when we read or listen to poems from previous eras, we are 'receiving' these *anachronistically*, that is: out of their time.

Defining a shifting genre

Poets use language to give value to how we live, whilst at the same time giving value to language itself. Being precise about this, in terms of defining characteristics of poetry, is extremely difficult: there are always exceptions, and there are many other forms which use poetic methods. Ultimately, poetry is an agreement between practitioners and audience, between poets and readers, poetry-performers and listeners in specific times and places that what is going on *is* poetry. The historical and contemporary thread of poetry is made up of thousands of these agreements. These become exposed at moments of change. One key moment in this history came in the nineteenth century when poets across the world started to break with the regularity of traditional verse, writing 'free verse' and 'prose poetry'. The fact that sufficient numbers of poets and audiences agreed that a good deal of this new poetry being produced was still poetry – despite its appearing to break all the rules previously used to define the genre – meant that the definition of poetry shifted and expanded.

This places poetry as a form of 'discourse', a very varied way for us to talk to each other and no matter what the 'rules' appear to be, these are in reality conventions and the making and breaking of them are in the hands of the users and receivers.

'English' poetry? A scavenging form

Traditionally, in the context of English studies, we study poetry written in English. This may seem uncontroversial unless we question whether the language spoken in England in the year 900, say, really was 'English'; or again, if we question whether, say, a sonnet written in English can really be described as 'English' given that the form was borrowed directly from those who wrote in Italian. In fact, through the world history of poetry, we can see that one of its defining features is the way in which poets have continually 'scavenged' poetic forms, motifs and methods from outside of their own cultural or linguistic group. Geoffrey Chaucer, often seen as a founding father of English poetry, borrowed rigorously and delightfully from traditions found in France and Italy. The form of the frame story which Chaucer uses in *The Canterbury Tales* is found originally in the Arab world. Over six hundred years later, a group of poets literally talking to each other (often in cafes and bars) or 'talking' to each other via their little magazines and books across the world, 'scavenged' from traditions found in, say, China or Japan to create new forms of poetry which we call the 'Modernist' tradition.

All this is by way of saying poetry as a whole is hybrid and intercultural.

The story of English poetry – a personal sketch

What follows is a brief sketch of some of the poetic movements or traditions of poetry composed in English, starting out from the time when the first Germanic speakers settled in the British Isles right up to the present day when English is spoken across the world. It's a deliberately eclectic selection, intended to pique your interest, to encourage you to read widely and adventurously, to follow your own path through this conversation.

Throughout this section, I have also highlighted some of the ways in which a particular poet or type of poetry influenced much later writing.

Old English poetry

Old English poetry was written in the language now referred to as 'Old English' or 'Anglo-Saxon'. Although English literature studies have focused on poetry produced in Anglo Saxon in both linguistic and cultural terms, it was a poetry that also drew on Latin (from texts central to the Christian religion) and Old Norse (from the 'Danish' or 'Viking' invasions). The forms it took included lyrics, riddles, charms and epics.

Mostly, it did not use the rhythm and rhyme schemes found in later poetry. Its main method of poetic cohesion came through the use of alliteration and assonance in half-lines attached in different ways to the stress of words.

Other features of this poetry that feel familiar today are its metaphorical methods and clear use of a voice or persona 'speaking' the poem. From its formulae (frequently repeated phrases), it's clear that early English poetry was rooted in an oral tradition, with poems written to be remembered by heart and recited. Some notable poets who have drawn on Old English poetry are Gerard Manley Hopkins in the nineteenth century, Dylan Thomas and Ted Hughes in the twentieth century and Seamus Heaney in the twentieth and twenty-first centuries.

Medieval religious and secular lyrics

A rich, European-wide 'lyric' tradition using regular rhythm, rhyme and in most cases melody (in other words they were songs) is found in both religious and secular lyrics during the medieval period. These poems drew on what were familiar symbols and emblems. Some of these are picked up and repeated through the history of poetry, as with say, the rose in the poetry of William Blake (late eighteenth century), Christina Rossetti (late nineteenth century) or Elizabeth Jennings (mid-twentieth century) – a concrete illustration of the way poems are 'in conversation with' earlier poems and traditions.

In the late medieval period some poets wrote long narratives: William Langland's *Piers the Plowman* (1367-86), the anonymous *Sir Gawain and the Green Knight* (late fourteenth century) and Geoffrey Chaucer's *The Canterbury Tales* (1387-1400) are often regarded as 'founding' texts of English Literature as they offer us panoramic views of society across classes and genders. One reason why Chaucer has his place in English studies is because he represents the moment when poets began writing in an 'English' which combined Middle English with words of French origin brought to England and the rest of the British Isles as a result of the Norman Invasion (Norman = French people from Normandy) of 1066.

Part of the Christian tradition was to translate parts or the whole Bible from Latin, Greek, or Hebrew into the vernacular or language spoken by the people (with the first full English translation of the New Testament being completed by William Tyndale in 1526). The translations of the *Psalms* and *Song of Solomon* are characterised by features we recognise as free verse. Many poets have drawn on the voices of the Bible for its imagery, language, and the rhythms set up by the translators, including Walt Whitman (a nineteenth-century American poet and one of the first writers of a freer form of verse in English).

Sixteenth-century sonnet writers

In the sixteenth century, English poets such as Thomas Wyatt (1503-1542), Sir Philip Sidney (1554-1586) and William Shakespeare (1564-1616) began to write sonnets, a form which originated in Italy. These fourteen-line poems are seemingly written to a lover but, it might be argued, are actually written for other poets, as a form of literary exhibitionism. The sonnet is one of the longest-lived and most flexible of forms, used and adapted through time by poets as diverse as John Donne (1572-1631), John Milton (1608-1674), Christina Rossetti (1830-1894), the American poet Edna St Vincent Millay (1892-1950), and Tony Harrison (1937-).

Popular ballad literature, 'dialect poetry' and 'chapbook poetry'

Popular traditions of poetry developed alongside these literary forms (as they continue to do today). From about 1450 onwards, poems were not only performed in the streets and at fairs but were also sold as single sheets. (We see a glimpse of this important, fertile tradition when the character Autolycus in Shakespeare's *A Winter's Tale* is shown selling ballads.) The political importance of poetry is often exemplified in this popular tradition. In the 1830s, for example, poets writing in their own dialect language wrote of the so-called 'cotton famine' in Lancashire.

The Metaphysicals and Augustans

The explosion of scientific, geographical, astronomical and medical discoveries in the late sixteenth and early seventeenth centuries equally expanded the world of poetry. The Metaphysical poets such as John Donne (1572-1631) and Andrew Marvell (1621-1678) took full advantage of this new knowledge, drawing on science, medicine, exploration and so on, as well as religion, art and the natural world, when searching for new ways to describe the world or express emotions. These poets are particularly associated with the conceit – a long, developed, often densely knotted, metaphor.

The exuberant, extravagant and playfully intellectual poetry of the Metaphysicals was followed in the eighteenth century by a tradition of poetry which owed a great deal to specific ideas and forms taken from Ancient Greece and Rome such as satires, epigrams, and epistles. Jonathan Swift, Alexander Pope, and John Dryden, often known as the Augustans, all wrote intellectual, difficult poems, many of which require an understanding of the period to be fully appreciated. Like newspaper cartoons or alternative comedy, this poetry references people, politics and scandals of the time. Many female poets engaged in the arguments expressed in these poems. It has not proved to be a popular tradition since.

Revolution!

Politically and poetically the end of the eighteenth century was a period of profound change. While the agricultural and industrial revolution destabilised old ways of working and living (and developed new ones), the American, then French revolutions radically altered the political landscape. Perhaps hard to believe today but these revolutions were reflected in a poetic revolution – enacted by poets from across Europe who themselves engaged in the political changes happening around them. These poets, who became known as the Romantics broke with the classical tradition by claiming that they would write in an ordinary language (see the manifesto of this in the 'Preface to the *Lyrical Ballads*'). They rejected the tyranny of 'reason' as an explanation for everything, choosing instead to celebrate what was natural and free. William Wordsworth (1770-1851), Samuel Taylor Coleridge (1772-1834), Percy Bysshe Shelley (1792-1822) and John Keats(1795-1821) are seen as the leading lights in this movement but women such as Anna Laetitia Barbauld (1743-1825) were also writing at the time.

It's a poetic revolution whose influence has been felt ever since, directly in the poetry which continues in the Romantic tradition, indirectly in the works of those who react against it, and in our notion of the poet and in poetry itself: solace in the pastoral, a belief in the innocence of nature, in 'the child', along with a turn away from the city, trade, and industry.

The poets John Clare (1793-1864), William Blake (1757-1827) and Robert Burns (1759-1796), all of whom were writing at this time, but somewhat outside the mainstream, express ideas related to Romanticism, but in unique ways, often showing the influence of the popular traditions mentioned above.

The Victorians

In the Victorian period – a time we think of as very rigidly structured, with clear ideas about the organisation of society, morals, religious beliefs – we also hear the first rumblings of doubt. In the second half of the nineteenth century, we find poets such as Matthew Arnold (1822-1888), Alfred Lord Tennyson (1809-1892), the American Walt Whitman (1819-1892), W.E. Henley (1849-1903), and Gerard Manley Hopkins (1844-1889) express ideas of doubt about the certainties of Victorian life (for example, religious beliefs) whilst at the same time using forms that break with the regularity and certainty of conventional verse. Edward Lear (1812-1888) and 'Lewis Carroll' (Charles Lutwidge Dodgson, 1832-1898) questioned the status quo in rather different ways. Nonsense poetry, though nominally for children, also deconstructed class, empire, reality, identity and poetry itself. They created a field which the later Surrealists would find useful.

Twentieth- and twenty-first-century developments

Throughout the twentieth and twenty-first centuries, poets have continued the poetry conversation in increasingly diverse forms (and anti-forms). The following overview gives you some glimpses of the different directions it has taken.

The social and political cataclysm that was World War One also affected poetry. The importance of this war in consolidating and pushing further both social doubts and poetic developments can be seen by comparing the early war poetry of someone like Rupert Brooke (1887-1915) and later war poetry by soldier-poets such as Wilfred Owen (1893-1918), Siegfried Sassoon (1886-1967) and Edward Thomas (1878-1917). The French poet Guillaume Apollinaire's (1880-1918) 'calligrammes' ('concrete poetry') anticipate the experiments of Modernism.

Responding to the horrors of the war and the social changes which came in its wake, a group of poets internationally made a theorised break with what had come before. Free verse, Imagism, chinoiserie, performance poetry, fragmentation, stream of consciousness led to Dada poetry, Surrealism and 'sound' poetry. Leading exponents include the British poets T.E. Hulme (1883-1917) and Arthur Waley (translator of Ancient Chinese poetry into free verse, 1889-1966), the Americans Ezra Pound (1885-1972), Amy Lowell (1874-1926) and HD (Hilda Doolittle, 1886-1961) and the French poet Benjamin Péret (1899-1959).

In the interwar period, we see poets all over the world consciously adopting some key ideas of modernity such as Freud's 'unconscious', speed, technology, film, human rights, the city as a place of dynamism but also of class oppression and so on. British poets D.H. Lawrence (1885-1930) and W.H. Auden (1907-1973) and American poets Langston Hughes (1902-1967) and Muriel Rukeyser (1913-1980) illustrate this poetic development.

In San Francisco poets were part of the social, political and cultural movement that stood opposed to the American 'way' whether that was war, the bourgeois norms of family life, formal etiquette and so on. Allen Ginsberg (1926-1997), Gregory Corso (1930-2001) and Lawrence Ferlinghetti (1919-) were amongst the first poets of this movement – the Beat poets. In Britain the 60s poets who were influenced in part by the US Beats but with a distinctive local tone, politics, feel and form were most famously the 'Mersey' poets, Roger McGough (1937-), Adrian Henri (1932-2000) and Brian Patten (1946-).

To one side of these were Ted Hughes (1930-1998) and Sylvia Plath (1932-1963), two poets who absorbed and used many 'traditional' forms and ideas of poetry but both in their own different ways. They created poems which seemed new in the way they dealt with trauma, sex and death. Their own intertwined and tragic lives have created a rich vein of stories, poetry and myth which, one might say, sees 'poetry' embedded in 'celebrity'.

In the second half of the twentieth century poetry continued to develop and diversify, while still echoing the poems of the past. Poetry in Britain has been enriched and invigorated by the impact of poets whose origins are in the Caribbean, for example Linton Kwesi Johnson (1952-), John Agard (1949-), Grace Nichols (1950-), Benjamin Zephaniah (1958-); poets such as John Cooper Clarke (1949-) whose work found a place in rock concerts, stand-up comedy venues and music festivals; poets like Tony Harrison (1937-), Carol Ann Duffy (1955-), Simon Armitage (1963-) and Seamus Heaney (1939-2013) who combine modernist ideas with classical and traditional forms; and by political performance poetry from poets such as Adrian Mitchell (1932-2008) and Liz Lochhead (1947-).

In the first decades of the twenty-first century both 'page poetry' and performance poetry continue to thrive, with poets like Kate Tempest (1985-), Hollie McNish (1984-), Inua Ellams (1984-) and Jacob Sam-La Rose (1976-) challenging the boundaries between the two. The anthology produced each year by the Forward Prize for Poetry is a good way of introducing yourself to interesting and significant poets (for example Sarah Howe (1983-), Don Paterson (1963-), Sinéad Morrissey (1972-), Hannah Lowe (1976), Raymond Antrobus (1986-)), as are features such as the *Guardian's* poem of the week. Digital forms of writing have also created new spaces for poetry: Twitter poets such as Brian Bilston and Instagram poets like Rupi Kaur (1992-) are using this new medium to write poems responding to current social and political issues, while Ian McMillan (1956-) tweets a daily prose poem based on his morning walk.

Poetry is being produced all the time, some of it in ways that seem new (for example as part of rap music, in poetry slams, or spoken word events and clubs) but actually recapitulate venues, situations and 'products' of the previous thousand years. Some Old English poems were a form of spoken word poetry, performed at social events. Street ballads were read aloud so that those who couldn't read could enjoy them. Poems have been put in books to be sold since at least Chaucer's time. Reading poetry silently to oneself was much practised by educated people in the sixteenth and seventeenth centuries and by many since then. What's new may in fact be very old.

The individual poem within the ongoing conversation

What does it mean to read an individual poem in the context of this ongoing poetic narrative? To explore this I'm going to look at the ways in which we might read William Wordsworth's 'Daffodils' (1807), one of the most famous poems in English, a poem which at the time was revolutionary in its language and its sentiment, but which has come to be a central part of the poetic canon.

I wander'd lonely as a cloud
That floats on high o'er vales and hills,
When all at once I saw a crowd,
A host of golden daffodils,
Beside the lake, beneath the trees
Fluttering and dancing in the breeze.

Continuous as the stars that shine
And twinkle on the milky way,
They stretch'd in never-ending line
Along the margin of a bay:
Ten thousand saw I at a glance
Tossing their heads in sprightly dance.

The waves beside them danced, but they
Out-did the sparkling waves in glee:
A poet could not but be gay
In such a jocund company!
I gazed – and gazed – but little thought
What wealth the show to me had brought:

For oft, when on my couch I lie
In vacant or in pensive mood,
They flash upon that inward eye
Which is the bliss of solitude;
And then my heart with pleasure fills
And dances with the daffodils.

It is quite possible to read the poem *anachronistically* (that is, out of time, without thinking about the time in which it was written or its place in a poetic tradition) and enjoy whatever first comes to mind. We might probe that enjoyment and make connections with our own lives and our own reading and see where it takes us. I might, say, remember a wood at a college where my mother taught, how it used to be full of daffodils in spring and that it was a sudden and amazing sight to come across them.

I might play a game which is to find non-stated connections in the poem according to its sound ('prosody') or its imagery where 'connections' can be a result of similarities or contrasts in the 'pictures' given to us by the poet (for example the series of contrasts: 'lonely' versus 'crowd'; 'ten thousand' versus 'I'; 'solitude' versus the 'host' of 'daffodils') to see if this helps me understand the poem's meaning.

But I might also approach it by asking questions about why the poet has written this particular poem in this particular way – that is, to read it *synchronically*, as a product of its time. This would require me to place the poet William Wordsworth in four different contexts: that of his family; his 'milieu'; the artistic, social and political movements of the time; and the traditions of language and poetry.

There isn't time or space to pursue all of these – so I will focus particularly on the artistic, social and political movements of the time and traditions of language and poetry. As you probably know, Wordsworth was indeed part of a movement. We call that movement the 'Romantics' and they took a committed social and political view towards 'nature', the arts and society. In broad terms, whatever the Romantics thought was 'natural' was good, whether that was inspiration, imagination, childhood, people who live in nature ('peasants'), rural folksongs and folk tales and 'freedom'. Freedom might equally mean the freedom to express oneself, the right for one's country to be free from rule by foreign powers, or equal human rights for all. All this was a reaction against some of the ideas and politics of the era that preceded them, that were held by people in power in Europe.

Amongst other things, we might wonder what a poem about walking in the countryside, looking at daffodils and thinking about them afterwards has to do with human rights or revolution. The connection, clear and apparent to the Romantics themselves is 'freedom'. The social and historical point about the daffodils, not expressed directly in the poem, is that they are wild and 'free'. They aren't in a garden or in a pot, in a window box in a city house or flat. They are beside a lake where they dance and they are described as being like a part of the most natural part of the universe we can see (the least touched by human hand): the Milky Way.

There are other synchronic aspects: do we have access to the exact place and time that Wordsworth lived through which we might say, 'triggered' or 'inspired' him? One way into this is through the diary that Wordsworth's sister, Dorothy kept. In it we find an entry for the exact day and place the pair of them (not Wordsworth alone!) went out and saw some daffodils which Dorothy recorded as dancing by the lake. She says they:

> ...tossed and reeled and danced and seemed as if they verily laughed with the wind that blew upon them over the lake, they looked so gay ever glancing ever changing.

What is striking here, of course, is how much William Wordsworth has borrowed from his sister. It raises interesting questions, including how 'original' the poem is (originality being a notion particularly associated with writers from the Romantic period onwards) and what it is that makes Wordsworth's a poem, while his sister's, though poetic, is not. The latter is a question which takes us back to those we first raised at the beginning of the chapter.

Another approach would be to look at the kind of poetic 'conversation' that Wordsworth was having with his literary, social and political contemporaries through his poetry and with the poems which had gone before. Any and every poem sits in and amongst these conversations and contributes to them. Every poem is both a reply and a provocation or an opening gambit.

But there's something missing here: the *diachronic* line – reading the poem in the context of our ongoing narrative of poetry. Where does the form of the poem, its motifs, its rhetoric, its style, its language come from? They can't have all sprung anew for the first time out of the Romantic movement, no matter how revolutionary it was. After all, it's not the first poem in English to rhyme, to use iambs (te-Tum 'feet') and tetrameter (four beats to the line). We might isolate some motifs: wandering out on your own in 'nature' at the time of year when things come into bloom – 'spring'; the idea of nature as inspiring and good; lying on your own in contemplation. Within this, there are many examples of figurative language – metaphor, simile and personification. Again, this is surely not the first poem in English to use such figurative language. We can also think about the form as a whole: a short (one page) expression of attitude and feeling attached (mostly) to a moment in time – or in this case two related moments. What is this form, where does it come from? (It's the lyric form.) All these aspects of a poem we can label as 'traditions' which lie within a poet's intertextual repertoire.

To take some of these: the 'going out in spring' in a poem has a long tradition in European poetry. No matter how revolutionary Wordsworth may have hoped he was being in writing this poem, he has adopted an idea from at least five hundred years before, probably originating in the songs sung by troubadours in France: the *reverdie* (literally the 're-greening') and the *chanson d'aventure* ('adventure-song'). Did he know he was using that old idea? Perhaps. Or perhaps he had just enjoyed poems or songs like that and 'borrowed' it rather as one might borrow some clothes. In using it, he has both included its original connotations and given it new, perhaps more political ones.

And why nature? The way we represent nature in the arts has a long history within the Judeo-Christian tradition stemming from the story of the Garden of Eden in Genesis. Eden is a perfect place that God created but it's a place that is spoiled because first Eve and then Adam were 'disobedient'. God told them not to eat the fruit of the Tree of Knowledge. But they did. Once they had 'knowledge' they had 'shame' of their natural bodies and clothed them. This is described in Christianity as the 'Fall'. Throughout Western culture there is the ongoing idea which suggests that 'nature' expresses some kind of goodness or perfection (before the Fall) and that what 'man' has done (because 'he' is fallen) is spoil it through anything from building cities to our sense of shame in our bodies, sex itself, any kind of 'sin', transgression, evil, badness or even naughtiness in children. Wordsworth's poem, we might say, expresses an aspect of that tradition, as if the persona of the poem has walked into the Garden of Eden and, as a result, finds 'bliss'. The poem, then, 'transforms' this source (the Eden story) into a lakeside scene.

Joining the conversation and taking your thinking further

This chapter offers you a personal story of poetry – both in my sweep through its history and in my reading of 'Daffodils'. Now it's over to you to start your own conversation with poetry – both reading and writing it. Rather than questions I've offered you some suggestions for how you might go about doing this.

Ways of approaching poems

- Cohesion – find the links created by the 'musicality' in a poem (rhythm, repetition, rhyme, alliteration, assonance) and by the patterns of imagery.

- Milieu – every poet and poem came out of a literary, philosophical and aesthetic 'moment' – a conversation between writers, thinkers and commentators. Placing a poet or poem in a milieu 'situates' it, and helps explain why and how it was written.

- Reinterpretation – writing a poem 'back' to a poem, creating a painting or a photo or a comic strip inspired by the poem, filming it, creating a mime or dance inspired by it – are all valid ways of exploring meanings in a poem.

- Poems 'unfold' or 'unroll' – they reveal themselves line by line, creating moods and changes; one way to 'track' these changes is to write a 'response' diary alongside the poem in which you record your spontaneous thoughts, puzzles, feelings and discoveries.

Reading list

Easthope, A. 2002. *Poetry as Discourse*. London: Routledge.

Fenton, J. 2003. *An Introduction to English Poetry*. London: Penguin.

Maxwell, G. 2016. *On Poetry*. Cambridge Mass.: Harvard University Press.

Padel, R. 52. 2004. *52 Ways of Looking at a Poem*. London: Vintage.

SHAKESPEARE AND HISTORICAL CONTEXT

Emma Smith

Looking at any work of literature in its historical context is an obvious readerly strategy. Clearly, the writer and his or her first audiences shared a set of cultural expectations that were historically specific, and we can be guilty of anachronistic thinking if we are not attentive to differences between then and now. On the other hand, the definition of a literary work worthy of our attention might precisely be that it transcends its own historical moment to speak to quite different ages and cultures. A classic, as Italo Calvino put it, 'is a book that has never finished saying what it has to say': a work, by definition, that is not limited to the period that produced it.

In this chapter, I want to add some complexity to the implied relationship between Shakespeare and his original historical context by asking some questions that are applicable when we consider any literary work historically. In particular I want to extend the vocabulary we have available for articulating aspects of this relationship of literature with its historical context. I want to suggest moving away from simple verbs suggesting a passive connection – words such as reflect, mirror, demonstrate, show, map, affirm – towards more argumentative verbs – such as interrogate, contradict, problematise, undermine, complicate, evade, reimagine. This more active vocabulary can help give us a more nuanced sense of the literary text as both a product of its historical situation and, crucially, something that is in certain ways independent of, or at an angle to, that situation.

What follows focuses around a few key reminders:

1. Shakespeare wrote entertainment, not documentary

2. Shakespeare's plays draw on previous literary texts as much as – or even more than – they do on real life

3. Shakespeare's plays are often part of contemporary debates, rather than separate from them

4. The theatre in the early modern period was not primarily realist

5. Shakespeare's plays have developed new, significant meanings in their long afterlife on stage and in criticism.

Shakespeare wrote entertainment, not documentary

The London theatre industry during Shakespeare's career was a highly profitable and popular entertainment business. It's not reductive to remind ourselves that it was this commercial environment that stimulated and supported Shakespeare's creativity. Being able to appeal to an audience is a key element of popular entertainment, and that means providing drama that treads the delicate balance between familiarity and novelty. Too much familiarity produces a play everyone feels they have already seen; too much novelty and it fails to land with its audience. We can see how Shakespeare reuses tropes and situations that have already proved popular: the female character who dresses in male clothing (in *The Two Gentlemen of Verona*, *As You Like It*, *The Merchant of Venice*, *Twelfth Night* and *Cymbeline*), the murder of a king or ruler (in *Richard II*, *Julius Caesar*, *Hamlet*, *Macbeth*), the misfit returning soldier (in *Macbeth*, *Coriolanus*, *Othello*, *Much Ado About Nothing*), or the jealous husband (in *Othello*, *The Merry Wives of Windsor*, *Much Ado About Nothing*, and *The Winter's Tale*). These repetitions and twists on familiar storylines embody that balance between the old and the new that was popular with audiences.

What audiences in the 1590s do not seem to have wanted from their theatre-going was anything approaching documentary. I'll talk more about the non-realist stage below, but for now we can observe that the plays of this period parade their fictional, exotic, or fairytale characteristics. To cross the Thames to the theatre was to go to a faraway place, not to encounter a familiar world. From plots to language, from male actors in female roles to the restricted dimensions of the stage itself, these are plays that revel in their own make-believe. Apart from, perhaps, *The Merry Wives of Windsor*, Shakespeare never sets a play in his own time and place: he is always drawing on the fictionality and distance of elsewhere. It's often said that the purpose of this is to avoid censorship or the problematic charge of political topicality, but Shakespeare's creative habits seem to exceed that possible practical motivation. Instead, we can characterise Shakespearean drama as highly inventive and fictional, even to its first audiences. That's to say, the people who went to the Globe to see Shakespeare's plays may well not have experienced them as having a direct relation to their own contemporary lives. Part of their popular allure may rather have been escapism.

In the early years of the seventeenth century, some playwrights developed a new genre of prose comedies set in contemporary London, often called city comedies. Ben Jonson, Thomas Dekker and Thomas Middleton produced plays bristling with topographical and contemporary references – about London for Londoners, peopled with a cast of merchants and prostitutes and spivs and innocents. They're not exactly documentary, but, like modern soap operas, more obviously organised around a recognisable place and time, with characters who may have seemed familiar to audiences from their own experience. The nearest Shakespeare gets to this popular genre is the gritty civic setting of *Measure for Measure*, but otherwise, it does not seem to have fired his imagination at all.

Shakespeare, then, seems to have little interest in representing his own time and place. Rather he is concerned to indulge his, and his audience's, imaginative appetite for escape from the mundane and everyday. But this itself may return us to historical context in some unexpected ways. We might see that escape is itself part of his own particular historical period. Looking to the historical past, as in his plays on English historical subjects, is often seen to be Shakespeare's, and his culture's, response to an uncertain future. Elizabeth I had no heir and the succession seemed potentially fraught with the political and religious upheavals that had preceded her long reign: looking backwards, rather than forwards, turns out to be a historically specific literary response. There are other examples too. We could see in Shakespeare's repeated representation of small-town or rural settings, in *A Midsummer Night's Dream*, for instance, or *As You Like It*, the city-dweller's nostalgic reminiscence for a rural past (a high proportion of London residents at the end of the sixteenth century had come, like Shakespeare, from provincial or rural communities to find work). So these settings can be understood in their historical context – in that they capture a particular retrospective cast to Elizabethan culture – but that relation to history is more oblique than is sometimes assumed.

Shakespeare's plays draw on previous literary texts as much as – or even more than – they do on real life

If you go to a creative writing course in the twenty-first century you may well be given the advice 'write about what you know'. In contemporary culture, personal experience is seen to give creative writing a valuable authenticity and a power – that's why the memoir is such a prominent genre right now. If you went on that same course in the sixteenth century (OK, they didn't exactly have them then, but bear with me), the advice would be 'write about what you have read'. The educational culture of the late sixteenth century was preoccupied with the learning and reusing of classical or continental literature. The aspiring writer made his or her name through skilfully retelling pre-existing stories, inserting him or herself prominently into a long and illustrious history of previous writers. This method of creativity was commonly referred to as *imitatio*.

We know that Shakespeare follows this cultural pattern, using pre-existing sources for just about all of his plays. Sometimes there is one major source – such as Holinshed's compendium of medieval history known as the *Chronicles*, which fuels *Macbeth* as well as the English history plays. Sometimes Shakespeare weaves together influences from a number of sources. Let's take one example: *King Lear*.

Shakespeare's most immediate source for *King Lear* appears to have been an anonymous play called *King Leir* (*imitatio* doesn't require authors to disguise their borrowings and influences), which had been performed in the early 1590s and printed in 1605, just prior to Shakespeare's work on his own play. In this drama, Leir's wife has died and he wants to marry off his youngest daughter Cordella.

She refuses and has her own choice of husband, the King of Gallia. Mistreated by his other two daughters Gonorill and Ragan, Leir regrets exiling Cordella and is reunited with her. He is reinstated as king by the Gallia army. In addition to this theatrical source, Shakespeare also used Holinshed's *Chronicles*, in which the king tests his daughters in order that the one who loves him most shall inherit his throne. Again, unrest in the kingdom divided between the older daughters is quelled by Cordeilla's husband and the Gallia army, who reinstate Lear to rule for another two years before he is succeeded by Cordeilla. There's also, further back in the gestation of Shakespeare's play, a kind of mythic Cinderella or 'as much as salt' story (in which a father asks how much his daughter loves him and gets a salty answer which he misinterprets: in fact salt, as a preservative, is fundamental to life, and it's therefore hard to think of a higher compliment). The title of the first published edition of *King Lear* in 1608 emphasises this folkloric inheritance: *The True Chronicle History of the Life and Death of King Lear and his Three Daughters*. This extended title sounds more like a fairy tale, whereas our preferred abbreviation, *King Lear*, establishes the play in the realm of singular, masculine tragedy.

There are other sources too – one is an item of contemporary gossip where the suggestive name of one of the key protagonists may well have prompted Shakespeare's memory of these other sources. In 1603 Grace, Lady Wildgosse, attempted to have her father Bryan Annesley certified mad so that she could take over his possessions. Her younger sister, named Cordell, disagreed, and barred the way to her father's house so that no inventory could be taken of his belongings. She appealed to the authorities to protect her father against her older sister, and this aristocratic family dispute, so coincidentally reminiscent of the dynastic complications of ancient Britain, was the cause of much general interest at the time.

From reviewing this material we can see that Shakespeare is heavily dependent on his source material, and that the majority of that material is literary or textual rather than observational. Even the Annesley case is unlikely to be something Shakespeare saw directly: he probably heard about it secondhand. There are some really interesting departures from that material, particularly in the shape of the ending of the play: all the literary and historical sources end with Lear's reinstatement on the throne, which makes Shakespeare's bleak conclusion with the death of Lear and of Cordelia all the more striking. But the main point to notice is that the plot and the characters are already delineated by prior texts. Lear's daughters perhaps have less to tell us about contemporary women, and more to tell us about women's role in stories about male rule. If we look at the fairytale element we can see that it would be unrealistic to expect the play to give us accurate or three-dimensional representations of complex female experience. Gonerill and Regan have no more character, psychological truth, or individual differentiation than the two Ugly Sisters who try to thwart the beautiful young

Cinderella (and, perhaps, Cordelia is similarly cardboardy). Women in traditional fairytales are innocent heroines or monstrous villains, simple as that.

Elsewhere, the genre of Shakespeare's plays makes a real difference to what kinds of material and characters they can discuss. The fact that the bodies of Gertrude, Claudius, Laertes and Hamlet all lie on the stage at the end of *Hamlet* is because that play is a revenge tragedy, a genre generating a high body count. It doesn't tell us anything about levels of, or attitudes towards, violence in early modern England. *Macbeth's* witches are performed for a metropolitan audience that is actually sceptical about whether witchcraft really is the work of the devil: deducing from the play something about what people actually believed would be like future historians concluding from the popularity of *Twilight* that vampire-belief was the dominant religion of young people in twenty-first century Britain. Women dressing as men probably was an occasional phenomenon in early modern London, but probably not with the frequency, or the guaranteed romantic payoff, that this behaviour carries in Shakespeare's comedies. We can recognise that these are generic imperatives rather than reportage, so we need to be careful of reading them too literally. That would be like viewing modern rom-coms, superhero films, and historical blockbusters as documentary accounts of life in the twenty-first century.

Shakespeare's plays are often part of contemporary debates, rather than separate from them

One of the crucial insights of the critical school known as New Historicism is that literature is a part of history. New Historicism, associated with Stephen Greenblatt in the late 1980s and 1990s, attempted to redraw a more dynamic relationship between literature and its historical context. That's to say, there isn't a stable and knowable 'history' against which we can compare literary texts: those texts are part of history, of debates and representations and cultural ideas, not separate from them. For example, one commonly-repeated critical idea about Shakespeare's histories in their historical context is that they work to reinforce the divine right of the Tudor monarchy – the so-called 'Tudor myth'. As evidence for this political ideology, a critic might cite the Elizabethan homilies, pieces of state propaganda appointed for regular reading in every church. One homily against 'disobedience and wilful rebellion' emphasised in particular that even if the monarch were a wicked tyrant it was still wrong for his subjects to disobey him, stressing that the first such rebellion was that of Satan against God, then Adam in the Garden of Eden (neither of which were conspicuous successes for the rebels).

Two objections to this interpretation immediately present themselves. The first is that all such public proclamations – think of the encouragement to eat 5-a-day in our own time, or to take time away from our smartphones – indicate not that everyone is signed up to a particular viewpoint, but quite the opposite. If we all automatically ate lots of vegetables, or all automatically believed that unswerving loyalty to the ruler was right, there would be no need to keep telling us to do it. Rather, the fact of the proclamations gives us evidence that the opposite view has at least some contemporary currency. The same scepticism can be applied to the conduct literature of this period that tells women how to behave (presumably it is evidence that at least some women were not at all convinced that this was how they wanted to behave), or to models of fixed social order like the so-called Chain of Being, that puts everyone in his place from angel to beetle (a rearguard defence of conservative ideas of social order in an age of rapid social mobility). Telling people to do or believe something is usually a sign that they don't.

If prescriptive writing such as official homilies or conduct books cannot be read as a simple description of how people did in fact behave, there's another objection to this model, too. Back to Shakespeare's histories. These plays are parables of regime change, of weak kings defeated by strong challengers, of rebellion and political turmoil. They understand that what's exciting in a history play is conflict and fighting, and that no-one wants to go to see a play all about people talking reasonably about their differences and supporting the legitimate monarch during a stable and peaceful reign. Bor-ing. But they also know that for a significant population, kings on stage are the only kings they know anything about. Most theatre-goers are probably not reading lengthy tomes on English history, or the extensive legal commentary about just rule and succession. Instead they are seeing partial, besieged, fallible royal figures in plays that therefore contribute to shaping their general ideas about monarchy and government. It's not that these ideas exist independently of theatre, it's that plays contribute to their audience's understanding of the issues they represent. To put it simply, weak kings in plays challenge the kind of propaganda represented by the homily against disobedience. History and literature are here interconnected: literature has an effect on history, rather than simply the other way around. If you wanted to give an account of how the early modern period viewed gender roles, the theatre, including Shakespeare's plays, would need to be part of the historical evidence.

The theatre in the early modern period was not primarily realist

In the early nineteenth century, the poet and critic Samuel Taylor Coleridge suggested that an enjoyment of Shakespeare's plays in the theatre demanded the 'willing suspension of disbelief': we had to overlook the unlikely or implausible elements of the plot or characters in order to enter the fiction of the play. It's been a compelling instruction with implications well beyond its original application, but I'm not sure it is particularly helpful when thinking about the playhouse for which Shakespeare wrote. Contrary to Coleridge, this theatre seems to have been designed to prompt disbelief, or, rather, to make spectators conscious that they were in a theatre. This fictional self-consciousness has an effect on the relation between plays and their own contemporary world.

Partly this is a feature of stage architecture. Outdoor theatres like the Globe performed plays in natural light, with the audience surrounding the action. There were none of the conventions that govern our more decorous theatrical culture: no spotlights to focus attention on the stage, no houselights to blank out the audience, no instructions to spectators to keep quiet. Accounts of early modern theatre-going suggest more relaxed audience behaviour and a greater onus on performers to retain the attention of the crowd. This has some interesting consequences. For example, criticism of Shakespeare's tragedies has spent much energy on the soliloquy, the moment when a character speaks alone on stage. For many critics this has been a privileged moment of access into the innermost private thoughts of the character: almost as if we were hardwired into his brain (women hardly ever soliloquise in Shakespeare). But the conditions of the theatre for which Shakespeare wrote make this an implausible reading. It seems more as if soliloquies would be moments of direct address to the audience: highly rhetorical, persuasive, you're-on-my-side-aren't-you claims that are public rather than private. That reading doesn't make soliloquies less important, but it does complicate their sincerity, because it acknowledges that they are designed, by Shakespeare and by their speakers, to prompt an audience reaction.

A non-realist theatre is the physical equivalent of Shakespeare's non-documentary style. If audiences are consistently being reminded that what they are seeing is a play, this may well serve to bracket the fiction off from everyday life. Shakespeare's plays are insistent about the fact that they are plays – from inset plays such as 'Pyramus and Thisbe' in *A Midsummer Night's Dream* or *Hamlet's* 'The Mousetrap', to theatrical imagery such as Macbeth's 'life's a poor player' or Jacques's famous 'All the world's a stage'. When Fabian says in the comedy *Twelfth Night,* 'If this were played upon a stage now, I could condemn it as an improbable fiction', we're all being encouraged to laugh along with the joke. We all know we are in the theatre. This self-consciousness contributes to the separation between Shakespearean fictions and the conventions of everyday life. It creates a distinct space where the rules are different. If men dressed in makeup and women's clothes in Cheapside, they'd probably be arrested: in the theatre they are applauded. Going to the theatre allows audiences to participate in an alternate universe, and while (like all alternative universes such as science fiction) this has some connection to the realities of Elizabethan life, they are complicated and disguised ones.

Shakespeare's plays have developed new, significant meanings in their long afterlife on stage and in criticism

The long and vital afterlife of Shakespearean drama means that the plays have multiple historical contexts, not just a single one relating to their date of composition and first performance. Seeing how different cultural expectations have been mapped onto Shakespeare's plays reveals their interpretative flexibility and their ongoing ability to speak to subsequent historical moments. The racial politics of *Othello*, for instance, have tracked general cultural attitudes. In the

American slave-owning South, the play seemed to corroborate the wicked fantasies of white supremacy, the demonised and oversexualised black male body, and of the impossibility of inter-racial marriage. In apartheid South Africa the play was performed to challenge racial segregation and in particular the racist prohibition on intimacies between different races. The play's ongoing life gives it serial, not single, historical resonances. Whenever a Shakespeare play is revived on stage, it is being made to say something relevant to our own time. These interpretations may have been unavailable to Shakespeare and his own time period: they are the evidence of each play's ongoing vitality and its ability to speak beyond its own moment. If, for example, we make Shakespeare about #MeToo and the ethics of consent, we are supplying a new historical context for his plays. In short, that's what makes Shakespeare worth reading and studying: he is not just talking from a world before enlightenment and toothpaste, but rather to a world which has changed unthinkably since his plays were first performed.

Thinking about Shakespeare in historical context is more difficult and more rewarding than seeing his plays as simple reflections of the culture which produced them. For the reasons I've discussed, it's always more complicated than that. We know this instinctively since we can see how absurd it would be to imagine that the television or film output of our own day simply reflects our everyday lives. As *The Hunger Games* or *The Lego Movie* are to the twenty-first century, so *Hamlet* and *Romeo and Juliet* were to the sixteenth: cultural products shaped by genre, imagination, and audience tastes, as well as by history.

Questions to take your thinking further

- How might you develop the verbs you use to describe the relationship between the historical context and the literary work?
- In what ways does your literary text seem to imagine different possibilities that are not necessarily deliverable in its contemporary world?
- What might early audiences or readers have most enjoyed about the text you're studying?
- Are there other parallels you might try to draw out between Shakespearean drama in its historical context, and modern film or television in ours?

Further reading

British Library. Discovering Literature. https://www.bl.uk/shakespeare

Barry, P. 2007. *Literature in Contexts*. Manchester: Manchester University Press.

Charry, B. 2017. *The Arden Guide to Renaissance Drama: An Introduction with Primary Sources*. London: Bloomsbury Arden Shakespeare.

Ryan, K. 2000. *Shakespeare: Texts and Contexts*. London: Macmillan Ltd.

Smith, E. 2007. *The Cambridge Introduction to Shakespeare*. Cambridge: Cambridge University Press.

THE RISE OF THE NOVEL: NARRATIVES OF VICE AND VIRTUE

Jenny Stevens

Introduction

> Novels are read right and left, above stairs and below, in town houses and in country parsonages, by young countesses and by farmers' daughters, by old lawyers and by young students. (Anthony Trollope, *An Autobiography*, 1883)

This chapter traces how the novel, a form which was not even a distinct genre at the start of the eighteenth century, grew to such ubiquity by the close of the Victorian era. Starting with a chronological overview of the social, economic and technological conditions in which novels were written, produced and received, the chapter then moves on to explore fiction's engagement with controversial questions around 'vice' and 'virtue'. These two extremes might be seen as bookending the novel's own progress: from teetering on the brink of respectability in its earliest days to being a major medium for debating the most urgent moral questions of the day.

While drama and poetry had long engaged with the idea of good and evil, the emergence of the novel in the early eighteenth century offered new ways of contemplating these abidingly fascinating concepts. Moving away from the unreal worlds and characters found in the traditional genres of romance and epic, novels placed readers in familiar situations, framing moral dilemmas that they could easily relate to their own lives. The narrative twists and turns, psychological realism and multiple perspectives made possible by the long fictional form all combined to create an unprecedented degree of verisimilitude. As such, the novel offered a highly personal, vivid readerly experience that could serve to raise moral consciousness, both in relation to the individual and to wider social concerns.

Scholarship and the 'rise' of the novel

A colossal corpus of academic writing has been produced on the history of the novel. However, one study stands out as seminal: Ian Watt's *The Rise of the Novel* (1957). A scholar-pioneer, Watt views fiction through the lens of historical, philosophical and socio-economic contexts, tracing the 'rise' of the novel alongside an emerging middle-class individualist culture, while emphasising its commitment to the 'texture of daily experience'. Inevitably, subsequent theoretical paradigms have challenged Watt's thesis. Nancy Armstrong's *Desire and Domestic Fiction*

(1987), for example, attended to female writers and readers as a corrective to Watt's undeniably masculinist account. More recently, Steven Moore's *The Novel: An Alternative History* (2010) charts the genre's ascendancy from as far back as the ancient Egyptian era. Nonetheless, Watt's survey remains a scholarly touchstone, its influence still discernible in the titles of some undergraduate modules and book chapters such as this one.

Materials, markets and mores

For much of the 1700s, novels were printed in small numbers on hand-presses, an artisanal process which made them prohibitively expensive. Such small-scale production changed radically in the course of the 1800s. Technological advances, such as the steam-powered printing press, enabled reading materials to be mass-produced and the arrival of the railway system (memorably depicted in Charles Dickens's *Dombey and Son*, 1848) ensured that these materials could be distributed speedily over a wide geographic area. Literacy rates rose steadily throughout the eighteenth century, and rapidly in the second half of the nineteenth century, with a concomitant rise in the demand for fiction. The establishment of free public libraries and 'circulating libraries' (which loaned books to paying subscribers), served to meet this demand, while improvements in lighting technology meant that readers could settle down with a novel for increasingly extended periods.

From the mid-to-late eighteenth century onwards, the kind of religious reading the zealous Mrs Pardiggle presses on the poor in Charles Dickens's *Bleak House* (1853) was steadily replaced by fiction, a shift in reading habits that did not meet with unanimous approval. Some feared the move from the religious to the secular, while others regretted what they perceived as a loss of intellectual rigour. Writing in 1859, the essayist William Rathbone Greg likened novels to 'soup or jelly [...] rapidly absorbed into the system' – a worrying substitution for the 'wholesome' food of non-fiction. Detractors like Greg were, though, in the minority by the mid-1800s, partly thanks to the genre's developing engagement with 'serious' subjects. Fiction-readers could learn about Roman history in Edward Bulwer Lytton's *Rienzi* (1835); the law of entail in George Eliot's *Felix Holt* (1866); or geometry in Edwin Abbott Abbot's *Flatland* (1884). Moreover, religious fictions such as *Darkness and Dawn* (1891), written by the prominent Anglican churchman F.W. Farrar, would, by the close of the century, offer novels the ultimate stamp of respectability.

Moralising the city

The city has always been the stuff of novelists, not least because of its dramatic extremes and the moral questions raised by them. This section focuses on representations of urban life in Daniel Defoe's *Moll Flanders* (1722), Jane Austen's *Persuasion* (1818) and Elizabeth Gaskell's *North and South* (1855). To read these three novels is also to track the changing face of the city itself: from Defoe's preindustrial London to Gaskell's mid-Victorian Manchester, transformed by the forces of industrialisation. Austen's depiction of Bath affords us a contrasting vision to the grit of London and Manchester life, as well as underscoring the protean nature of urban identities. Bath's reputation in the early eighteenth century as England's second most 'fashion-forward' city after London, is quite far removed from how it is commonly regarded today: a relatively sedate location, prized primarily for its classical past.

Characteristic of its time, the title-page of *Moll Flanders* gestures towards a 'true life' account of a whore, wife, thief, and *'Penitent'*, though what follows is a work of great fictional sophistication. A retrospective narrator, Moll is both teller and the told, and Defoe leaves it to the reader to decide how far her vice-to-virtue narrative is to be trusted. It is in London that she becomes most mired in criminality and we view urban life through the perspective of someone on whom 'Poverty presses' and whose pickpocketing prowess depends on an intimate knowledge of the capital's topography. Nowhere does her voice seem so subjectively 'real' as when she names the city streets through which she travels:

> I went thro' into *Batholomew Close*, and then turn'd round to another Passage that goes into *Long-lane*, so away into *Charterhouse-Yard* and out into *St. John's-street*, then crossing into *Smithfield*, went down *Chick-lane* and into *Field-lane* to *Holbourn-bridge*.

Describing here her swift departure after stealing a little girl's necklace, she later reflects that she had not harmed the child; rather, she 'had given the Parents a just Reproof for [...] leaving the poor little Lamb to come home by itself'. The deftness of her casuistry matches her deft navigation of the urban landscape.

As Moll's thieving grows more expert and lucrative, so she becomes prone to the vice of avarice. Soon 'ingulph'd in Labyrinths of Trouble' – Defoe's metaphor here mirroring the cityscape itself – she is eventually caught and incarcerated in Newgate prison. London's 'Emblem of Hell' marks the end of her criminal life, the start of her spiritual renewal, and the return to her birthplace. A century or so later, Dickens's Oliver Twist would have the same start in life and move in a similarly subterranean London, though his unworldly virtue made him less credible, and perhaps less sympathetic, than Defoe's flawed urban warrior.

In *Moll*, London's cosmopolitan glamour is glimpsed only through the luxury goods stolen by a criminal underclass. In *Persuasion*, however, Austen represents Bath primarily through its wealthy, privileged society. Focalising the narrative predominantly through the novel's mature, sensitive heroine, Anne Elliot, Austen's razor-sharp gaze rests on the hypocrisy, conceit and vacuity of Bath's elite. If *Northanger Abbey* (1818) maps the city in guidebook detail, *Persuasion* activates the location to delineate character. The 'conceited, silly' Sir Walter, and his snobbish eldest daughter, Elizabeth, choose to 'retrench' to Bath, a city that Anne 'disliked' and whose 'white glare' she dreads.

When Anne's 'very determined [...] disinclination for Bath' is overridden by family pressures, her relationship with the city becomes more complex. While it is here she despairs of her father's fawning over the aristocratic Dalrymples, it is also where she finds the courage to resist his snobbery. She insists on visiting her invalid friend, Mrs Smith, in 'Westgate Buildings', an address Sir Walter considers beyond the social pale. And while the city holds one villainous suitor, the scheming William Walter Elliot, it is also visited by Frederick Wentworth, the man whom, eight years previously, she was persuaded to reject – a decision she comes to regret greatly. Anne's 'undeviating' suitor's renewed proposal takes place in the 'comparatively quiet and retired gravel walk' of outdoor Bath, rather than its intimate indoor spaces, so that while the city is the site for romantic fulfilment, the couple's attachment to it remains questionable.

If *Persuasion* focuses on the failings of the wealthy, Gaskell's *North and South* (1855) examines the 'vices' and 'virtues' of both rich and poor. Before appearing in serial form in Dickens's *Household Words*, the novel took its title from the heroine 'Margaret Hale'. The titular shift to *North and South*, made at the editor's suggestion, signposts the fiction's identity as a 'condition-of-England' novel, a sub-genre that explored the impact of industrialisation on the urban poor, and which included Benjamin Disraeli's *Sybil* (1845), Charles Kingsley's *Alton Locke* (1850) and Dickens's *Hard Times* (1854).

North and South is set in England's industrial capital, Manchester (named Milton-Northern in the novel). Gaskell lived in Manchester, witnessing at first-hand how the city's layout enabled the prosperous to bypass the workers' squalid living quarters. In *North and South,* we see her heroine break through this socio-economic apartheid, maturing in self-knowledge in the process – the industrial novel meets female *Bildungsroman*. Gaskell might have privileged place over personage when finalising her title, but she nonetheless exploits to the full the novel's capacity to portray the complexities of personal experiences, relationships and emotions over a sustained period.

When Margaret's father decides to step down as a Church of England minister, the family move from a hamlet in the south to Manchester. Initially, Margaret is shocked by the city's 'taste and smell of smoke' and the 'bold, fearless faces' of the factory workers; however, she soon becomes invigorated by its 'human interest', much of it centred on John Thornton, a working-class boy who has risen to be one of Milton's chief businessmen. As the novel moves towards a marriage (typical of what Henry James sneeringly termed the 'wind-up' of Victorian fiction), Gaskell reveals some harsh truths about factory conditions through Margaret's friendship with Bessy Higgins, who dies aged 19, 'poisoned by the fluff' that flies off the cotton machines. We also see the human cost of *laissez-faire* economics through the rather less sentimentalised John Boucher, an impoverished strike-breaker, whose desperation drives him to commit suicide in just inches of water. Gaskell's image of the dead man's skin, 'stained by the water in the brook [...] used for dyeing purposes', strikingly fuses industrial process and its consequences.

Yet, if Margaret initially equates 'north and south' with 'vice' and 'virtue', her creator seems ultimately set on deconstructing such binaries. Factory labour is hard, but so too is agricultural work: as Margaret warns Nicholas Higgins, workers in the South are 'out in all weathers', prone to rheumatism and worse. And if Milton's industrial growth has brought evils, it has also, as Margaret's father acknowledges, brought 'something dazzling' in its technological invention and power.

Complicating the villain

Despite postmodernist cautions about responding to fictional characters as 'real people', one of the pleasures of reading a novel is 'getting to know' its inhabitants, the vicarious thrill of walking alongside the 'baddy' proving especially compelling. This section turns its attention to how certain authors sought to destabilise prevailing notions of the villain, harnessing the novel's potential to present psychologically realistic portraits of evil-doers. Focusing on Mary Shelley's *Frankenstein* (1818), Emily Brontë's *Wuthering Heights* (1847) and Charles Dickens's *Great Expectations* (1861), it considers how the perpetrators of criminal acts, often extremely violent, are presented to readers in ways that make them too humanly compelling to be dismissed as innately 'bad'. The brutal misdeeds of Shelley's Creature, Brontë's Heathcliff and Dickens's Magwitch might be recounted in graphic detail, but readers are in turn shown the inhumane treatment that these wrongdoers have themselves endured – and are thereby invited to question how far 'villains' are born or made. Moreover, the storytelling voices employed across these three novels hinder any simple judgement, as readers are obliged to adjudicate between the sometimes contradictory perspectives generated by the authors' manipulation of frame narratives and retrospective viewpoints.

In *Frankenstein*, Shelley demonstrates the capacity of the novel to explore some 'big' questions. Is there an 'essential' self? How is a sense of morality formed? Is a propensity for evil part of the human condition or an aberrance? Labelled retrospectively as a Gothic novel or a prototypical work of science fiction, *Frankenstein* is also a narratological experiment, whereby the indeterminacy created by its layering of three first-person narratives complicates moral judgement. The Creature is one of fiction's most bizarre narrators. An unholy patchwork of materials stolen from the 'dissecting room and the slaughter-house', he also appears to possess a human consciousness that enables him to speak, question and reflect.

How far we consider the Creature a 'villain' largely depends on the degree of 'humanness' we grant him. Like any human, he develops from neonate to speaking subject, capable of feeling emotion and voicing the existential question 'What was I?'

Yet the Creature does not look like most men and his rebarbative appearance means that he is rejected by everyone who encounters him, including his own creator. Enraged by this treatment, he declares 'everlasting war against the species' and learns, like any fictional villain, how to 'work mischief'. As he embarks on a campaign of wanton destruction and murder, the reader is compelled to consider how far the Creature's sentience includes understanding the moral imperatives earthly villains usually attempt to override.

The Creature tells Victor: 'I am malicious because I am miserable', an assertion of nurture over nature that might equally apply to *Wuthering Heights*' Heathcliff, whose ill-treatment in youth by implication underlies his brutal behaviour in adulthood. However, contemporary commentators often located the seeds of Heathcliff's villainy not in his mistreatment by others, but in his inability to curb his own 'passions'. The novelist's sister, Charlotte, for instance, read Heathcliff's trajectory as that of a downright villain, 'never once swerving in his arrow-straight course to perdition' (Preface, 1850 edition).

Heathcliff certainly commits acts that most would deem villainous. His abuse of his wife, Isabella, begins with his hanging her dog until it almost expires, and culminates in his hurling a knife at her; little surprise, then, that she describes him as 'a monster, and not a human being!'. And it is Isabella who recounts in graphic detail how Heathcliff 'kicked and trampled on [Hindley]'. Such brutality extends to Heathcliff's own offspring, the terminally-ill Linton, whose fear of his father knows no bounds. In an intriguing article, entitled 'Is Heathcliff a murderer?' (1996), John Sutherland regards the narrative lacuna of Heathcliff's three-year absence as marking his transition from 'humane stable-lad' to 'gentleman psychopath': his newfound gentility brings with it a newfound cruelty.

Ultimately, the novel resists any finite reading of Heathcliff. He might, as Sutherland argues, have been responsible for Hindley's death; on the other hand, it is his 'natural impulse' to save the infant Hareton, when he is accidentally dropped by his drunken father. His essential humanity might also reside in his unerring love for Cathy – yet even she determines him a 'fierce, pitiless, wolfish man'.

In *Great Expectations*, Magwitch, mistreated in childhood and socially excluded, returns from years abroad a wealthy man and, as such, has much in common with Heathcliff. One significant point of departure, however, is that Magwitch is a felon, and thus as far as some Victorians were concerned, a 'villain'. Sentenced to fourteen years, double that given to the public-school-educated Compeyson, accused along with him, Magwitch is left angry and resentful at the egregious inequity of the judicial decision. His accumulated rage bursts into the novel's first chapter when Pip, the narrative's controlling consciousness, recalls the terror felt by his six-year-old self when confronted by a 'fearful man, all in coarse grey'. Licking his lips at Pip's 'fat cheeks' and threatening to tear out and consume his internal organs, Magwitch seems every bit the villain, albeit one with fairy-tale touches:

the big bad wolf in convict's clothing. But aspects of Pip's account complicate such a reading. He recalls how the escapee 'had been soaked in water, and smothered in mud, and lamed by stones, and cut by flints, and stung by nettles, and torn by briars', the grammatical parallelism positioning him as the victim rather than the perpetrator of physical harm, certain phrases redolent of the crucified Christ. And though Pip is petrified, he nevertheless stays while Magwitch devours the stolen Christmas food, an act of communion that underlines the humanity of both child and criminal.

When Magwitch returns, Pip, now acculturated – however uneasily – to genteel society, has lost his childhood innocence and recoils from his 'second father'. Drawing on Shelley's *Frankenstein* to express his feelings towards his newly-revealed benefactor, Pip casts Magwitch as the 'creature who had made me', assigning to him the villainous impiety of Victor Frankenstein. Here, Dickens's intertextual manoeuvre resists a wholescale whitewashing of the criminal: the motivation behind Pip's 'great expectations' is as much a desire for revenge as it is a desire to repay an act of kindness. And if Pip's eventual acceptance of Magwitch as a man more sinned against than sinning steers readers to respond in kind, his death-bed scene, managed with more than a touch of the author's hallmark sentimentality, nonetheless takes place behind bars.

Redefining the 'pure woman'

In the period covered in this chapter, female 'virtue' was closely aligned with female chastity. This section features novels which all tackle the vexed question of a woman's sexuality in ways that aroused a good deal of debate and controversy at the time of their publication and beyond: Samuel Richardson's *Pamela* (1740), George Eliot's *Adam Bede* (1859), Thomas Hardy's *Tess of the D'Urbervilles* (1891) and George Moore's *Esther Waters* (1894). Read across time, the authors' avowed intentions for composing their novels demonstrate fiction's movement towards ever more radical treatments of socio-sexual issues. Richardson desired to 'promote the cause of religion and virtue'; more than a century later, Eliot committed herself to creating 'real breathing men and women'; and finally, as we move towards the twentieth century, Moore pronounced his determination to 'write as grown-up men and women talk of life's passions'.

The female employee sexually harassed by a male boss is an age-old story. Richardson's *Pamela* takes just such a storyline but follows it to a revolutionary conclusion: the woman's 'virtue' remains intact, the predator reforms, and the maid marries 'her beloved, gracious master'. In common with most fictions of the period, the novel has a subtitle, *Virtue Rewarded*, which guaranteed its original consumers a decorous outcome and a 'respectable' read. The twists and turns involved in the preservation of Pamela's 'virtue' are told entirely through letters, most authored by the heroine herself. Richardson's manipulation of the popular epistolary form and a style which he described as 'writing to the moment', results in a brilliantly authentic interior voice. Readers surely feel 'in the moment' when Pamela recounts:

> I found his Hand in my Bosom, and when my Fright let me know it, I was ready to die; and I sighed, and scream'd, and fainted away. And still he had his Arms about my Neck [...] And all in a cold, clammy Sweat was I.

It was moments such as this which led some readers to question the 'virtue' of Pamela's story. Some denounced Richardson's depictions of Mr B.'s lubricious onslaughts as pornographic, with others regarding Pamela's protracted defence of her virginity as no more than a ploy to raise her social status. Henry Fielding's witty parody *Shamela* (1741), described by one recent scholar as *Pamela's* 'evil twin', reads Richardson's heroine as more devious than devout, more shamming than saintly.

Pamela's eventual happiness is, of course, far from ordinary. Most 'real' women in her situation were left to bear the consequences of 'seduction' or rape, and many nineteenth-century novelists employed fiction to represent their plight. Treating sexual issues at a time when publishers were highly averse to offending what George Bernard Shaw branded 'middle-class morality' was no easy venture. Authors were obliged to develop their own semiotic code: lighted cigars, loosened hair, carriages (especially when bound for London) could all signify the erotic, while seasonal changes could indicate the stages of pregnancy as surely as medical textbooks.

Adam Bede relates the story of Hetty Sorrel who, after bearing a child outside of marriage, is subsequently accused of its murder – a daunting scenario for a novelist devoted to literary realism. Eliot eschews the 'rakish-gentleman-pursuing-innocent-country-maiden' cliché: she presents Hetty as coquettish, patting her 'pound of butter with quite a self-possessed [...] air' and her lover, Squire Arthur Donnithorne, as guilty of some 'egoism', but by no means a 'courtier of Vice'. As a consequence of mutual attraction, the two 'roll to meet each other like two velvet peaches', though the consequences of this meeting are anything but equally shared; extricating himself from the relationship by letter, Donnithorne sets off for Ireland, leaving Hetty pregnant and penniless.

Hetty gives birth without medical assistance, leaving her baby in the woods, where it is later discovered dead – tragic events which are only revealed to the reader shortly before the mother's trial for infanticide. The accused tells the Methodist preacher, Dinah:

> 'I don't know how I felt about the baby. I seemed to hate it – it was like a heavy weight hanging around my neck; and yet its crying went through me, and I daredn't look at its little hands and face.'

From Gaskell's *Ruth* (1853) to Hardy's *Tess of the D'Urbervilles* (1891), the 'vices' of unmarried mothers are, to varying degrees, exculpated by 'natural' maternal feelings. So in giving Hetty equivocal feelings towards her own baby, Eliot presents a rare fictional challenge to normative perceptions of motherly 'instincts'. But Eliot does not go so far as sparing Hetty the harsh punishment typically meted out to transgressive females. Though she is spared execution, her transportation to New South Wales, where she dies a few years later, is hardly a reprieve.

Thirty years on from *Adam Bede*, the heroine of Thomas Hardy's *Tess of the D'Urbervilles* would not offend essentialist notions of womanhood as Hetty had done. While Tess might look at the 'bastard gift of shameless Nature' that results from her rape with 'a gloomy indifference that was almost dislike', the sentimental account of her dying baby's make-shift baptism leaves the reader in no doubt of her maternal virtue. Here, Tess, the fallen Eve, takes on the 'immaculate beauty' of a grieving Madonna – the ultimate icon of the 'pure woman' captured in the novel's subtitle, 'A Pure Woman Faithfully Presented'.

The controversies sparked by Hardy's last-minute addition of this sub-title are frequently discussed in critical writing about the novel. The debates generated by George Moore's novel *Esther Waters* are now far less well-known. Published only three years after *Tess,* this is possibly the most candid 'fallen woman' novel of the Victorian era. Influenced by French literary Naturalism, Moore's novel represents a significant departure from earlier fictionalising of the unmarried mother: the heroine loses her 'virtue' willingly to a working-class man; her 'punishment' extends only as far as having to struggle with bleak socio-economic circumstances; and she survives to see her son grow into healthy manhood. A dedicated controversialist, Moore depicts Esther's first sexual experience with unprecedented candour, clearly signalling the moment of penetration – and the 'awakening in pain' that follows.

In the Preface to *The Picture of Dorian Gray* (1890), Moore's boyhood friend, Oscar Wilde, wrote 'There is no such thing as a moral or an immoral book. Books are well written, or badly written. That is all.' An oft-quoted aphorism, it serves as an apt coda to the first two hundred years of the novel, as well as a rallying cry for fiction to break through the *cordon sanitaire* of Victorian censorship.

Reading the past: present and future

The bestselling Victorian novelist, Mrs Humphry Ward, rated the novel 'the most elastic' of genres and, indeed, those featured here have all proven 'elastic' enough to accommodate the radically different 'moral' outlooks of the twenty-first-century reader. Nowadays, we might read *Pamela* through the lens of the #MeToo movement; be considered 'snowflakes' for regarding Shelley's 'Creature' a victim; or take up the opportunity offered at the 2018 Cheltenham Literature Festival to debate 'Heathcliff vs Darcy: Who's the Bigger Sh*t?' As Frank Kermode observes, successful fictions help us 'make sense of the here and now' (*The Sense of an Ending*, 1967).

Creative artists, as well as readers, continue to breathe new life into centuries-old fictions. The so-called 'classics' are a popular choice for screen adaptations and are frequently reworked in a range of other media; twenty-first-century examples include works as diverse as Paula Rego's lithographs of *Jane Eyre* (2001); Will Self's *Dorian: An Imitation* (2002), a fictional updating of Wilde's *Picture of Dorian Gray*; and, most recently, Martin Crimp's *When We Have Sufficiently Tortured Each Other* (2019), a drama modelled on Richardson's *Pamela*. Changes to how past novels are read in the academy have also brought fresh perspectives. Literary-critical areas such as narratology (the study of narrative technique), have identified what might be considered 'modernist' or 'postmodernist' characteristics in the literary techniques of long-dead authors, their insights militating against a straightforwardly linear chronicling of the 'rise of the novel'.

The powerful cultural and aesthetic influence of fictions past will doubtless be felt for generations to come. Equally likely is that they will be received in transmediated forms, shaped to socio-cultural circumstances yet unknown. With Jane Austen's novels already inhabiting the virtual world of role-play games, who knows what might be around the corner?

Questions to take your thinking further

- The contemporary novelist, Milan Kundera, defines the genre as one which 'searches and poses questions.' How far is this true of the novels featured here or the eighteenth- and nineteenth-century novels you have read?
- If 'novel' is a word linked to newness, why do you think the 'classics' of the eighteenth and nineteenth centuries continue to hold such influence?
- What 'blind spots' might we have when reading novels of the distant past?
- Could any aspect of the novel be considered 'universal'?

Reading list

Altick, R.D. 1957. *The English Common Reader: A Social History of the Mass Reading Public, 1800-1900*. Chicago: University of Chicago Press.

McKeon, M. 1987. *The Origins of the English Novel 1600-1740*. Baltimore: The John Hopkins University Press.

Mullan, J. 2006. *How Novels Work*. Oxford: Oxford University Press.

Richetti, J. ed. 1996. *The Cambridge Companion to the Eighteenth-Century Novel*. Cambridge: Cambridge University Press.

Rodensky, L. ed. 2013. *The Oxford Handbook of the Victorian Novel*. Oxford: Oxford University Press.

Seager, N. 2012. *The Rise of the Novel*. Basingstoke: Palgrave Macmillan.

THE ROMANTICS

Malcolm Hebron

Wordsworth's 'Daffodils', Coleridge's 'The Rime of the Ancient Mariner', Blake's 'The Tyger', Keats's 'Ode on to Autumn', Shelley's 'To a Skylark', Byron's 'We'll go no more a-roving': six poems, still widely read today, all written between 1789 and 1819. Poetry flourished during the late eighteenth and early nineteenth centuries.

Contextualising Romanticism

Romanticism is a term applied to the period c.1780-1830 and refers to literature, art and philosophy across Europe. Although the word 'Romantic' was used in these years, the label 'Romanticism' is retrospective. The term denotes a set of concerns shared by leading figures. Key among these are an insistence on the importance of emotion, and a fascination with the sources of creative expression. Romantic poetry, our focus here, explores subjectivity – the inner world of feelings and imagination.

Romanticism is best understood in two contexts: cultural and political. Culturally, it marked a break from eighteenth-century Neoclassicism. In Neoclassicism, the arts were based on an imitation of the visual art and literature of ancient Greece and Rome. These were held to represent the finest achievements of the human mind, and followed rules of symmetry and harmony, expressing order in the universe. Romanticism was a turn away from this idea of culture. Where Neoclassicism favoured discipline and balance, Romanticism preferred wildness, spontaneity and inspiration, a preference reflected as much in the style as the content; and where Neoclassicism placed reason as the highest human value, Romanticism emphasised the primary importance of the emotions.

Politically, Romanticism belonged to the age of revolutions. Like the American Revolution (1776) and the French Revolution (1789), it represented a liberation from the old order: the individual was exalted above society, and the common man was viewed with a new dignity, capable of the profoundest feelings.

The poetry

It's not the case, of course, that one day all poets were writing witty, formal verse celebrating reason and intellect or describing the sun rising as 'reddening Phoebus lifts his golden fire' and the next they were all about nature, feeling and the ordinary man. The melancholy 'Graveyard School' of poets (Thomas Gray and Edward Young, for example), with their interest in folk tales, the sublime and the uncanny, anticipate many of the features we associate with Romantic poetry. Still, it is true that there was a profound shift in the style, subject matter and intent of poets writing in the mid-eighteenth century and those writing at the end of it. The two extracts below show this difference. Both are about nature but where Alexander Pope writes in rhyming verse about improving nature, William Wordsworth in his conversational blank verse looks to nature to be his guide.

Alexander Pope: Essay on Criticism (published anonymously 1711)
Those RULES of old discover'd, not devis'd,
Are Nature still, but Nature methodis'd;
Nature, like liberty, is but restrain'd
By the same laws which first herself ordain'd.
Hear how learn'd Greece her useful rules indites,
When to repress and when indulge our flights...

William Wordsworth: Lines composed a few miles above Tintern Abbey, On Revisiting the Banks of the Wye during a Tour, July 13, 1798
Therefore am I still
A lover of the meadows and the woods
And mountains; and of all that we behold
From this green earth; of all the mighty world
Of eye, and ear, – both what they half create,
And what perceive; well pleased to recognise
In nature and the language of the sense
The anchor of my purest thoughts, the nurse,
The guide, the guardian of my heart, and soul
Of all my moral being.

For the poets of the first half of the eighteenth century, nature was something to be tamed and controlled. The period saw a vogue for formal landscaped gardens, while wealthy travellers viewed nature from inside their carriages. They would carry with them a 'claude' glass, a small mirror which, when looked through, made the countryside look like a landscape by the Italian painter Claude Lorrain. Poets like Wordsworth and Coleridge, on the other hand, tramped through the mountainous landscapes of the Lake District and the Quantock Hills. Where the Neoclassical poets of the eighteenth century sought beauty, the Romantics sought the sublime – wild and desolate landscapes, storms, raging torrents and cloud-capped mountains. The sense of being completely overwhelmed by the incomprehensible, something much bigger than oneself, replaced the balanced, symmetrical, reasoned beauty of the Neoclassicists.

A wild landscape, untouched by man, was seen as aesthetically more pleasing, as a moral guide and a source of spiritual renewal. Coleridge hails Nature (with a capital N) as 'Great universal teacher' ('Frost at Midnight'), while Wordsworth urges 'Let nature be your teacher' ('The Tables Turned'). Even an urban poet like Blake turned to an image of the countryside as a symbol of freedom, innocence and natural religion, contrasting it with constraints – walls, locks, rules and laws – imposed by man. This Romantic view of nature not only placed it above civilisation (seen as alienating and corrupting) but even above traditional religion – a provocative and controversial belief, embraced by the atheist Percy Bysshe Shelley.

If untamed nature was venerated because it was uncivilised, so too was childhood. Before the mid-eighteenth century, children were seen as being in a state of 'original sin'. Only through religious instruction and the civilising influence of society could they be 'saved'. As with so much during this period, the late eighteenth-century turned these beliefs on their head: childhood became associated with innocence, freedom, imagination, spontaneity – a natural state before children were constrained and corrupted by society. In the short poem 'My Heart Leaps Up When I Behold', Wordsworth declares 'The Child is Father of the Man' – a tricky paradox to grasp but one which gets to the heart of the late eighteenth/early nineteenth-century belief that adults have much to learn from children.

The six writers of the poems mentioned in the introductory paragraph dominate the Romantic period. Often categorised into two generations, the first is represented by William Blake, William Wordsworth and Samuel Taylor Coleridge; the second by John Keats, Percy Bysshe Shelley and Lord Byron. They were by no means the only poets writing in this period. These six poets give you a sense of what the ideas explored above looked like in practice and offer you some starting points for your own explorations.

First generation

William Blake (1757-1827)

William Blake was not well known as a poet during his lifetime. He earned his living as an engraver, illustrating his own poems with hand-coloured engravings, the images becoming part of the meaning, in dialogue with the poem. A visionary and mystic who lived all his life in or near London, Blake stands apart from the mainstream, including the other Romantic poets. What he shares with them, however, is a fierce opposition to the corruption of contemporary society, a rejection of conventional values and morals and a belief in imagination.

Blake's *Songs of Innocence* (1789) presents humanity in its pure state, open to the joys of life, while 'Songs of Experience', published five years later in *Songs of Innocence and Experience*, marks the damaging impact of a society that stifled the imagination and corrupted the soul. Written in a verse form which recalls both children's nursery rhymes and well-known hymns, poems such as 'London', 'The Garden of Love' and 'The Human Abstract' expose the hypocrisy of society and organised religion, which represses and corrupts man's innocence. Although a fervent supporter of the French Revolution (long after the poets William Wordsworth and Samuel Taylor Coleridge had lost their revolutionary idealism), Blake's poems illustrate more than a call for political change. They exemplify the need for a revolution in thinking and feeling, and a fresh appraisal of the true source of fulfilment in human life.

On one level, the language of the *Songs* is simple and child-like. However, it is also heavily symbolic. While the symbolism might draw on shared meanings (the lamb as a symbol of Christ), it might also be highly personal (as in the rose in 'The Sick Rose'). In other writings, Blake goes further into this highly personal language. *The Marriage of Heaven and Hell* (c.1790-3) is a torrent of utterances conveying powerful and sometimes shocking content: 'Sooner strangle an infant in its cradle than nurse unacted desires' ('Proverbs of Hell'). Blake's longer works, like *Vision of the Daughters of Albion*, continue the theme of revolt, expressed through an obscure private mythology. They represent an extreme of Romantic subjectivity, loaded with strong feeling but deeply, even inaccessibly, private.

William Wordsworth (1770-1850)

> Bliss was it in that dawn to be alive,
> But to be young was very heaven!

So Wordsworth, writing in 1805, captured the heady radicalism of being in France during the French Revolution. It was this sort of sentiment which inspired his early poetry, particularly *Lyrical Ballads* (1798). In this collection, written with his friend Samuel Taylor Coleridge, he sought to shake up the poetry world.

Wordsworth explained his and Coleridge's beliefs in the 'Preface' to the second edition in 1800:

> Low and rustic life was generally chosen, because in that condition the essential passions of the heart find a better soil in which they can attain their maturity.

If 'low and rustic life' is the ideal subject for poetry, so too is 'the real language of men in a state of vivid sensation' – a rejection of the artificial trappings of the eighteenth-century's belief in a special poetic diction. Wordsworth explained that their aim was to write poetry using ordinary language:

> The principal object, then, proposed in these *Poems* was to choose incidents and situations from common life, and to relate or describe them, throughout, as far as was possible in a selection of language really used by men, and, at the same time, to throw over them a certain colouring of imagination, whereby ordinary things should be presented to the mind in an unusual aspect.

This was a revolutionary moment in poetry. For the Augustan poet of the previous century, the task of the poet was to contemplate some general truth – that all beauty fades, for example – and then convey it in eloquent language to the common, educated reader. Feelings will accompany the thought, but they are not the starting point. In Wordsworth's conception, the feeling *is* the starting point. In *Lyrical Ballads* we see the beginnings of what many of us assume a poem to be – the intimate communication of a special private experience.

Wordsworth's masterpiece is perhaps *The Prelude,* a long autobiographical poem in blank verse. His preoccupation with the ways in which our personal experiences shape us is brought to life in the intense descriptions of experiences such as stealing a boat and skating at night – experiences the poet called 'spots of time'. Begun in 1798 and revised throughout his life, *The Prelude* was finally published in 1850. The version of the poem you are most likely to read today is the one from 1805.

Samuel Taylor Coleridge (1772-1834)

Where Wordsworth draws on scenes from common life, Coleridge's inspiration lies in the ballad tradition, travellers' tales, and above all the intensifying, strange and often nightmarish world of the imagination. His best known works catch imagination on the wing: in the conversational 'Frost at Midnight', in the music and fantastical imagery of 'Kubla Khan', which explores creativity as a beguiling, dangerous force; in the supernatural world of 'Christabel', and in the terrifying sublimity of 'The Rime of the Ancient Mariner', Coleridge's only contribution to the *Lyrical Ballads*.

Coleridge's writings are often incomplete – 'Kubla Khan' was famously interrupted by 'the person from Porlock'. That impression of an inner chaos scarcely held at bay is part of the depth and energy that Coleridge's fragmented, deeply lived work conveys.

As well as writing poetry, Coleridge wrote literary criticism, lectured and studied the Romantic ideas of German philosophers. In his prose work *Biographia Literaria* (1817) he works out a theory of the poetic imagination. This, he holds, goes beyond 'Fancy' (or imagination) as was commonly understood, and becomes an echo of the divine creation itself. As might be expected from someone famous for his incomplete poems, the book does not really present a complete or coherent theory.

The second generation

In the 1810s a new generation of poets brought fresh energy to English writing. With the ending of the Napoleonic wars at the battle of Waterloo (1815), the powers across Europe, determined to prevent any further popular movements, implemented a series of repressive measures, including restrictions on free speech. It was partly opposition to this reactionary politics that inspired the second generation of Romantic poets who, though not even born at the time of the French Revolution, embraced its early idealism. Lord Byron, Percy Bysshe Shelley and John Keats also all died young, creating the image of the Romantic artist as a tragic figure, a fount of creativity in opposition to a heartless world.

George Gordon, Lord Byron (1788-1824)

Byron inherited an aristocratic title, and lived the life of a libertine nobleman, seeking adventure and sensation. Unlike the other Romantics, who were fairly obscure in their own lifetime, Byron became the centre of a personality cult. He burst onto the literary scene with *Childe Harold's Pilgrimage* (1812), a verse narrative describing the adventures of a libertine clearly based on himself. The book was a bestseller: five hundred copies were sold in just three days, 4500 in six months. 'I awoke one morning and found myself famous,' Byron said. His celebrity took a different turn when, in 1814, he was suspected of incest with his half-sister. Ostracised from society, in 1816 he left England permanently, first staying with the Shelleys in their house on the banks of Lake Geneva, then moving to Italy. Where the first generation Romantics looked to English countryside and German thinking for their inspiration, the later poets were drawn to southern Europe and the cultures of ancient Greece and Rome.

Byron wrote many shorter lyrics, but his most famous work is *Don Juan* (1819-24) another long verse narrative, about the legendary womaniser who is also the subject of *Don Giovanni*, Mozart's opera of 1787. *Don Juan* is interesting for the speaker's voice – ironic, witty, piercing hypocrisy and false sentiment in brilliant rhyming verse. Byron in some ways embodied perfectly the image of the Romantic poet – dashing, reckless, living for the moment, and seemingly capable of spontaneous, effortless genius. He also represented the poet as politically engaged, a reputation sealed when he died assisting the Greeks in their struggle for liberty against the Turks. Yet, in other ways, Byron is an uncomfortable fit with Romanticism. He did not believe that feeling comes before reason, and in his satirical wit he belongs in the eighteenth-century tradition of Pope. Where Wordsworth and Coleridge were fascinated by subjectivity and the authentic self, Byron's poetry deliberately strikes a series of brilliant poses. It is interesting to compare the self-presentation of his verse with the personal voice that comes across in his sparkling letters.

Percy Bysshe Shelley (1792-1822)

Of all the Romantic poets, Shelley most resists a short summary. Like Byron, he was an aristocrat and pursued his urges with complete indifference to society's opinion. His own views seem strikingly modern: he was an atheist, a pacifist, and believed in vegetarianism, free love and sexual equality. His complicated domestic life brought scandal and personal tragedy. After early years as a political activist, in 1814 he retreated to Geneva with Mary Wollstonecraft Godwin, later Mary Shelley, author of *Frankenstein* (1818). Mary's father, William Godwin, was a radical thinker who influenced Shelley in his belief that man, and society, were capable of progress, and even perfectible. His political engagement in writing is illustrated by 'The Masque of Anarchy', written in the wake of the Peterloo Massacre of 1819, in which leading politicians are excoriated: 'I met Murder on the way – / He had a face like Castlereagh'.[1]

Shelley was a philosophical poet, with an excellent knowledge of Greek. He was a Platonist, believing in the Greek philosopher Plato's theory that true reality lies beyond the visible world in the realm of ideas. His imagination was charged by pagan mythology, modern science and political theory. The poetic result is a remarkable variety of forms, styles and rich, elaborate imagery, thick with allusions and metaphoric constructions. He is most read today for his lyrics, but was also the author of Gothic novels, verse epistles, philosophical poems, and poetic dramas. He also wrote an impassioned *Defence of Poetry* (1821), holding that poetry can develop the finer feelings and direct them to moral ends for the wider good, famously claiming that, 'Poets are the unacknowledged legislators of the World.' In his time, his work was admired by a small circle but had no impact on wider society. His death by drowning made Shelley the epitome of the tragic Romantic hero, the intense and short-lived flame.

John Keats (1795-1821)

Unlike Byron and Shelley, Keats was born without privileges. He left school at fifteen, was apprenticed to an apothecary and qualified as an apothecary surgeon, but chose to devote himself to poetry. He died aged 24 from tuberculosis, the illness which had already killed his mother and brother. Keats's poetry is full of forebodings of death and a sense of the ephemerality of life.

Like the other second generation Romantics, Keats was involved with radical politics, joining the circle in London, based around Leigh Hunt, atheist and editor of the radical newspaper *The Examiner*. But his poetry does not address politics directly. Instead it expresses the encounter of a profoundly sensitive imagination with beauty – the beauties of art, nature, and the stories drawn from antiquity and medieval chivalry. Keats is the most sensuous of the Romantic poets. 'Season of mists and mellow fruitfulness', the first line of 'To Autumn', takes in not just the sight of mist and the feel of ripening fruit, but the musical pleasures of the language itself, in its rich alliteration and cadences. The effect can be magical, but also cloying, and his poetry is at its best when this acutely developed sensitivity is harnessed to a line of thought and disciplined by a demanding verse form, as it is in the *Odes*, written in a burst of creativity in 1819. Next to his poetry, Keats's letters are deeply revealing of his processes and preoccupations, and his capacity for deep human attachments.

---

[1] Viscount Castlereagh, leader of the Tories in the Commons, was a spokesman for the harsh measures of political repression that followed the Peterloo massacre. (John Mullan, *The Guardian*, 2013)

Long influence

The Romantics were more than poets: they revolutionised the notion of poetry itself. From being a voice speaking of universal themes to a general reader, a poem became a vehicle for self-expression. The writer becomes a distinct individual, conveying personal thoughts and experiences directly to an individual reader. Where an earlier poet Milton writes, like a prophet, of man's relationship to God, Wordsworth whispers of the loss of a mysterious 'Lucy' and Keats shares an individual's rapturous contemplation of a Grecian urn. They speak not in an artificial specialised language of poetry, but in something close to the language of speech (or, very often, a mixture of the two). We read today more to be moved by a shared experience than to be enlightened by a moral message – indeed it is interesting that while exams tell us to write about a poem's 'effects on the reader', they do not require any appreciation of a text's moral or philosophical purpose. That, too, is the legacy of the Romantics.

Poetry since the Romantics has characteristically been intimate (although, of course, some poets have reacted against this), and the personality of the poet an essential part of our perception of the art. The cult of personality – illustrated by the second generation Romantics in particular – is alive and well in modern culture: Jim Morrison, Tupac, Kurt Cobain, Ian Curtis, and Amy Winehouse are modern examples of the figure of the Romantic hero, a creative life touched by personal problems and ending far too early. The Romantic cult of personality is also problematic, putting the life before the work: it was resisted by the poet and critic T.S. Eliot and the Modernists, though today, in the age of poetry slams and readings which can be immediately shared on the internet, it is undoubtedly an important aspect of the literary scene. The contemporary attachment to subjectivity – 'I want to find the real me' – derives from Romanticism, positively when it stresses the rights and dignity of the individual, but negatively – one might argue – when it encourages self-indulgence, narcissism and irresponsibility. The relationship between rights and duties, the individual and society, remains fraught with ambiguity.

Romanticism's fascination with the imagination remains a live presence in our thinking today. It lies behind our general belief in the benefits of creativity, though a closer look at the Romantics might suggest that creativity can be fierce and destructive as well as healing and enriching. The Romantic theme of nature, and critique of materialism, speaks directly to today's world, facing the challenge of climate change and the rapid diminution of biodiversity on earth. In this context, the works of the Romantics can seem strikingly prescient.

Questions to take your thinking further

- How useful are the ideas associated with the 'Romantic' movement in helping us to appreciate the poets from this period?
- Can the context of the time help us to understand how six major poets emerged during such a short period (about twenty years)?
- Is there anything to be said for Shelley's assertion that 'poets are the unacknowledged legislators of the world'?
- What influences of Romanticism can you see in today's culture? As well as literature, think of film, television, music, advertising, and art.

Reading list

Blanning, T. 2010. *The Romantic Revolution*. London: Weidenfeld and Nicolson.

Butler, M. 1985. *Romantics, Rebels and Reactionaries: English Literature and its Background*. Oxford: Oxford University Press.

Chandler, J., ed. 2008. *The Cambridge Companion to British Romantic Poetry*. Cambridge: Cambridge University Press.

Ferber, M. 2012. *The Cambridge Introduction to British Romantic Poetry*. Cambridge: Cambridge University Press.

Wu, D., ed. 1994. *Romanticism: An Anthology*. Oxford: Blackwell.

MODERNISM

Stephen Donovan

This chapter provides an overview of Modernism, a movement lasting from around 1890 to 1945 whose influence on all forms of cultural production has been pervasive and enduring. It offers a definition of Modernism in literature, an account of its historical origins, and an explanation for why Modernist writing differs so spectacularly from its nineteenth-century predecessors. Two short case studies consider how Modernist writers responded to the impact of World War One and new philosophical and scientific ideas. The chapter concludes with a consideration of how the scope of Modernism has been re-evaluated in recent years, and suggests examples for further reading on the critical approaches and resources for research that are now driving Modernist studies.

Definition

Modernism is largely a retrospective label. In 1927, Robert Graves and Laura Riding published *A Survey of Modernist Poetry* in which they discussed recent work by T.S. Eliot, Ezra Pound, Hilda Doolittle ('H.D.'), e.e. cummings, and other contemporary poets writing in English. Yet the term was used only rarely during these years. In their own lifetimes, Modernist writers were more likely to identify with a 'little' magazine, a literary manifesto, a publishing house, or one of the period's ephemeral sub-groupings, such as Wyndham Lewis's Vorticism or Amy Lowell's Imagism. Even so, they were united in seeing themselves as part of a broader movement in the arts that was committed to making a radical break with mainstream culture. 'I am *modern*,' insisted Joseph Conrad in 1902, 'and I would rather recall Wagner the musician and Rodin the sculptor [...] and Whistler the painter [...]. They too had to suffer for being 'new.''

By their very nature, avant-garde and experimental writers have always considered themselves subversive, radical, and countercultural. But Modernist writers were unique, both in the kind of 'new' which they advocated and in its historical impact. Modernist works in any medium are also surprisingly easy to identify when set alongside their late-nineteenth-century equivalents.

Take the fine arts, for example. Pierre-Auguste Cot's *La Tempête* (1880) is an oil painting of two classical nymphs sheltering under a cloak, while Sybil Andrews's *The Gale* (c.1930) is a woodcut cartoon of two men leaning into umbrellas against parallel lines of swirling raindrops. Both images have the roughly same subject-matter, but where Cot has portrayed the nymphs with near-photographic realism, Andrews has created an abstract geometric pattern of interconnected bodies, umbrellas, and clouds.

Pierre-Auguste Cot: La *Tempête* (1880)

Sybil Andrews: *The Gale* (c.1930)

Or sculpture. Frederick Leighton's *Athlete Wrestling with a Python* (1877) and Umberto Boccioni's *Forme uniche della continuà nello spazio* (*Unique Forms of Continuity in Space*) (1913) both depict muscular male figures in dynamic movement. Yet where Leighton has rendered his athlete with such precise detail that it might almost be a cast of the model's own body, Boccioni's footballer, with his strangely flowing metallic lines, looks rather like a 3D rendering of a blurry film still. And where Leighton's title is plainly descriptive, Boccioni's sounds like a caption from a book on astrophysics.

Frederick Leighton's *Athlete Wrestling with a Python* (1877)

Umberto Boccioni's *Forme uniche della continuà nello spazio* (*Unique Forms of Continuity in Space*) (1913)

Or architecture. A suburban house from nineteenth-century Britain is typically made of red brick, with wood-framed windows centred around a front door, and capped by a roof in slate or tile. Its traditional style stands in stark contrast to a high Modernist building such as the Villa Savoye (1928-31) by French-Swiss architect Le Corbusier. Barely recognisable as a house, this 'machine for living' – as its designer called it – is a severe, near-symmetrical box in gleaming white concrete, its second-floor living area held up by thin stilts and illuminated by rows of steel-framed windows.

A nineteenth-century house

Le Corbusier: Villa Savoye (1928-31)

Or this chapter's focus, literature. Elizabeth Barrett Browning's 'My Heart and I' (1862), a lament by a bereaved lover, begins as follows:

> Enough! we're tired, my heart and I.
> We sit beside the headstone thus,
> And wish that name were carved for us.
> The moss reprints more tenderly
> The hard types of the mason's knife,
> As heaven's sweet life renews earth's life
> With which we're tired, my heart and I.

T.S. Eliot's 'The Love Song of J. Alfred Prufrock' (1915), also a lament by a solitary lover, opens with an Italian epigraph from Dante before proceeding:

> Let us go then, you and I,
> When the evening is spread out against the sky
> Like a patient etherized upon a table;
> Let us go, through certain half-deserted streets,
> The muttering retreats
> Of restless nights in one-night cheap hotels
> And sawdust restaurants with oyster-shells:
> Streets that follow like a tedious argument
> Of insidious intent
> To lead you to an overwhelming question...
> Oh, do not ask, 'What is it?'
> Let us go and make our visit.

Both poems are melancholic in tone, both are introspective, and both offer a glimpse of painful and deeply felt emotions. Yet where 'My Heart and I' is relatively straightforward in its meaning, 'Prufrock' is frustratingly obscure. How on earth can an evening be like an anaesthetised hospital patient? In what way do streets resemble tedious arguments? With its cryptic ellipses ('...') and unexplained 'What is it?', this is a poem that deliberately resists easy explanation or paraphrase.

And the contrast is reinforced by their versification. The coherence of 'My Heart and I' is matched by the regularity of its seven-line iambic pentameter (the ten 'feet' of da-DUM stresses), which identifies the poem as a variant of an older verse form known as *rhyme royal*. The ambiguity and difficulty of 'Prufrock' are likewise matched by its verse form, which is neither free (the poem is mostly rhymed) nor fixed (each line has a different metre). Eliot instead draws on a range of poetic modes and styles, making for a more disjunctive and demanding experience for the reader.

Before and after. In each pairing the difference between Modernism and its predecessors is clear enough. But what exactly is that difference?

In a famous lecture titled 'Mr. Bennett and Mrs Brown' (1924), Virginia Woolf answered this question by imagining how two kinds of novelists might describe an ordinary railway passenger. A realist writer like Arnold Bennett, she explained, would provide a vast amount of meticulously observed data – those stable material facts on which narrative realism depends – so as to let his readers 'see' the hypothetical Mrs Brown, as if she existed in the real world. And yet, Woolf argued, such a portrait would not merely be incomplete, it would fail utterly to convey the extraordinary richness of another person's mind. Woolf did not pretend to have the formula for a more truthful kind of representation, but she insisted that now was a time for ceaseless experimenting. In the present 'season of failures and fragments', she predicted, 'Georgians' (her term for what we would call Modernist writers) would need to continue 'smashing' all the worn-out conventions of literary realism.

What makes Modernism so unmistakeably different from its predecessors, then, is *form*. More precisely, a special relationship to form. Modernists were not calling for a new style of painting, a new model for poetry, or a new principle of sculpture, as previous avant-gardes had done. Nor were they suggesting that anything was now admissible as art, or that an artist could have only solipsistic knowledge of his or her private reality. On the contrary, they often disagreed violently over formal issues which today seem inconsequential.

For Modernists, it went far deeper: innovating in form was the primary duty of the artist or writer. This task was more important than finding original subject matter or conveying a political perspective. It was more important even than any particular set of artistic principles, such as the 'scientific' or 'naturalist' realism of writers like Arnold Bennett and Frank Norris, which aimed to show how the material realities of the world determined the lives of ordinary people.

Modernism had an infinitely grander ambition. It would find a representational form capable of presenting the world as we actually experience it. Look again at our examples. Andrews's woodcut is less an image of rain, than an idea of what rain is like. Boccioni's sculpture replicates not the human physique, but the perception of movement in a solid body. Le Corbusier's villa is not a space-efficient home, but a reimagining of what a house should be. And Eliot's poem is not a lonely man's speech put into verse, but a simulation of someone thinking in and through language.

In each case, the form is predominant, impossible to ignore. Precisely because it is so radically new, the form of Modernist works cannot be separated from their subject. These are texts, images, and objects whose ultimate concern is the way we see, touch, think, and speak about the world. Like scientists trying to find an underlying code or organising structure of reality, Modernists pursued this preoccupation with form into ever-greater extremes of abstraction: the white-on-white shape paintings of Ben Nicholson; the blockish reclining sculptures of Henry Moore; the multilingual, crossword-like 'night language' of James Joyce's *Finnegans Wake* (1939); and the unpunctuated, repetitious syntax of Gertrude Stein's *Patriarchal Poetry* (1927):

> Next to vast which is why do I be behind the chair because of a chimney fire and higher why do I beside belie what is it when is it which is it well all to be tell all to be well all to be never do do the difference between effort and be in be in within be mine be in be within be within in.

Modernists were convinced that there existed an undiscovered formal solution – a new vocabulary, a new syntax, a new perspective, a new temporal and spatial framework – to the seemingly insuperable challenge of conveying reality. Modernism, we might say, describes the collective efforts of artists across a range of media to use innovations in form as a way to represent, with an unprecedented degree of fidelity, the physical and mental complexity of human experience.

Origins

Where did this impulse come from? What prompted Modernist writers, artists, musicians, and thinkers to experiment so radically with form?

The clue is in the timing. During these decades, the social, technological, and, above all, economic conditions of life, particularly in cities in Europe and the United States, underwent a series of revolutionary transformations. Sometimes called modernisation, this shift involved an intensification of capitalist development, whose effects were especially pronounced in the area of cultural production. The years around 1900 saw the emergence of a mass leisure industry, including new media such as cinema and radio, and the rapid proliferation of advertisements in an increasingly bold visual and linguistic idiom.

The impact was most spectacular in the field of publishing, particular newspapers and magazines. Not only did serial publications grow exponentially in number and circulation, they vastly expanded the scope of their coverage and, in the process, changed their style and format beyond recognition. When, in 1895, Frank Munsey reduced the price of *Munsey's Magazine* to fifteen cents, below its printing cost, and used advertising revenue to make up the shortfall, he unleashed an economic model for truly mass cultural production which eventually led to the 'free' content of our own digital era.

Literary modernism began in the magazines, Robert Scholes has declared, and the claim is true in two senses. Most obviously, Modernist writers first published many of the works for which they are now remembered in 'little' magazines: *The English Review*, *The Dial*, *The New Age*, *The Egoist*, *The Blue Review*, *transition*, and dozens like them. Wyndham Lewis included his drama *Enemy of the Stars* in his own short-lived magazine *BLAST* in June 1914; Langston Hughes submitted his first poem, 'The Negro Speaks of Rivers', to *The Crisis* in June 1921; and James Joyce's novel *Ulysses* (1922) was serialised monthly in the *Little Review* from March 1918 until December 1920, when it was suppressed as obscene by the U.S. Post Office. Modernism was also made possible by the manifestoes, editorial work, reviewing, and essay writing of key magazine editors such as Harriet Monroe (*Poetry*), Hilda Doolittle (*Close Up*), Marianne Moore (*Others*), and Jane Heap and Margaret Anderson (*Little Review*).

But Modernism also emerged as a response to the legions of popular and middlebrow magazines of this period, which continually needed new literary material, especially short fiction. The handsome rates of payment and special prizes offered by *Tit-Bits*, a penny magazine of snippets, jokes, and advice, elicited submissions from plenty of fledgling writers, including Woolf, Conrad, and Joyce. Joyce made his literary debut with 'The Sisters' in a journal for pig farmers, the *Irish Homestead*, in August 1904; Katherine Mansfield made hers with 'Vignettes' in an Australian literary magazine, *The Native Companion*, in October 1907; and D.H. Lawrence's first publication, 'A Prelude', won a short-story competition held by the *Nottingham Guardian* in December 1907.

For many years, critics were in broad agreement that Modernist writers had been firmly hostile to mass culture, and dealt with popular periodicals only from economic necessity. The reality is more complex. Early-twentieth-century commercial magazines could be highly conventional and conformist, turning the plots, narratives, style, and language of literary works into generic commodities. At the same time, they also embodied the energy, diversity, and innovativeness of modern life, and they spoke to their readers in brash and effective new voices. Modernist writers were experimenting with form in order to break through the commodification of literature and language, in accordance with Ezra Pound's famous instruction to 'MAKE IT NEW'. Yet much of their inspiration and source material was drawn from precisely those mass cultural publications.

More than just opposites, Modernism and mass culture thus existed in a dialectical relationship, a creative two-way street. Indeed, there is a curious parallel between the commodifying logic of the marketplace and the way that the formal experiments of Modernist writers began to resolve themselves, almost like brands, into what we now instantly recognise as a 'Hemingwayesque', 'Conradian', 'Eliotic', or 'Steinian' style.

New perspectives

First published in *Rhythm* magazine in September 1912, Katherine Mansfield's 'How Pearl Button Was Kidnapped' relates the day-long adventure of a young Pakeha (white New Zealander) girl who falls in with two Maori women. She follows them, first to their home and then to the seaside, where uniformed police officers suddenly arrive to take her away.

Barely three pages long, the story has a deceptively simple style and is narrated in a third-person voice which overlaps intermittently with Pearl's own perspective, as here in its opening and closing lines:

> Pearl Button swung on the little gate in front of the House of Boxes. It was the early afternoon of a sunshiny day with little winds playing hide-and-seek in it. They blew Pearl Button's pinafore frill into her mouth and they blew the street dust all over the House of Boxes. Pearl watched it – like a cloud – like when mother peppered her fish and the top of the pepper-pot came off.
>
> [...]
>
> Suddenly the girl gave a frightful scream. The woman raised herself and Pearl slipped down on the sand and looked towards the land. Little men in blue coats – little blue men came running, running towards her with shouts and whistlings – a crowd of little blue men to carry her back to the House of Boxes.

The fragmentary story ends, as it has begun, with ambiguity and uncertainty for the reader. Has Pearl really been kidnapped, as the title suggests? Why is her home called the House of Boxes? Is Pearl Button even her real name?

Colour is strikingly prominent in this story, whose style is in other regards extremely spare. A few years earlier, the Fauvist group of artists, including André Derain and Henri Matisse, had begun experimenting with landscapes and portraits made up of solid blocks of intense colours. And Mansfield, too, repeatedly describes objects in terms of colours, invariably very simple. Washing is 'pink and red and blue'; the Maori women are 'dressed in blue and [...] dressed in yellow and green'; their cart is drawn by 'a red pony and a black pony'; and the sea is 'a great big piece of blue water' whose 'white tops came leaping over the blue'. In turn, handkerchiefs are 'pink'; Pearl's neck is 'white'; her teeth 'very white', and her curls 'yellow'; the woman's ornament is 'green' and hair 'black'; dogs are 'yellow'; grass is 'brown'; a cup is 'green'; fields are full of 'white flowers and pink briar'. And so on, insistently.

Yet despite Mansfield's emphasis upon visible attributes, the sense of sight has here become strangely unreliable. Look again at the story's stylistically odd final sentence, in which 'Little men in blue coats' becomes 'little blue men' and then 'a crowd of little blue men'. The policemen are of course neither little (this is an effect of perspective) nor blue (except metonymically as uniformed) nor perhaps even a crowd (a term, in any case, that is never used of police officers). This is, rather, the world as seen from a child's perspective, but a perspective that has somehow also merged with that of an omniscient, narrating adult. In paradigmatic Modernist fashion, Mansfield forces her readers to see, not so much the policemen, as the child's seeing of the policemen, and, in the process, to become aware of how our visual sense, in tandem with language, seeks to give coherence to our sensory experience of the world.

If Mansfield's underlying subject is the visual sense, then that of Rebecca West's *The Return of the Soldier* (1918) is time. Set in an English country house, it explores the shattering impact of World War One upon civilians and combatants alike. The novella's eponymous soldier, Chris Baldry, returns to his wife Kitty and cousin Jenny in a state of calm shell-shock that has relocated his consciousness to a period fifteen years before. Baldry does not recognise Kitty, is unaware of the tragic death of their child, and believes himself still in love with an old flame, Margaret. All three women are compassionate in their treatment of Chris, who, with the help of a psychoanalyst, is eventually restored to his former traumatised state. Yet West's off-kilter narrative leaves the reader wholly uncertain as to what kind of redemption has taken place, not least since Chris is now eligible for duty in 'that No-Man's-Land where bullets fall like rain on the rotting faces of the dead'.

In a pivotal scene, the women observe Chris becoming overwhelmed while ascending the staircase of a house that he remembers as 'different'. The house has indeed been renovated in the last fifteen years, but, as the women are agonisingly aware, there is a double absence in that the structural changes which so startle Chris were made to create a nursery for his and Kitty's now-dead child. Where a realist novelist would have stopped there, West offers the following description of how Jenny's own experience of reality has also been strangely affected:

> The dusk flowed in wet and cool from the garden, as if to put out the fire of confusion lighted on our hearthstone, and the furniture, very visible through that soft evening opacity with the observant brightness of old, well-polished wood, seemed terribly aware. Strangeness had come into the house, and everything was appalled by it, even time.

In characteristically Modernist fashion, West here extends to the material world the same kind of uncertainty that has come to define the relations between human beings and their past. The words of the text are quite ordinary – 'the furniture [...] seemed terribly aware', 'everything was appalled by it, even time' – yet their meaning is elusive and the ideas underlying them are as abstract as any shapes in a Modernist artwork.

What makes *The Return of the Soldier* so remarkable as a work of fiction is how it uses the phenomenon of shell-shock, a thoroughly modern kind of psychological injury caused by mechanised mass warfare, to dramatise the complexity of memory, identity, and time as experienced by all human beings. In so doing, West was responding to a succession of recent and epochal intellectual developments. In psychology, Sigmund Freud had shown that the human psyche is organised around a division between conscious and unconscious realms, the former actively repressing the latter. In philosophy, Henri Bergson had explored the idea that the human experience of time is structured by two distinct elements: *durée* or lived time, and *temps* or measured time. And in physics, Albert Einstein had demonstrated, sensationally, that time itself is relational and changes speed depending on the observer's movement relative to an object. More than just a meditation upon the domestic impact of the war, then, West's novella attempts to find a narrative mode adequate to this deepened understanding of the nature of reality.

Conclusion

Where did Modernism go? The short answer is that Modernism is still with us, not only in our museums and libraries but also in our public spaces and even our very forms of cultural expression. Just as many Modernist writers came to work for Hollywood – William Faulkner scripted several films, including *The Big Sleep* (1946), and Salvador Dali designed the sets for Alfred Hitchcock's *Spellbound* (1945) – so, too, can Modernism's impact be detected in the look and sound of mass cultural texts as diverse as Disney's *Dumbo* (1941) and Stanley Kubrick's *2001: A Space Odyssey* (1968). And while Modernism in literature may not have become a dominant mode – in prose fiction, for example, realism continues to rule – its innovations changed the literary field irrevocably. Indeed, so established had the narrative techniques and formal innovations of Modernism become by mid-century that they eventually provoked a post-Modernist reaction in the postwar period by writers such as John Barth, J.G. Ballard, Kathy Acker, Toni Morrison, Angela Carter, and Thomas Pynchon.

Today, the study of Modernism – or, more usually, Modernism*s*, plural – reflects this broadened understanding of the movement's origins and impact. No longer limited to what Wyndham Lewis once approvingly called 'the Men of 1914', Modernism is now seen for what it is: a truly transnational, transmedial, and culturally diverse movement that encompassed Harlem Renaissance poets and novelists such as Nella Larsen and Zora Neale Hurston, chroniclers of British proletarian life such as James Hanley and Henry Green, and so-called 'middlebrow' writers such as Rose Macaulay and Elizabeth Bowen. James Joyce, who long dreamt that experimental writing would find its place in posterity among a large readership, would surely have been delighted.

Questions to take your thinking further

- What makes a literary work Modernist?
- What factors lay behind Modernism as a movement in the arts?
- Who were the audiences, intended and actual, of Modernist writing?
- To what extent was Modernism an elitist or a democratising impulse?
- What influence has Modernism had on subsequent literary writing and even mass culture itself?

Reading list

The Modern Journals Project. Database of Modernist journals, created by Robert Scholes and digitised by Brown University and The University of Tulsa. URL: modjourn.org

Howarth, P. 2011. *The Cambridge Introduction to Modernist Poetry*. Cambridge: Cambridge University Press.

Kenner, H. 1987. *The Mechanic Muse*. Oxford: Oxford University Press.

Scott, Bonnie Kime (ed.) 2007. *Gender in Modernism: New Geographies, Complex Intersections*. Champaign, IL: University of Illinois Press.

Tew, P., and A. Murray (eds.) 2009. *The Modernism Handbook*. London: Continuum.

MODERN BRITISH AND IRISH DRAMA

Sean McEvoy

As the nineteenth century gave way to the twentieth, drama in Britain and Ireland was in a pretty bad way. Melodrama and plays that owed more to spectacular sets and effects had dominated the stage for some time. It is no accident that plays written in English between 1780 and 1890 are very rarely studied today. But things were about to change. When change came, it came from abroad: first from Scandinavia, and later from Germany, amongst other places. This chapter explores the ways in which, throughout the twentieth century, the different European influences were developed and adapted by playwrights in Britain and Ireland. The legacy of these changes? A flourishing (if sometimes precarious) theatre, in which playwrights from increasingly diverse backgrounds are able to stage plays which interrogate contemporary life with energy, depth and skill.

From well-made play to realist drama

It's a broad but not untruthful characterisation of most nineteenth-century European theatre to say that it was concerned primarily with the production and manipulation of the audience's emotional response. The 'well-made play' as it was known (after the French dramatist Eugène Scribe's formulaic *pièce bien faite*) worked towards a resolution where justice was seen to be done or a Christian virtue vindicated. The pleasure of the spectacle (in terms of set and costume), even when the stage aimed at a 'realistic' depiction, was also regarded as an important part of what theatre should be. This is the theatrical context in which the plays of the Norwegian dramatist Henrik Ibsen were first staged.

Between 1875 and 1882 Ibsen revolutionised theatre with plays which destabilised and challenged, rather than confirmed, the audience's values and expectations. Instead of seeking to elicit emotional response and engagement, Ibsen dramatised uncomfortable and difficult issues facing contemporary society – and at the end of the play left his audience without a comforting resolution. In *A Doll's House* (1879), for example, marriage is presented as a trap from which a young woman needs to escape. In *An Enemy of the People* (1883) local political corruption and hypocrisy are examined. Characters' problems and sufferings are located in a wider social, political or even philosophical context, rather than being simply the result of personal failings.

The plays are realist not only in terms of their subject matter, but also their form and style, particularly when compared with the emotion-based, melodramatic mode of much nineteenth-century drama. 'Realist' doesn't mean characters talked and behaved exactly as they would in real life (there was a short-lived nineteenth-century movement called 'Naturalism' that attempted that). Rather, they spoke in a way recognisably like 'real' life but crafted and shaped. This is still drama with action structured into dramatically satisfying units employing suspense, revelation and climax.

In Britain, the Irish writer George Bernard Shaw saw himself as the champion of 'Ibsenism'. A very popular playwright in the first decades of the twentieth century, Shaw was a socialist with many outspoken views. Characters in his plays openly debate moral and political issues with each other with great wit and energy. *Mrs Warren's Profession* (first staged 1902) set out to be honest about Victorian prostitution; *John Bull's Other Island* (1904) examined the relations between Britain and Ireland; *Major Barbara* (1905) looked at the ethics of the arms trade. In Shaw's plays, unlike in Ibsen's, coherence of characterisation and plot can sometimes come second to the presentation of ideas. However, although ideas are central to his plays, his main mode was comedy, with the funny and the serious mixed much more promiscuously than in earlier plays.

As Realism became the dominant genre of 'serious' theatre in Britain in the twentieth century, it became more subtle in its presentation of ideas – without Shaw's overt debate. Playwrights sought to comment on the condition of the country, by creating dramas which situated ideas in particular historical and political moments. Noël Coward's *This Happy Breed* (1943) illustrates this approach. His drama of an ordinary English family in the interwar years both expresses the English preoccupation with class and reflects the spirit of national resilience and optimism which Coward found in wartime Britain.

Thirteen years later, John Osborne's realist play *Look Back in Anger* (1956) shook the theatrical world anew through the way it articulated the deep sense of frustration felt by young people growing up in post-war Britain. What was particularly new was that the play's protagonist, Jimmy Porter, was a highly-articulate working-class man with much to say about class and nation (and about women, it turns out). The play gave rise to the term 'angry young man', an influential phrase which came to symbolise a particular type of disillusioned protagonist. The idea of the 'state of the nation play' became established, and contemporary social comment of some sort has been the staple of much of the expressive realist writing of the last sixty years.

If British and Irish drama were shaped by developments in European theatre, they were also shaped by political and social developments in the UK. In the thirty years after 1945 the expansion of further and higher education enabled people to become writers, directors and actors, who would never before have had the chance. In the same period, national and local government bodies began sponsoring the arts, funding plays that would not necessarily have been put on by a commercial theatre that needed to make a profit. Until 1968, all plays had to be licensed by the Office of the Lord Chamberlain, a situation which led to some plays being censored – including plays by Ibsen and Strindberg and Edward Bond's *Saved*, a play refused a license in 1965 for its scenes of extreme violence (see page 88). The ending of censorship allowed writers and directors to stage politically and socially challenging plays in publicly-funded theatres.

This socially-engaged theatre is exemplified in the late twentieth century by playwrights such as David Hare. *Skylight* (1995) shows the attempted reunion of two lovers, one a successful businessman, the other an inner-city primary teacher, and alongside the emotional tangles plays out a conflict between the values of the private and public sectors in the last years of the century. Hare has gone on to write 'documentary' plays such as *Stuff Happens* (2004), presenting the build-up to the US-led attack on Iraq in 2003 using only the recorded words of the participants. Such documentary reconstructions, crafted by employing all the conventions of drama, have become a new mode of realism. In a globalised world there is also a new focus beyond the state of the nation.

In the twenty-first century there has been something of a turn away from the contained kinds of expressive realism once more to present more explicit debate of global issues. Lucy Kirkwood's *Chimerica* (2013) looks at a future dominated by the US and China; Lucy Prebble's *Enron* (2009), set in Texas, shows the instability and mendacity of a destructive form of global capitalism.

Absurdism and Postmodernism

Immediately after World War Two there developed a very different, recognisably modernist form of theatre. If realist drama challenged audience expectations of theatre in the nineteenth century, now Absurdism destabilised those who had grown used to Realism.

Writing in the context of the Holocaust, the bombing of Nagasaki and Hiroshima and the looming threat of nuclear war, and influenced by Existentialism, a contemporary French philosophical movement which saw human existence as essentially purposeless and the universe as hostile, dramatists such as Eugène Ionesco and Samuel Beckett used drama to draw attention to the absurdity of humanity. In plays such as Ionesco's 1958 *Rhinocéros* the logic of everyday life is suspended and the impossible becomes unexceptionable: this is a world in which people can turn into rhinos.

When Samuel Beckett's play *Waiting for Godot* was first performed in the English theatre in 1955 (having been written in French and first staged in Paris) it provoked walkouts. The theatre critic Vivian Mercier's famous review captures the essence of the play – both its absurdity and its power:

[*Waiting for Godot*] has achieved a theoretical impossibility – a play in which nothing happens, that yet keeps audiences glued to their seats. What's more, since the second act is a subtly different reprise of the first, he has written a play in which nothing happens, twice.

Two tramps, Vladimir and Estragon stand upon a stage which is bare apart from a tree. They joke, argue, mess around, weep and laugh as they wait for Godot, a mysterious, seemingly powerful, person who never comes but who they believe (with differing degrees of confidence) will solve an unspecified predicament. In each act of the play they are visited by the tyrannical Pozzo and his slave Lucky. The second time he comes Pozzo is blind. Sometimes Vladimir and Estragon tease the audience about the whole falseness of the play they are watching: the audience are also engaged in a pointless killing of time. But as Pozzo puts it, we 'give birth astride of a grave, the light gleams an instant, then it's night once more'.

The Theatre of the Absurd (a term coined by the theatre critic Martin Esslin to describe these absurdist plays) was perhaps most influential in breaking the spell of conventional Realism and opening up more productive possibilities.

Harold Pinter's early plays were initially assumed to be part of the absurdist movement. In *The Birthday Party* (1958) a super-smooth and self-possessed Jew and an anxious and violent Irishman arrive unannounced in a seaside boarding house where they reveal that it is the birthday of Stanley, the moody and unprepossessing lodger who feels far from his original home. They throw him a party, but also interrogate and, it seems, torture him before taking him off to 'Uncle Monty' for 'special treatment'. Who any of these characters really are or why they are doing this remains unexplained. In its absurdity, *The Birthday Party* dramatises fears provoked by a world (for example, East Germany, the Soviet Union) in which people in authority could turn up at your door, take you away and torture you for no good reason: for your race, nationality or beliefs. The play's treatment of being a 'foreigner' at a time of significant immigration into Britain is also thought-provoking and far from absurd.

The influence of absurdist theatre, with its foregrounding of the meaningless, the illogical or incomprehensible and hostile universe, is clear in plays we call postmodern. Tom Stoppard's *Rosencrantz and Guildenstern are Dead* (1966), often classed as absurdist, can rather be seen as a forerunner of this postmodern theatre. In this play Stoppard takes two minor characters from Shakespeare's *Hamlet* and turns them into recognisably modern men, killing time and trying to work out what's going on between moments of being thrust, bafflingly, into the action of Shakespeare's play. If the characters' lack of control over their own destiny and the foregrounding of the randomness of the world might be seen as absurdist, the drama's playfulness, self-consciousness, irreverent quotation from other plays and its constant comic awareness of itself as theatre are all characteristic of the 'all surface no depth' model of Postmodernism.

Martin Crimp's *Attempts on her Life* (1997) consists of seventeen very different, sometimes parodic scenes whose only link is the identity of 'Anne', who turns out to be a car, or, it seems, an art-object at different points. Even if, as one character says, 'the point is that the search for a point is pointless' contemporary fears about terrorism and ethnic violence are held up for examination and juxtaposed in a rapid sequence which might be seen to mirror the chaos of an information-overloaded world.

Martin McDonagh's *The Lieutenant of Inishmore* (2001) turns Irish republican terrorism into a murderous and hilarious blood-soaked farce whose plot concerns a cat which has been run over by mistake. His *A Very Very Dark Matter* (2018) involves vengeful ghosts, time travel, and the nineteenth-century writers Hans Christian Andersen and Charles Dickens, both of whom keep African pygmy sisters in cages to secretly write their work. Not actually absurd, this twenty-first century play uses the possibilities of theatre to depict a 'postmodern' modern world in which technology has shrunk time and space, where the status of the comic and the serious has been eroded if not reversed at times, and where spectacle and image have more authority and impact than truth.

'Epic' theatre

A further strand of European theatre which profoundly influenced British and Irish theatre in the post-war period is the 'Epic theatre' of the German playwright Bertolt Brecht. A life-long communist who struggled against the rise of Nazism in Germany, from where he was forced to flee in 1933, Brecht had developed a style of play and performance dedicated to making the audience engage intellectually with the political issues being presented.

Brecht believed that in realist drama the audience becomes so emotionally caught up in the world of the play that they are unable to question why the action unfolding before them on stage happens in this way. He wanted the audience to be 'alienated' from the action so that they could see the political and social forces at work in his fundamentally anti-capitalist plays. The plays themselves present episodic scenes which require the audience to work out the causal connections between them. Captions at the side of the stage offer a perspective on the action. Characters speak (or sing) to the audience explaining themselves or their dilemmas. Importantly, there was no attempt to maintain an illusion that the audience were watching a slice of reality. The actors could be seen changing costume at the back of the stage, and the style of performance made it clear that we were seeing an impersonation of the character by the actor, not a naturalistic inhabiting of the role.

Although Brecht had been developing this form of theatre since the 1920s, it was not until the 1956 German Berliner Ensemble theatre company production of *Mother Courage* at the Palace Theatre in London that his influence was really felt in Britain.

The working-class dramatist Edward Bond was one of the first to adapt Brecht's ideas successfully to the English stage. *Saved* (1965), initially banned from public performance, showed a group of disaffected, inarticulate young men stone a baby to death in a pram. The other scenes in the play show how their lives have brought them to a point where they are capable of committing this atrocity. In his early plays Bond developed his own 'aggro effect' with the same purpose as Brecht's 'alienation effect': putting violence on stage which would shock the audience into asking what point it was making. Taking on what he considered the enormous conservative power of Shakespeare, in his *Lear* (1971) Bond rewrote Shakespeare's tragedy as an ultra-violent Cold War fable about the terrible violence that underwrites modern societies and the capacity for revolution to go horribly astray if it does not put humanity at its core. When Lear sees the body of his daughter Fontanelle, who had rebelled against him and overthrown him, dissected on stage, he is astonished to see no sign of the cruel 'beast' that she was to him inside her 'beautiful' organs. He sees a 'body made by the hand of a child [...] if I had known this beauty and patience and care, how I would have loved her.' The horror is used to foreground a reflection on Lear's understanding of the implications of recognising our shared human vulnerability.

Epic techniques, which prevent the audience from simply 'escaping' into the drama can also serve avowedly feminist theatre. The central act of Caryl Churchill's *Top Girls* (1982) superbly employs Brechtian montage, where short scenes that are not directly related to each other are juxtaposed to bring out the connections between them to a political purpose. As in Brecht's theatre the audience is forced to make connections between a series of scenes showing the lives of different women. Putting all these scenes next to each other insistently brings forward questions about the challenges faced by women in a society where the expectations placed upon them as wives, mothers and lovers affect their ability to operate and even to grasp their own situation in the world of business and employment in comparison to men.

Timberlake Wertenbaker's *Our Country's Good* (1988), which tells the story of a play put on in the first convict settlement in Australia, shows how far Brechtian alienation conventions have become embedded in British drama. Each scene has a projected title which can direct the audience as to the issue to be considered: 'The Authorities Discuss the Merits of Theatre', 'The Science of Hanging' or 'The Meaning of Plays'. In the first production of this self-consciously theatrical play about the value of the theatre, the conventions of contemporary realistic theatre were blatantly abandoned. Today casting the black actress Alphonsia Emmanuel as a white convict and as a white British officer might be regarded as colour- and gender-blind casting, but in 1988 it would have been seen as an alienation device underlining the absurdity of the racial and gender hierarchies through which oppressive power in the play is constructed.

Expressionism

One further strand of European theatre with a significant influence on the development of twentieth-century drama is Expressionism. In drama Expressionism describes a type of early-twentieth theatre in which both characters and production represent emotional states and abstract concepts on stage. The Swedish dramatist August Strindberg in his 1907 play *The Ghost Sonata* used a multi-level house in which were presented characters representing and embodying corruption in the different levels of society. In 1920s Germany Expressionism formed the basis of a political approach to theatre, with people standing on stage for political classes or embodying a particular social crisis.

The techniques of expressionist theatre are evident in the plays of dramatists such as the American Tennessee Williams. In British and Irish theatre, Expressionism had a particular impact on late twentieth-century experimental writing by playwrights such as Sarah Kane, Caryl Churchill and debbie tucker green.

The first half of Sarah Kane's *Blasted* (1995) is a piece of social realism, showing the violent and abusive relationship between Cate and the much older Ian. A bomb explosion suddenly tears apart the hotel room in Leeds where the action of the play takes place, and they find themselves graphically brutalised as a civil war erupts. The final shocking scenes, featuring taboos such as cannibalism, are a series of tableaux of the dying (then resurrected) Ian. The play's second half gives physical, visual expression of the continuity, in Kane's own view, between violence in personal relationships between men and women and the waging of war. But – and this is where the influence of expressionist techniques is clearly evident – it also presents powerful visual metaphors for the psychological damage wrought to both Cate and Ian by their own relationship and by the violent society in which they live. The internal becomes external.

Caryl Churchill's *The Skriker* (1994) mixes outlandish figures from folklore with a 'realistic' social situation involving the teenage Josie, who has killed her baby, and her pregnant friend Lily. They each encounter the needy shape-shifting Skriker who can effect apparent magic and who can transport them to a strange underworld. The Skriker represents nature and the material world seeking vengeance on humanity for the terrible despoliation now visited upon the planet, or is perhaps a dramatised representation of our damaged psychological relationship with nature.

In debbie tucker green's work the characters, unnamed, can stand for a whole class of person: in *Trade* (2005) they represent the exploitative Western sex tourist, while in *Stoning Mary* (2005) representative characters standing for 'African' problems such as the AIDS epidemic or child soldiers are transposed to the West. In this play, actors playing each character's ego stand next to them, undercutting and commenting on what their character is saying. As with Strindberg and Toller, Expressionism allows green to critique the way we live by making it physically, often jarringly, visible.

In the future

This chapter has concentrated on the different ways in which developments in European drama shook up and reinvigorated what had become a tired, conventional and comfortable form of entertainment. Alongside this, it has highlighted two other significant developments of recent years: the major growth in women's work being staged, and a much greater diversity of voices from different communities among playwrights.

The chapter has focused on plays performed on fixed stages. Looking to the future it will be interesting to see how technological developments and the movement of theatre outside of traditional spaces will shape both new writing and the production of existing texts.

Though it still remains rather niche and academic, there has also arisen a radical 'post-dramatic' theatre which disposes of all conventional categories of character and plot and focuses on the relationship between performer and audience. By their very nature, I suspect these developments will have limited impact on the written dramatic texts which are studied on literature courses, but they may eventually lead to an increasing divide between performance and text-based theatre.

Questions to take your thinking further

- Are some kinds of theatre better suited to certain subjects and time periods than others?
- How does the contemporary theatre tell stories and engage its audience differently to on-screen drama?
- Is any theatre ever actually 'realistic'?
- Why is theatre, as an art form, so engaged with people as social and political creatures?
- Why might there be a future for theatre in a digital, virtual reality world?

Reading list

Billington, M. 2007. *State of the Nation: British Theatre Since 1945*. London: Faber and Faber.

Shellard, D. 1999. *British Theatre Since The War*. New Haven CT and London: Yale University Press.

Shepherd, S. 2009. *The Cambridge Introduction to Modern British Theatre*. Cambridge: Cambridge University Press.

Shepherd-Barr, K. 2016. *Modern Theatre: A Very Short Introduction*. Oxford: Oxford University Press.

THE NOVEL IN THE 20TH AND 21ST CENTURIES

Pamela Bickley

Introduction

During the twentieth century the novel established itself as a vibrant and essential part of modern culture. The great novelists of the nineteenth century had undoubtedly paved the way, developing flexible narrative structures to address significant issues of the day, while exploring the inner lives of their protagonists. The Victorian legacy modelled realist fiction: a believable and coherent world proceeding according to rational notions of cause and effect; characterisation which, equally, seems consistent and credible; above all, perhaps, plots that progress towards an acceptable and just closure. By the end of the twentieth century, the novel had evolved in radical and challenging ways, both in content and form. Hybridity is perhaps the defining concept: contemporary fiction can engage with urgent social and moral issues or it can evoke one individual's distinctive interior world. Context might be the seemingly unremarkable world of the everyday or it might be an alternative, fantastical universe. Language might be heightened and poetical or brutal and demotic; structure might be sequential or fragmented. Late twentieth-century novels retain an ability to shock and disturb, indeed, to divide public opinion: James Kelman's *How Late It Was, How Late* and Salman Rushdie's *The Satanic Verses* won major literary awards but, at the same time, were seen as deliberately courting outrage and controversy.

This chapter will focus on British and Irish fiction with some reference to American writing.

Modernism

The innovative creativity of twentieth-century fiction derives, first, from the radicalism of the great writers of Modernism: Conrad, Woolf, Joyce and, later, Beckett. From the earliest years of the twentieth century, D.H. Lawrence was dismantling Victorian notions of propriety, experimenting with symbolism as a way of denoting character, concluding his novels in open-ended ways. *Women in Love* (1921) inherits Victorian traditions of writing about a society through key families, class, work and relationships. But Lawrence approaches sexuality with a new frankness: sexual relations outside marriage do not incur the inevitable downfall of the heroine; sexual relations between men are proposed as part of a more complete human experience of love. And the end of the novel resists conventional closure: Ursula and Birkin experience shared passionate love, but for Birkin the death of Gerald is the loss of 'another kind of love', one that Ursula cannot understand:

> 'You can't have two kinds of love. Why should you!'
> 'It seems as if I can't,' he said. 'Yet I wanted it.'
> 'You can't have it, because it's false, impossible,' she said.
> 'I don't believe that,' he answered.

With this irresolution, the novel ends. Virginia Woolf experimented more radically with narrative structure, believing that art must capture life in all its randomness and complexity:

> Examine for a moment an ordinary mind on an ordinary day. The mind receives a myriad impressions – trivial, fantastic, evanescent, or engraved with the sharpness of steel. From all sides they come, an incessant shower of innumerable atoms … Is it not the task of the novelist to convey this varying, this unknown and uncircumscribed spirit, whatever aberration or complexity it may display …?
>
> ('Modern Fiction', 1919)

Mrs Dalloway (1925) is, famously, a novel organised around the events, significant or otherwise, of a single day. Clarissa's past emotions dominate her thoughts as she proceeds through her decorous tasks; the London setting – the anonymous, bustling city – brings her in close proximity to an individual she will never know, Septimus Smith. For Septimus, time and place lack any conventional meaning; he is frozen, traumatised by his experiences of the war. Yet Woolf establishes an undercurrent of melancholy solitariness that links the two characters: Clarissa too is haunted by death – the tragic accident that killed her sister; the knowledge that she is drawing towards her own end. Like Mrs Ramsay, in Woolf's *To the Lighthouse* (1927), Clarissa believes in bringing people together; she has evolved 'this atheist's religion of doing good for the sake of goodness'. Both women epitomise the Modernist turning away from a theocentric universe:

> How could any Lord have made this world? [Mrs Ramsay] asked. With her mind she had always seized the fact that there is no reason, order, justice: but suffering, death, the poor. There was no treachery too base for the world to commit; she knew that. No happiness lasted; she knew that.

In Woolf's novels reality is shifting and impermanent, the totemic lighthouse is seen to be both 'a silvery misty looking tower with a yellow eye' and 'a stark tower on a bare rock' because, as James Ramsay discovers, 'nothing was simply one thing'.

James Joyce used what T.S. Eliot termed a 'mythical method' in *Ulysses* (1922) where a single day in Dublin (16 June, 1904) is portrayed through the central consciousness of Leopold Bloom, paralleling and parodying the epic journey of Odysseus. *Ulysses* was subject to numerous obscenity prosecutions and widely banned: the novel graphically describes bodily functions, employs language then regarded as pornographic, satirises the Roman Catholic church, and mocks the British royal family. Joyce's carnivalesque *tour de force*, richly ironic and stylistically innovative, was far in advance of its time. It was, perhaps, the quintessential text of the Modernist era, greeted by its earliest readers with incomprehension and, at times, fury.

The 'death of the novel'?

After the seismic shock of Modernism, the novel resumed more familiar territories with recognisable worlds and structures, often lamenting past certainties and ideals (Graham Greene, Evelyn Waugh, Elizabeth Bowen) or pursuing complex psychological states and intellectual uncertainties (Iris Murdoch, John Fowles, William Golding). There is, undoubtedly, compelling and rewarding fiction to be found in the mid-twentieth century but, to many writers of the time, the novel seemed threatened with extinction. British novelist John Fowles, writing in 1979, complained that 'a lot of contemporary English fiction is abysmally parochial and of no conceivable interest to anyone who is not English and middle class'. Yet by the beginning of the twenty-first century, Dominic Head, in a study of contemporary fiction, described the novel as 'phenomenally rich and inventive, a genre in a state of creative expansion, and as far removed from terminal decline as it is possible to imagine'. How had this change come about? Literary academic Lorna Sage observed in 1980 that where the 'English' novel 'appeared to be strangling in its own decorous and unappetising repressions', new voices were energising the genre from outside, notably women's writing and postcolonial perspectives. One of the defining features of late twentieth- and twenty-first-century fiction is its engagement with problematic, even disturbing, concerns of the day: writing such as Lionel Shriver's *We Need to Talk About Kevin* (2003) addressed head-on the troubling issue of American school shootings. Modern fiction has also cast an unflinching searchlight on troubling areas of the past; slavery and its legacy in Toni Morrison's *Beloved* (1987); the dark shadows over Ireland's history in Seamus Deane's *Reading in the Dark* (1996).

Warfare and conflict

Fiction is an ideal means of negotiating and coming to terms with historical events. This is particularly true of the two world wars of the twentieth century, the Holocaust, and colonialism and its legacies. The relaxation of censorship laws together with increasing tolerance of difficult subject matter has meant that material that would have been deemed offensive or improper can now be published.

The brutal realities of trench warfare and the initial conspiracy of silence around World War One seem particularly relevant here. As the last British survivors died, towards the final years of the twentieth century, a number of profound and searching novels appeared, notably Pat Barker's *Regeneration* trilogy. Barker writes with a licence not permitted to earlier novelists such as Aldington (*Death of a Hero*, 1929), blending fact and fiction, confronting the immediacy of mutilation, and death, all the while refracting her material through an incisive critique of the English class system. There is no sepia-tinted nostalgia in her interrogation of class: warfare has not eroded the barriers between 'officers and men'; women continue to suffer physical abuse and die from backstreet abortions. The primary focus of the first novel of the trilogy, *Regeneration* (1991), is the Craiglockhart Hospital and the treatment of trauma and repression by the anthropologist and psychiatrist Rivers. Fusing factual details with the dreams and hallucinatory terrors of the individuals depicted creates a dislocating effect for the reader. We know the listed battles or the poetry of Owen and Sassoon who meet for the first time at Craiglockhart. But the structure of the novel, leading the reader through Rivers's encounters with his patients, introduces fragmented narratives that take the reader into individual horrors, graphically evoked. These young men are lost in a personal hell that often defies the limits of language. This is notably the case in Barker's decision to conclude the novel with Dr Yealland's treatments – a disturbing scene of sanctioned torture. The patient, Callan, has suffered a complete breakdown, manifested in mutism. He is, quite literally, speechless from his experiences. Yealland, who believes that 'men who [break] down are degenerates', locks his patient into the treatment room and then applies increasing electrical shocks until he is satisfied that there is discernible improvement. Callan suffers agonising pain; at one point, there is no sound in the room but his terrified sobbing. Yealland's greatest cruelty, however, is his insistence that, 'You must speak, but I shall not listen to anything you have to say'. The voiceless sufferer is a fitting conclusion to a work that treats silence and repression in the face of the indescribable: 'Armageddon, Golgotha, there were no words ...'

Approaching historically verifiable material through narrative experiment is also a characteristic of the body of fiction that explores World War Two and the Holocaust. There have been numerous mis-quotations, or mis-translations, of cultural theorist Adorno's famous assertion that it is 'barbaric to write poetry after Auschwitz', taken generally to mean that no form of artistic expression is possible following the reality of the Holocaust. In fact, the early testimonies of survivors such as Elie Wiesel and Primo Levi have resulted in a strong commitment to fiction that bears witness to the truth. Novelists have, correspondingly, employed a number of different narrative strategies to approach the subject. Keneally's *Schindler's Ark* (1982), like Barker's novels, insists on its factuality; Oskar Schindler was indeed 'real' – a Nazi profiteer but, seemingly, a man who determined to protect Jewish workers in his factories. One of the most striking attempts to 'novelise' the Holocaust is Martin Amis's *Time's Arrow* (1991) which rewinds a man's life backwards from the moment of his death – a narrative device suggested by a passage in Vonnegut's

Slaughterhouse 5 where a sequence of film depicts a bombing mission in reverse. In Amis's novel, a sardonic narrator emerges with the death of the protagonist, elderly American doctor, 'Tod Friendly', revisiting and reversing the events of his life. In his American persona, the doctor is seen wounding his patients; in his earlier life, as Dr Odilo Unverdorben, he has performed unspeakable atrocities at Auschwitz but, in this bizarre reverse chronology, he sees himself restoring life and healing pain. So the novel not only reverses time but also offers an antithesis to the truth. At times this results in a blackly comic effect, at odds with the subject. The surrealism of the narrative provokes a different type of engagement, however, forcing the reader to question assumptions and conventions about the novel itself; whether there are subjects that defy fiction; what forms of narrative could ever be appropriate to the Holocaust. By contrast, the Canadian novelist Anne Michaels, in *Fugitive Pieces* (1997), crafts a densely poetic work which draws on ideas of buried truths. The child Jakob, the first-person narrator at the opening of the novel, escapes the Nazi destruction of his home – his parents are murdered, his sister taken away. He seeks refuge in an archaeological site, Biskupin, where he becomes a 'bog-boy' until rescued by Greek archaeologist Athos, an academic who is attempting to counter Nazi falsification of the past. Biskupin, known as the 'Polish Pompeii', was already famous: 'But Biskupin was proof of an advanced culture that wasn't German; Himmler ordered its obliteration.' For decades Jakob seems to inhabit a liminal world, haunted by recurrent nightmares; summoning memories and inventing stories of his lost sister, Bella. The second narrator, Ben, is the son of holocaust survivors, born four years after their liberation. He too is marked by their experiences of trauma and loss – there can be no 'ordinariness' in their lives. The 'fugitive pieces' of the novel are finally drawn together by Ben's quest to find Jakob's poetic notebooks, the testimony to survival.

Further reading:

Louis Begley, *Wartime Lies* (1991)

Sebastian Faulks, *Birdsong* (1993)

Michael Ondaatje, *The English Patient* (1992)

Postcolonial identities

For writers at the end of the twentieth century and beginning of the twenty-first, questions of historical and cultural identity are both insistent and complex. As critic Elleke Boehmer has established, this new writing is not, simply, the writing that 'comes after' empire: postcolonial literature is 'that which critically or subversively scrutinises the colonial relationship'. The novel is an ideal genre to explore the complex perspectives of this postcolonial situation: different settings, time-scales and characters can be effectively juxtaposed and the nuances of dialogue between different voices can create a sense of dramatic immediacy. Andrea Levy's *Small Island* (2004) is an excellent example: the experiences of

Gilbert Joseph, a Jamaican who serves in the RAF during the war, reveal depths of racism and exclusion. Gilbert's sole wartime encounter with personal violence is from American GIs, stationed in Britain. When Gilbert returns to England in 1948, on the Windrush, he finds a cold reception: 'Let me count the doors that opened slow and shut quick.' His Jamaican wife, Hortense, who has idealised the 'Mother Country', is infinitely disillusioned when she discovers that her teaching qualifications are rejected – even derided. As the novel ends, Gilbert and Hortense are asked to adopt the biracial baby of their friend and landlady, Queenie, who fears the prejudice her illegitimate child will experience. In the turbulent emotion of this poignant scene, Gilbert makes an impassioned appeal against British racism:

> 'Listen to me, man, we both just finish fighting a war – a bloody war – for the better world we wan' see. And on the same side [...] You and me, fighting for empire, fighting for peace. But still, after all that we suffer together, you wan' tell me that I am worthless and you are not.'

For Levy, the experiences of the war and its immediate aftermath, intensify ideas of race, empire, and identity.

In Monica Ali's *Brick Lane* (2003), the postcolonial context is that of a later generation. Chanu is an educated Bangladeshi who expects to succeed in England but who fails to achieve his ambitions. His wife, Nazneen, has joined him as a young bride from her village; she speaks no English and initially struggles with the challenges of London life. But when Chanu desires to return to Dhaka, Nazneen feels she can never go back:

> 'I can't go with you,' she said.
> 'I can't stay,' said Chanu, and they clung to each other inside a sadness that went beyond words and tears, beyond that place [...] to travel with them wherever they went.

But where London has offered Hortense only a painful process of readjustment, Nazneen discovers new possibilities. At the end of the novel, when her daughters take her ice-skating, she is initially hesitant, 'you can't skate in a sari.' Her daughter replied, 'This is England,' [...] 'You can do whatever you like.'

Further reading:

J.M. Coetzee, *Disgrace* (1999)

Hanif Kureishi, *The Buddha of Suburbia* (1990)

Zadie Smith, *White Teeth* (2000)

America post 9/11: 'Ground Zero literature'

For a novelist such as Mohsin Hamid, the postcolonial experience is radically altered by 9/11 and the attacks on New York and Washington. In *The Reluctant Fundamentalist* (2007), the first-person narrator, Changez, unfolds his story in the form of a monologue to a silent listener. He has been the archetypal ambitious and successful Princeton student, wholeheartedly embracing American culture and winning a much-coveted position as a financial analyst, until jolted violently out of his preconceptions about himself and the society he has adopted when he sees television reportage of the attacks on the World Trade Center: 'I smiled. Yes, despicable as it may sound, my initial reaction was to be remarkably pleased.' Changez finds his life altered completely; he is now a 'foreigner' amongst his work colleagues and in his New York social life. Looking at America through different eyes, he rejects his lucrative and prestigious career and returns to Pakistan. The restrained, somewhat pedantic, register of Changez's idiolect is an effective means for establishing the cultural divide that separates him from his uneasy listener. DeLillo's *Falling Man* (2007) is a novel written from within the dominant culture, responding to an ethical imperative to find meaning through the process of melding fiction and traumatic reality. DeLillo's novel seeks to comprehend events through the different narratives interwoven through the work, recreating experience through the memories of Keith and Florence who escape from the First Tower, and charting the attempts of others in the community to use language as a means of transcending the disorientation and fear that is the new reality. The novel begins abruptly with the diminishing roar of impact, 'a world, a time and space of falling ash and near night'. Keith Neudecker walks away from the falling tower and arrives at the door of his former wife, Lianne. He is carrying a briefcase that turns out to belong to a woman, Florence, who had worked on the floor below him. Returning the briefcase unites the two survivors in a constant loop of memory; Florence, first, recounting her experience of the stairwell – 'going through it again' because she feels 'I'm still on the stairs'. They become lovers; they also sit watching videotape of the planes. The climax of the novel returns to the moment of impact and Keith's memories: the chaos of his escape and his desperate attempts to rescue a dying colleague bring the novel full circle with the opening description of 'figures in windows a thousand feet up, dropping into free space'. Threaded through the narrative is 'Falling Man' himself – a performance artist who plunges headfirst in imitation of the iconic photograph of 9/11 and who thereby re-enacts the horror of that first fall. Falling Man's near suicidal acrobatic display is bizarre – but so, of course, is New York itself where 'everything now is measured by after'.

Further reading:

Jonathan Safran Foer, *Extremely Loud and Incredibly Close* (2005)

Jay McInerney, *The Good Life* (2006)

Joseph O'Neill, *Netherland* (2008)

Dystopia and apocalypse

Apocalyptic pessimism is perhaps the inevitable corollary of the warfare and terrorism that has marked the turn of the new century. The novel has long been the genre of dystopian new worlds from H.G. Wells in the 1890s through Orwell's *Nineteen Eighty-Four* and Huxley's *Brave New World* in the mid-twentieth century, to Atwood's *The Handmaid's Tale* (1989). In Kazuo Ishiguro's *Never Let Me Go* (2005), the first-person narrator, Kathy H, introduces the reader to a seemingly normal world, but, by degrees, it becomes apparent that Kathy and her friends inhabit an unimaginable universe. They are clones, created in order to supply vital organs; as such, they can only survive into early adulthood. Ishiguro controls the reader's response brilliantly: the most haunting question is why the characters never attempt to escape from their destinies. They wander freely around an English city; they even appear to question whether they might be able to postpone their fate; they fall in love. But, horrifyingly, they never reject the future mapped out for them. Cormac McCarthy's *The Road* (2006) offers a vision of a devastated wasteland, where a few survivors compete for scant resources, attempting to avoid the predatory cannibals who roam unchecked. Sentences lack finite verbs to convey the absence of life in this desolation; apocalypse brings anarchy.

Further reading:

Margaret Atwood, *Oryx and Crake* (2003)

J.G. Ballard, *The Drowned World* (1962); *Millenium People* (2003)

Taboo

Academic critic Linden Peach has written of late twentieth-century writing that it is preoccupied with 'exhaustion, excess, limit and transgression', and tackling taboo head on has certainly been a feature of contemporary fiction. It could be argued that the Gothic is a genre which has altered and developed according to changing social circumstances while remaining a means of exploring disturbing, psychotic states of mind. Irish writer Patrick McCabe treats madness and alienation in *The Dead School* (1995) and *The Butcher Boy* (1992) to an extent which might be seen as repelling rather than engaging readers. *The Butcher Boy* is a means of approaching the difficult area of paedophilia – the child, Francie Brady, has been abused by a priest. He is also told by his neighbour, Mrs Nugent, that he is a pig. So Francie, horrifyingly, identifies himself with pigs and with slaughter, describing a violent revenge on Mrs Nugent. It is also characteristic of contemporary writing that Francie is an unreliable narrator, to the extent that readers cannot identify how far his retrospective narrative is entirely delusional. Areas of taboo might also encompass subject content or questions of language: Irving Welsh's *Trainspotting* (1993) provoked reactions of disgust and alarm when first published, as much for its style and language as for its subject matter. But as the subject of the novel is desensitisation, the seeming indifference to violence and degradation is crucially relevant to the effect of the writing. In other instances, writers have used the novel as a means of exposing the hypocrisies or abuses of a society. Roddy Doyle's *The Woman Who Walked Into Doors* (1996) is a novel adapted from an RTÉ/BBC miniseries, *Family,* which had caused outrage in its first appearance as a television play: Irish Catholic family life could not be depicted as abusive. Doyle went on to publish the novel as a means of exploring more fully the perspective of the abused wife, Paula Spencer, in particular the fact that Paula does not leave her husband. The first-person voice here is one that attempts to make sense of her own story, '[r]ewriting history' but, finally, accepting the reality of her husband's sadism and the complicity of a society where doctors, nurses, priests, family collude in silence rather than question her injuries.

Taboos, of course, can change: in 1928, Radclyffe Hall's lesbian novel, *The Well of Loneliness*, was tried for obscenity and all published copies were ordered to be destroyed. Jeanette Winterson's *Oranges Are Not The Only Fruit* (1985) fuses Victorian *bildungsroman*, complete with biblical scaffolding, with the young protagonist's growing knowledge of her gay identity. Had LGBT issues become mainstream? In Alan Hollinghurst's *The Line of Beauty* (2004), gay relations are certainly taboo in the moneyed world of Margaret Thatcher's 1980s' political admirers, and in the context of the emerging HIV/AIDS crisis. Hollinghurst's novel illustrates the ways in which an older generation's homophobia coexists with the casual sex and cocaine lifestyles of the primary narrator and his circle. The formerly taboo had become Booker prize winner.

Further reading:

James Kelman, *How Late it Was, How Late* (1994)

Ian McEwan, *The Cement Garden* (1993)

Colm Tóibín, *The Blackwater Lightship* (1998)

Conclusion: the future

Professor of modern literature, Peter Boxall, suggests a fascinating theory of the novel – that it can often be ahead of the culture that it encompasses, developing 'futural forms which it alone is able to summon into existence'. Undoubtedly, society in the twenty-first century will continue to undergo profound change, and fiction in its capacity for experiment can be expected to reflect, even anticipate, newness. Perhaps the novelist Salman Rushdie – threatened with death for his fiction – could be allowed the final word:

> I do not believe that novels are trivial matters. The ones I care most about are those which attempt radical reformulations of language, form and ideas, those that attempt to do what the word novel seems to insist upon: to see the world anew.

Prompts and questions to take your thinking further

- How does contemporary fiction address the politics of identity?
- Explore ways in which novels engage with everyday existence.
- Consider any text that might be judged as experimental in form and/or language and analyse its narrative purpose and effects.
- Compare novels based on specific historic events, considering how texts negotiate with the past.
- Study ways in which any one author approaches the taboo or transgressive.

Reading list

Boxall, P. 2015. *The Value of the Novel.* Cambridge: Cambridge University Press.

Caserio, R.L. 2009. *The Cambridge Companion to the Twentieth-Century English Novel.* Cambridge: Cambridge University Press.

Head, D. 2002. *The Cambridge Introduction to Modern British Fiction, 1950-2000.* Cambridge: Cambridge University Press.

Morrison, J. 2003. *Contemporary Fiction.* London: Routledge.

Tew, P. 2007. *The Contemporary British Novel.* London: Continuum.

DECLARATION AND DREAM: AMERICAN LITERATURE 1776-2018

Nicolas Tredell

Introduction

The USA is a nation founded on a literary text: the Declaration of Independence of 4 July 1776. This is not primarily a piece of fiction, poetry or drama, though it has elements of all three; it was born in the heat of revolution against the British crown, to justify an act of treason punishable by execution; as Benjamin Franklin, himself a prolific author, was said to have remarked to his fellow-signatories: 'We must all hang together or assuredly we shall all hang separately.'

Words were crucial in cementing this unity. The Declaration is a stirring piece of rhetoric that offers a vision of human nature in striking formulations – perhaps most notably, its assertion of a human right to 'Life, Liberty and the pursuit of Happiness' – and a series of indictments of the Old World, as represented by Britain.

The idea that words define a nation persists in American culture. Thomas Jefferson, who drafted the Declaration of Independence, and later became the third President of the United States, might not have liked the literary style of the 45th President in Twitter mode; but both use language in the idiom of their time, adapted to their envisaged audiences, to try to construct and reinforce an idea and narrative of a nation.

The Declaration of Independence is also the founding document of the American Dream, although the phrase itself does not seem to appear in print until 1931 in James Truslow Adams's book *The Epic of America*. Even in the Declaration, however, two forms of otherness already shadow the Dream: one from the Old World, one from the New. The Old World otherness is that of Britain, the colonial power; the New World otherness is that of Native Americans. The final item in the Declaration's denunciation of Old World iniquities combines these two threatening others: 'the present King of Great Britain', George III, has 'endeavoured to bring on the inhabitants of our frontiers, the merciless Indian Savages, whose known rule of warfare, is an undistinguished destruction of all ages, sexes and conditions.'

This sense of perceived threats from the Old World and from indigenous and neighbouring inhabitants will persist in American culture and literature.

The importance of words in American identity gives a special significance to its literature, which now has a long, rich and various history. This essay offers a compressed account of its development and considers its present and its possible future.

Looking to the past

1607-1849

From 1607 and the founding of Jamestown[1] to 1776 and the Declaration of Independence, America was a British colony and its writers emulated British examples to a significant extent – for instance, Anne Bradstreet, with her poetry collection *The Tenth Muse Lately Sprung Up in America* (1650) and Phillis Wheatley, who wrote *Poems on Various Subjects, Religious and Moral* (1773).[2]

This imitation of European models continued to some degree in the decades immediately after independence; the novelist James Fenimore Cooper, for example, drew on the historical fiction of Sir Walter Scott, though he was acutely aware of the presence of Native Americans, as in his novel *The Last of the Mohicans* (1826).

In the 1830s and 1840s, the work of Edgar Allan Poe made an impact in its own right and helped to inaugurate the strand of writing later dubbed Southern Gothic, which explored decay, transgression and horror. But Poe died in 1849, just before a series of works appeared that seemed more distinctively American than any previous ones.

The 1850s

The most prominent literary events in 1850s America were three novels, Nathaniel Hawthorne's *The Scarlet Letter* (1850), Herman Melville's *Moby-Dick* (1851), Harriet Beecher Stowe's *Uncle Tom's Cabin* (1852), and a poetry collection, Walt Whitman's *Leaves of Grass* (1855).

The Scarlet Letter, A Romance was in one sense an historical novel, going back to seventeenth-century Boston to evoke the mixture of desire, guilt, transgression and compulsion that characterised early Puritan America; in another sense Hawthorne's novel was, as its subtitle announces, a romance rather than an example of realism; its primary concern was to engage with human desires and dilemmas through symbolism and it might, in a realist perspective, seem extravagant, exotic, improbable and melodramatic.

Melville's *Moby-Dick* partly anticipates Naturalism – it is a huge databank of information about whaling – and it also, with its seafaring exploits, partakes of the adventure story genre; but its primary force is symbolic: it powerfully dramatises

---

[1] Jamestown: America's first English colony
[2] The first published book by an African American writer

the human capacity for self-destructive obsession, embodied in the figure of Captain Ahab and his quest for the great whale of the novel's title.

The Scarlet Letter and *Moby-Dick* establish a prototype for a certain kind of American novel that will become known as The Great American Novel, which mixes realism and symbolism to tackle 'big' themes that seem both particularly American and universal, applying to all humanity.

Harriet Beecher Stowe's *Uncle Tom's Cabin* is less innovative but its propaganda for the abolition of slavery proved powerful; the sixteenth President of the United States, Abraham Lincoln, supposedly said that it started the American Civil War. This was an obvious exaggeration, but it did arise from and reinforce an idea that would persist in later American writing: that literature could make things happen.

Walt Whitman's poem collection *Leaves of Grass* breaks with the genteel conventions of English mid-Victorian poetry and its American imitators. It is a celebration of the self but not in an enclosed egotistical sense; Whitman applauds an expansive American self, open to experience and variety: 'I am large, I contain multitudes'. Whitman accumulates lines to create a sense of multiplicity and democracy: his poems are a vast American agora[3] in which a wide range of phenomena meet and jostle.

Whitman's poetry would take on a more sombre tone, however, under the pressure of public events – above all, the American Civil War and Lincoln's assassination on 14 April 1865. Serving as a part-time medical orderly in the Civil War brought Whitman into physical contact with the trauma of a whole nation.

The American Civil War

The American Civil War (1861-5) was a trauma for the whole nation because it revealed, all too painfully, that the nation was not a whole. It fractured the founding myth of the original unity of the USA and split its history into two epochs, the antebellum and postbellum. The Civil War left profound marks on politics, culture and literature and many unresolved problems that would persist through the twentieth and into the twenty-first century, as recent controversies about statues of Confederate leaders demonstrate.

In literary terms, the Civil War and the defeat of the South gave a greater eccentricity and intensity to the genre of Southern Gothic, which would brilliantly combine with Modernism in the work of William Faulkner and continue to feed into literature and drama, for instance in the fiction of Carson McCullers, the plays of Tennessee Williams and the novels of Cormac McCarthy. It also produced a war novel, Stephen Crane's *The Red Badge of Courage* (1895), whose author had never seen military action but who set a standard for later American war writing.

---

[3] Assembly or gathering place

The later nineteenth century

Perhaps the most distinctively American novel that appeared in the decades after the Civil War, though significantly set in the antebellum epoch, was Mark Twain's *The Adventures of Huckleberry Finn* (UK, 1884; US, 1885), which sustains a vernacular narrative voice over its whole length and touches on key themes of American literature: the relationship between white and African Americans, male bonding free of supposedly repressive female control, and escape from the constraints of civilisation.

This last element became especially important after 1890, when the Superintendent of the US Census declared that:

> Up to and including 1880 the country had a frontier of settlement, but at present the unsettled area has been so broken into by isolated bodies of settlement that there can hardly be said to be a frontier line.

Frederick Jackson Turner's influential essay, 'The Significance of the Frontier in American History' (1893), argued that the Frontier had been crucial in shaping American identity and distinguishing it from that of Europe, offering

> a new field of opportunity, a gate of escape from the bondage of the past; and freshness, and confidence, and scorn of older society, impatience of its restraints and its ideas, and indifference to its lessons.

Turner concluded that the disappearance of the frontier closed the first period of American history. It was no longer so easy to light out for a territory supposedly outside the constraints of civilisation, as Huck Finn does at the end of Twain's novel.

Not all American writers wanted to 'light out for the Territory', however; Henry James lit out for a more rather than less constrained zone, settling in Britain, which he felt had the traditions necessary to a novelist that the USA lacked. The major focus of his fiction was on Americans encountering Europe and England, what he called the international theme, as in *Daisy Miller* (1879) or *The Portrait of a Lady* (1881).

James's friend and fellow author Edith Wharton shared his love of an elaborate style and of high society, but more often located her fiction in America itself, as in *Ethan Frome* (1911), set in an imaginary Massachusetts town, or *The Age of Innocence* (1920), which unfolds mainly in New York City.

In American poetry, a chastened but still exuberant Whitman embodied one important direction; Emily Dickinson exemplified another, though a proper appreciation of her work only developed as the twentieth century progressed, in light of Modernism and then of Feminism. Where Whitman was expansive, using many words, Dickinson was economical, using few words but packing them with power, as in the second stanza of 'There's a certain slant...', a poem that evokes the inward effect of a particular kind of winter afternoon light:

Heavenly Hurt, it gives us –
We can find no scar,
But internal difference,
Where the Meanings, are –

The two contrasting dynamics of capacious and concentrated poetry, epitomised in Whitman and Dickinson respectively, would continue to energise American literature throughout the twentieth century and into the present day.

The early twentieth century

If American literature in the later nineteenth-century moved away from British models, one European movement, primarily exemplified by the French writer Émile Zola, found its US counterpart: Naturalism. American novelists made major contributions to this genre, for example, Frank Norris and, above all, Theodore Dreiser. Dreiser's strong sense of the extent to which people were not free agents but subject to pressures from their instincts and from society, could make his novels seem amoral and degrading; but from his perspective, he was telling it like it is.

The title character of Dreiser's first novel, *Sister Carrie* (1900), frankly chases life's pleasures, living out the right to 'the pursuit of Happiness' enshrined in the Declaration of Independence; without any taint of authorial disapproval. Clyde Griffiths, in Dreiser's *An American Tragedy* (1925), is remorselessly enmeshed in instinctual and social webs and the novel, true to its title, ends grimly and implies that its tragic pattern is not just personal to its protagonist but representative of a wider society, the USA itself; 'the pursuit of Happiness' may end very unhappily; the American Dream can turn to nightmare. But in between *Sister Carrie* and *An American Tragedy*, America would enter a European nightmare.

World War One

In the early twentieth century, nearly fifty years after the American Civil War ended, the USA became embroiled in another murderous conflict: World War One. America did not join in until 6 April 1917; the AEF, the American Expeditionary Force, then fought its major battle in September to November 1918, in the Meuse-Argonne offensive in which the title character of F. Scott Fitzgerald's *The Great Gatsby* (1925) claims to have proved a hero.

World War One had a major impact on American writing, for example in John Dos Passos's novel *Three Soldiers* (1921) and, most notably, in Ernest Hemingway's novel *A Farewell to Arms* (1929), with its taciturn, understated style that evoked trauma perhaps more powerfully than elaborate language might have done.

The 1920s

America emerged from the trauma of World War One, however, as the dominant global power. Scott Fitzgerald recalled the triumphant mood in his essay 'Echoes of the Jazz Age' (1931): 'We were the most powerful nation. Who could tell us any longer what was fashionable and what was fun?' Fun seemed to be the priority: as Fitzgerald put it in another retrospective essay, 'Early Success' (1937), 'America was going on the greatest, gaudiest spree in history.'

Three legislative changes helped to complicate and characterise this spree: the Eighteenth Amendment, ratified on 16 January 1919, prohibited the manufacture, sale, or transportation of intoxicating liquors; the Nineteenth Amendment, ratified on 18 August 1920, affirmed that the right of American citizens to vote should not be denied or abridged by the United States or by any State on account of sex – in other words, it gave women the vote; and the Emergency Quota Act that came into effect on 19 May 1921 placed restrictions on immigration.

Prohibition had unintended consequences; people drank more rather than less intoxicating liquor – as a character in John Dos Passos's *Manhattan Transfer* (1925) says, 'the difficulty under prohibition is keeping sober' – and organised crime boomed; bootlegging is one of the sources of Jay Gatsby's immense fortune, and an apparently limitless flow of alcohol lubricates his lavish parties. This widespread flouting of the law under Prohibition contributed to a licentious atmosphere.

The Nineteenth Amendment encouraged the emancipation of women but a range of other changes in fashion and behaviour more visibly fostered this, epitomised in the figure Scott and Zelda Fitzgerald helped to make famous: the flapper.

The Emergency Quota Act arose from and exacerbated hostility to immigration. The immediate postwar social and industrial unrest in the USA, often blamed on foreign agitators, had intensified fears of immigrants from Europe and further afield. America's previous immigration policy had been relatively 'open-door' and one result of this was a significant body of literature by and about Russian and East European immigrants who became part of American society: for instance, Abraham Cahan's *The Rise of David Levinsky* (1917) and Willa Cather's *My Ántonia* (1918). Now this phase of literature began to fade.

The legislative and social changes of the 1920s criss-crossed with the artistic innovations of Modernism – or as we might say now, to highlight their plurality, Modernisms. We have, for example, a novel that emerged during the great cultural starburst of the African American Harlem Renaissance, Jean Toomer's *Cane* (1923), with its discontinuous mixture of verse and prose; John Dos Passos's *Manhattan Transfer* (1925), with its crosscutting between different characters and its prose poetry; and William Faulkner's *The Sound and the Fury* (1929), with its immersive interior monologues and complex chronological shifts.

Two other novels that appeared during the Harlem Renaissance, Nella Larsen's *Quicksand* (1928) and *Passing* (1929), mixed realism and a strong narrative line with modernist techniques of fragmentation and ellipsis, like Fitzgerald's *The Great Gatsby*, but kept their focus firmly on their female mixed-race protagonists.

The spree of the 1920s ended, however, with the Wall Street Crash in October 1929.

The 1930s

The Wall Street Crash was followed by the Great Depression of the 1930s and the emergence of fiction that combined some of the elements of Naturalism with radical politics, often influenced by socialism or Marxism. For instance, John Dos Passos's massive trilogy *USA*, made up of *The 42nd Parallel* (1930), *1919* (1932) and *The Big Money* (1936), develops and extends the modernist techniques he had used in the 1920s in *Manhattan Transfer* in an epic that aims, as its overall title suggests, to encompass, through a range of representative fictional and real-life stories, the immensity, variety, energy and corruption of America.

Coming at the end of the decade, John Steinbeck's *The Grapes of Wrath* (1939) is another epic interweaving the family saga of the Joads with a sense of wider collective behaviour. Although Steinbeck was condemned as a communist at the time, his vision was closer to that of Thomas Jefferson than of Marx; he believed in a nation of individual small property owners working the land and he opposed big banks and corporations.

Marxism was a greater influence on Richard Wright's *Native Son* (1940), with its powerful study of an African American who kills two women; but Wright's novel also had elements of Dreiser's Naturalism in *An American Tragedy* and of the genre called Urban Realism, and converged with the French Existentialism that would feed back into postwar American literature and culture.

Zora Neale Hurston had offered an alternative vision to Wright in her novel *Their Eyes Were Watching God* (1937), which focuses on the experience of its female protagonist, Janie Mae Crawford, from her childhood, when she becomes suddenly aware of her ethnicity, through her successive relationships with three men in one of the all-black townships that existed in America at this time. *Their Eyes Were Watching God* is alert to oppression and trauma, particularly that of women, but it is also celebratory in its lyrical prose and joyful mingling of genres. Its qualities, however, went largely unrecognised until the 1980s.

World War Two

When the Japanese surprise air attack on the American naval base at Pearl Harbour on 7 December 1941 provoked the USA to enter World War Two, the sense of being enmeshed in inescapable collective processes evident in Steinbeck, Dos Passos and Wright increased. It is summed up in Randall Jarrell's five-line poem 'The Death of the Ball Turret Gunner' (1945), which starts 'From my mother's sleep I fell into the State' and ends 'When I died they washed me out of the turret with a hose.'

Two later novels that also express this sense of a sometimes lethal enmeshment are Joseph Heller's *Catch-22* (1961) and Kurt Vonnegut's *Slaughterhouse-Five* (1969), but they did not appear until the 1960s, where their absurdism and anti-war tendencies seemed to match the mood of that decade.

In contrast, Norman Mailer's *The Naked and the Dead* (1948), published only three years after the war's end, is also critical of war and American society but adopts a grimly realistic approach from its arresting opening onwards when the soldiers sail towards an assault on a Pacific island:

> All over the ship, all through the convoy, there was a knowledge that in a few hours some of them were going to be dead.

American soldiers who did survive World War Two returned to a different America.

The 1950s

Postwar America enjoyed an economic boom that seemed to make the American Dream come true and the Great Depression of the 1930s a distant memory. But nightmares troubled the Dream: fears of nuclear war and Communist infiltration created a strong sense of unease that pulsed in the literature of the period.

Arthur Miller interrogated the American Dream in his plays, most centrally *Death of a Salesman* (1949). American novelists produced a rich crop of fiction that was often linked with, though not confined to, specific ethnicities. Jewish American writing encompassed Saul Bellow's *The Adventures of Augie March* (1953), Bernard Malamud's *The Assistant* (1957) and Philip Roth's *Goodbye, Columbus* (1959); all these authors would have prolific careers. African American writing included Ralph Ellison's *Invisible Man* (1952), which used modified modernist techniques to dramatise the disorientations of its protagonist, and James Baldwin's *Go Tell It On the Mountain* (1953), which evokes the son of a preacher man wrestling with his father's contradictions.

In the later 1950s the Beat writers emerged, rebelling against what cultural commentators such as David Reisman, Vance Packard and William H. Whyte saw as a growing conformity in American society. The most prominent Beats were the novelist William S. Burroughs and Jack Kerouac, and the poet Allen Ginsberg. Burroughs's *Naked Lunch* (1959) is a comic, hard-edged phantasmagoria existing in an interzone between reality, dream, hallucination and vision. Kerouac's *On the Road* (1957), in an American tradition going back at least to *Huckleberry Finn*, evokes its protagonist's travels with his buddy around the USA and into Mexico. Ginsberg's *Howl* (1956) is a poetic journey through trauma. The Beats anticipated key themes and attitudes of the 1960s counterculture, though only Ginsberg identified wholeheartedly with this.

The 1960s

In the 1960s, domestic and global tumults, especially the Vietnam War, and the increasing erosion of the boundaries of 'high' and 'popular' culture were matched in American literature by a growing discontent with traditional forms and attitudes. This was evident in, for example, the 'confessional' poetry of Anne Sexton and Robert Lowell, and in the development of the nonfiction novel that applied narrative techniques such as dialogue, dramatised scenes, and internal monologue to documented events: notable nonfiction novels included Truman Capote's *In Cold Blood* (1966), recreating the story of the seemingly motiveless murder of a Kansas family, and Norman Mailer's *The Armies of the Night* (1968), about the 1967 anti-Vietnam march on the Pentagon.

After the 1960s

After the 1960s many literary possibilities proliferated, from postmodernist playfulness to a revived realism. Major women writers emerged, for instance Alice Walker with *The Color Purple* (1982), reanimating the form of the epistolary novel, the novel told in letters, to focus on male abuse of women while maintaining an ultimately affirmative outlook, and Toni Morrison, with *Beloved* (1987), which, in a heightened, intense prose echoing Faulkner and George Eliot but emerging as a distinctive style in its own right, evokes the plight of a mother who kills her baby so that it should not be brought up in slavery.

Perhaps the author who came closest to writing the Great American Novel of the later twentieth century was Don DeLillo, whose *Underworld* (1997) stretches non-chronologically from the 1950s to the 1990s, encompasses a rich range of historical and personal themes, and sustains over its great length a style that is both hard-edged and poetic. It showed how far American literature had come since its early imitation of English and European models. But today the timespan it covers may still seem, in a sense, an age of innocence.

The present

The fall from this end-of-century innocence came early in the new millennium with the traumas of 9/11 and the Iraq war, which posed particularly strong questions about what kind of literary response might be possible or appropriate. The reconfiguration effected by the emergence of new women writers and the rediscovery of past ones (such as Hurston) in the late twentieth century was further reshaped in the early twenty-first century by the increased visibility, in literature, culture and society, of different sexual and gender orientations (for instance, LGBTQ, QTIPOC) and ethnicities (for example, Asian American, Chicano, Latino/a, Native American).

These traumas and transformations have generated a creative ferment in American literature that is volatile but often invigorating. Key recent works would include Lisa Halliday's novel *Asymmetry* (2018) which takes in intergenerational relationships, immigration and the Iraq war and its aftermath, and Wendy Chen's poetry collection *Unearthings* (2018) which explores, in spare language, her family history and complex identity as an Asian American woman, born in a small 'red house / On the Connecticut River' but still perceived through an eroticised Orientalist prism as from 'no country / but the East, / my body fragrant / as star anise.'

The future

To predict the future of American literature, especially at present, is risky. It seems likely, however, that electronic media, especially in the country that gave birth to the GUI, Mac, iPhone and iPad, will continue to impact upon every aspect of literary production, from the act of creation to the process of dissemination. Themes of the past, such as ethnic and gender imbalance and ecological and martial devastation, seem more pressing than ever, and writers of fiction, drama and poetry will want to pursue them further. Issues of national identity and their intersection with issues of ethnic and gender identity will be explored more fully. Above all, the American Dream enshrined in the Declaration of Independence, however chastened by abrasive realities, will continue to animate American literature, even as the ever-growing weight of history pulls it back towards the past.

Questions to take your thinking further

- Why should we study American Literature?
- What are the differences and similarities between American Literature and English Literature?
- How far is a knowledge of American history helpful in understanding American Literature?
- Is it possible today to write a Great American Novel, Poem or Play?
- What is the relationship between American Literature and digital media?

Reading list

Adams, B. 2008. *Asian American Literature*. Edinburgh: Edinburgh University Press.

Gray, R. 2011. *A History of American Literature*. 2nd edn. Oxford: Wiley-Blackwell.

Miller, D. Quentin. 2016. *The Routledge Introduction to African American Literature*. London: Routledge.

Morley, C. 2012. *Modern American Literature*. Edinburgh: Edinburgh University Press.

Wirth-Nesher, H. 2019. *The Cambridge History of Jewish American Literature*. Cambridge: Cambridge University Press.

POSTCOLONIALISM
Leila Kamali

What is 'postcolonial' literature?

'Postcolonial literature' in its most conventional sense refers to the literature written by peoples of formerly colonised territories, lands which have been occupied and governed by another nation. A well-known example of colonialism is the British occupation of India. 'Postcolonial literature' is also used to describe writing which responds explicitly to the relationship between a colonising power and colonised peoples. So in the example of literature by Indian authors, 'postcolonial' elements might comment upon the relationship between British influence and the Indian people, even long after the country has regained its political independence. In fact, the critics Bill Ashcroft, Gareth Griffiths and Helen Tiffin suggest that the term 'postcolonial' can 'cover all the culture affected by the imperial process from the moment of colonisation to the present day' (*The Empire Writes Back*, 2002). 'Postcolonial literature' can also be understood to refer to a far wider literature than simply the texts emerging from former colonies. It is specifically interested in questions of power, culture and race which underpin colonial process, but which also extend far beyond formal colonial arrangements, arguably to all segments of today's society.

Orientalism and naming the postcolonial

The 1960s saw rapid decolonisation of much of the former British Empire, with nations across Africa and the Caribbean claiming their independence. As a result of these high-profile independence movements, a public appetite grew for what came to be known as 'postcolonial literature' in English, and this eventually became established as a field of study. The term 'postcolonial literature' only came to be commonly used in the 1990s, but it named a way of understanding texts that is most often thought of as having originated in the 1970s with Edward Said's work *Orientalism* (1978). This text helped to define the literature of the former British Empire as being specifically interested in structures of power.

Importantly, postcolonial literature is written from the position of those who have in many ways been 'othered' by a dominant discourse (for example, the point of view of Algerians rather than of French colonisers, or of the Indian population rather than of the British). Interestingly one of the things that postcolonial literature also reveals is the way in which the national identity of the colonisers is formed in part through their relationship with the people and cultures it colonises: the colonisers identify themselves against this 'Other'. So in writing about 'the Orient's special place in European Western experience', Said comments:

The Orient is not only adjacent to Europe; it is also the place of Europe's greatest and richest and oldest colonies, the source of its civilisations and languages [...] and one of its deepest and most recurring images of the Other. In addition, the Orient has helped to define Europe (or the West) as its contrasting image, idea, personality, experience.

Naming and narrative

A central argument in Said's *Orientalism* is that European nations maintained their cultural and political power through their continued capacity to name and define Middle Eastern and Asian peoples. This is an argument which could be applied to European attitudes to all non-white peoples. The power to name is often linked closely, in postcolonial literature, to the power to decide what is true, at every level of a nation's story. This is an idea brought to life in Salman Rushdie's 1981 novel *Midnight's Children*, which opens with the birth of its protagonist Saleem Sinai, at midnight on the day of India's independence from Britain. Making a case for the importance of storytelling not only to the Indian/Pakistani cultural backdrop against which Saleem's narrative is set, but to postcolonial processes of power themselves, the protagonist emphasises, 'I am the sum total of everything that went before me, of all I have been seen done, of everything done-to-me. I am everyone everything whose being-in-the-world affected was affected by mine.' Postcolonial literature explores the ways in which the cultural identity of the less powerful is shaped by stories that are told by the dominant sections of society (think white, male, middle-class). Equally importantly, postcolonial literature highlights the importance of the stories of the less powerful which challenge such dominant positions.

The coloniser's truth: Frantz Fanon's legacy

This emphasis in postcolonial literature upon truth and its relationship to power – or whose truth carries most power in the world – is read through the lens of psychopathology in the work of Frantz Fanon. Fanon was a Martinique-born psychiatrist who wrote *Black Skin, White Masks* (1952) and *The Wretched of the Earth* (1961) in the context of French colonialism and the Algerian revolution. Writing long before 'postcolonial literature' was formalised as a critical position, Fanon nevertheless offered clear-sighted theorisations of the colonised (and racialised) condition based upon observations from his clinical practice and in his encounters with everyday colonial society. In *Black Skin, White Masks*, Fanon writes:

> Every colonised people – in other words, every people in whose soul an inferiority complex has been created by the death and burial of its local cultural originality – finds itself face to face with the language of the civilising nation; that is, with the culture of the mother country.

In this work Fanon explains the ways in which colonial racism objectifies and defines the black man's identity, in the process alienating him from his own consciousness and his capacity to define himself. A similar logic, fascinatingly, was described as early as 1903, against the American historical backdrop of slavery and segregation by African American thinker W.E.B. Du Bois, as 'double consciousness'.

Fanon's later work *The Wretched of the Earth*, born in the cradle of the Algerian revolution, extends the analysis of the psychological consequences of colonial oppression into something of a manifesto for the overturning of colonial power and the establishment of decolonised nations. Fanon's striking contention is that the process of decolonisation must be a violent one. He argues that colonialism 'is violence in its natural state, and it will only yield when confronted with greater violence.' Fanon writes that because colonialism 'turns to the past of the oppressed people, and distorts, disfigures and destroys it', a precise value must also be placed upon a distinctive national culture as a key part of the overthrow and transfer of power. He writes: 'A national culture is the whole body of efforts made by a people in the sphere of thought to describe, justify and praise the action through which that people has created itself and keeps itself in existence.' Implicit in this argument is the importance of postcolonial literature itself, then, in the maintenance and equally the reversal of the major structures of power which govern society.

Power and tradition

For colonised people, the relationship with colonial power is rarely simple. Chinua Achebe's *Things Fall Apart* (1958) is one of the earliest works of postcolonial African literature to appear in English, and was actually published well before the formalising of 'postcolonial literature' as an area of study. The novel tells the story of Okonkwo, a wrestler from the Igbo (or Ibo) people in Nigeria, and shows how the workings of colonial power can be complex. Okonkwo is a man motivated by the belief that his father was a weak man and that he must therefore prove himself as a great warrior. This personal struggle puts him at odds with the customs of his village, a struggle which is only intensified when European colonialism arrives:

> Okonkwo felt a cold shudder run through him [...] He saw himself and his father crowding round their ancestral shrine waiting in vain for worship and sacrifice and finding nothing but ashes of bygone days, and his children the while praying to the white man's god.

Okonkwo is struck here by what postcolonial critic Homi Bhabha has called 'mimicry', a process of imitating the coloniser which quickly endangers the cultures of colonised peoples (1994). When Okonkwo finds that his village cannot be wholly defended against infringements by European custom, his frustrations reach crisis point and he takes his own life. His clansman Obeirika comments that the white man 'has put a knife on the things that held us together and we have fallen apart.' Achebe's tale shows clearly that the roles of coloniser and colonised must not be mistaken as falling into any simple relationship between 'bad' and 'good'. Instead, the novel shows how colonial power works insidiously with instabilities which may already be present in any society, always ready to exploit them in their own interests.

Gender in postcolonial contexts

So it's clear that in a postcolonial context, the question of power is much more complex than a simple struggle between a colonising European nation, and a colonised place or culture. Even before European colonialism, within the context of a traditional society, questions of gender, tradition and rights are shown to contain the potential for conflict. Critics reading texts from a postcolonial perspective need to be alert to the subtleties of these conflicts and what they reveal about power relationships. Gayatri Spivak addresses this in her seminal essay 'Can the Subaltern Speak?' (1988). In this essay she writes about 'the story of the mythic Sati', which tells of a classical Hindu practice where a widow commits suicide by placing her body onto her husband's funeral pyre. Spivak emphasises that a postcolonial reading of this practice must be alive to the conflicting dynamics of power it represents. For Spivak, the narrative in which the widow self-immolates is not only about the loss of the individual's life. The way in which this act is interpreted (or read) reveals a great deal about the society doing the interpreting. So it will be read differently from a patriarchal Indian cultural perspective than from a colonialist British one. In and against these narratives about the Indian woman, Spivak's point is that the voice of the woman as 'subaltern' is mostly unheard. Her work makes us think about how important it is to treat such a silenced historical figure's story with a greater sensitivity.

Tsitsi Dangarembga's 1988 novel *Nervous Conditions* takes its title from Frantz Fanon's famous pronouncement in *The Wretched of the Earth* that 'the condition of the native is a nervous condition'. Her novel tells the story of Tambu, a young girl growing up in 1970s rural Rhodesia (now Zimbabwe). Hungry for education she encounters restrictions both in her traditional family and in her British colonial schooling. Resistant to the message given to her by her parents, to 'Accept your lot', Tambu persists in her ambitions. Interestingly, the power of education - whether given or withheld - is shown not only to create alliances between women but also divisions. Tambu's aunt Maiguru, who herself achieved a Master's degree only to give up her ambitions for the sake of children and family, says, 'People were prejudiced against educated women. Prejudiced. That's why they said we weren't decent. That was in the fifties. Now we are into the seventies. I am disappointed that people still believe the same things.' The conflict between the pull toward personal fulfilment that is represented by education, the traditional pressures of home, and the restricted education of the British system is perceptively represented in this novel as providing the source of a 'nervous condition' suffered acutely by Tambu's cousin Nyasha:

> She began to rock, her body quivering tensely. 'I won't grovel. Oh no, I won't. I'm not a good girl. I'm evil. I'm not a good girl.' I touched her to comfort her and that was the trigger. 'I won't grovel, I won't die,' she raged and crouched like a cat ready to spring.

Like Achebe and Spivak, Dangarembga is interested in humanising and making visible the complex interplay of power in gender and generational relationships in which the colonial dynamic operates.

Story as a vehicle for power

Postcolonial literature, it may be said, has a particularly vested interest in story as a vehicle of power. In his essay 'The National Longing for Form' (1989), Tim Brennan argues that it is stories which form the foundation of nations, and which help to craft the direction in which political and economic power flow. He writes:

> It was the novel that historically accompanied the rise of nations by objectifying the 'one, yet many' of national life, and by mimicking the structure of the nation, a clearly bordered jumble of languages and styles.

Discussion of postcolonial literature in an English language context can create a cloak of invisibility around the multilingual contexts of postcolonial literature, and the processes of translation which are inherent to the texts we read. In this way, issues of power in postcolonial literature are absolutely bound up with questions of language and its relationship to what gets published.

An ongoing discussion between Chinua Achebe and the Kenyan author Ngũgĩ wa Thiong'o encapsulates these debates about postcolonial literature and the practice of writing in English, the language of the former coloniser. In a 1975 speech entitled 'The African Writer and the English Language', Achebe made the case for English as a suitable vehicle in which to situate a modern African literature:

> I feel that the English language will be able to carry the weight of my African experience. But it will have to be a new English, still in full communion with its ancestral home but altered to suit new African surroundings.

Ngũgĩ, writing in *Decolonising the Mind: The Politics of Language in African Literature* (1981), counters Achebe's position, making a stern critique of the kind of view which embraces the hybrid potential of English for postcolonial literature:

> How did we, as African writers, come to be so feeble towards the claims of our languages on us and so aggressive in our claims on other languages, particularly the languages of our colonisation? [...] Language carries culture, and culture carries, particularly through orature and literature, the entire body of values by which we come to perceive ourselves and our place in the world.

Not to be outdone, Achebe describes Ngũgĩ's attachment to his own mother tongue Gikuyu as a 'pastoral idyll' (1989). He offers a retort which he claims is grounded not in compromise and obeisance to the English coloniser, but in pragmatism, and an interest in the unity of modern African nation-states:

> As long as Nigeria wishes to exist as a nation it has no choice in the foreseeable future but to hold its more than two hundred component nationalities together through an alien language, English. [...] It would seem then that the culprit for Africa's language difficulties was not imperialism, as Ngũgĩ would have us believe, but the linguistic plurality of modern African states.

The particular dilemma of the appropriateness or not of writing postcolonial (and often anti-colonial) literature in the language of the coloniser, continues today to inform African writers' use of language, and is a debate which does not find easy resolution.

Creolising the language

The relationship with the former coloniser's language is a significant question also raised in the postcolonial context of the Caribbean, where writers have typically found it impossible to represent their own experience in standard English. In 1984, poet Kamau Brathwaite wrote:

> It is nation language in the Caribbean that, in fact, largely ignores the [English poetic form of the] pentameter. Nation language is the language which is influenced very strongly by the African model, the African aspect of our New World/Caribbean heritage. English it may be in terms of some of its lexical features. But in its contours, its rhythm and timbre, its sound explosions, it is not English.

A key example of something resembling nation language, or what is also referred to as a 'creolised' approach to English typical of postcolonial Caribbean literature, is Sam Selvon's novel *The Lonely Londoners*, published in 1956, and a key text of what is now known as the 'Windrush experience'. Selvon anticipates the approach of many writers of postcolonial and diaspora experience to the task of self-representation in English literary form. Having initially attempted to write a novel in standard English, he abandoned it as not appropriate to the story that needed to be told. Writing in a creolised English, a 'nation language' bearing the flavour of Caribbean language not only in reported speech but also in descriptive passages, was ground-breaking at the time:

> One grim winter evening, when it had a kind of unrealness about London, with a fog sleeping restlessly over the city and the lights showing in the blur as if is not London at all but some strange place on another planet, Moses Aloetta hop on a number 46 bus at the corner of Chepstow Road and Westbourne Grove to go to Waterloo to meet a fellar who was coming from Trinidad on the boat-train.

Postcolonial and diaspora literature

Caribbean writing in and about Britain, because it occurs against older histories of migration from Africa, India and elsewhere to the Caribbean, as well as a more recent migration to Britain, begins to cross the border between 'postcolonial literature' and the 'literature of diaspora' (a term meaning dispersal or scattering of peoples). James Clifford wrote in 1988:

> This century has seen a drastic expansion of mobility, including tourism, migrant labor, immigration, urban sprawl. More and more people 'dwell' with the help of mass transit, automobiles, airplanes. In cities on six continents foreign populations have come to stay – mixing in but often in partial, specific fashions. The 'exotic' is uncannily close. [...] 'Cultural difference' is no longer a stable, exotic otherness; self-other relations are matters of power and rhetoric rather than of essence.

Postcolonial literature today begins to encompass narratives which represent both arrival in the cities of the colonising country (for example, London), and the subsequent entrenchment of diverse cultures of formerly colonised people in these imperial centres. As we move into twenty-first century literature, the result is often the kind of community that is depicted in Zadie Smith's *White Teeth* (2000) – a patchwork of first, second, and third-generation migrants and beyond, their cultures mingling in diverse and often celebratory fashion:

> This has been the century of strangers, brown, yellow and white. This has been the century of the great immigrant experiment. It is only this late in the day that you can walk into a playground and find Isaac Leung by the fish pond, Danny Rahman in the football cage, Quang O'Rourke bouncing a basketball, and Irie Jones humming a tune. Children with first and last names on a direct collision course. Names that secrete within them mass exodus, cramped boats and planes, cold arrivals, medical checks. It is only this late in the day, and possibly only in Willesden, that you can find best friends Sita and Sharon, constantly mistaken for each other because Sita is white (her mother liked the name) and Sharon is Pakistani (her mother thought it best – less trouble).

This mingling of cultures is something the theorist Homi Bhabha commented upon, suggesting that late-twentieth-century cultural identity was fluid and always changing, shaped in what he called the 'Third Space of enunciation', where it was impossible to imagine that there was any such thing as racial or cultural 'purity'.

Read today (in 2019), the rather triumphant tone of Smith's turn-of-the-century postcolonial multiculturalism contains within it hints of something very much more sinister. In the current era of far-right nationalisms, 'trouble' seems nothing to joke about, and the figure of the refugee that Smith associates above with the dim and distant twentieth-century past, is situated with increasing regularity on our television screens and in our daily lives. Contemporary Kenyan-born Somali-

British poet Warsan Shire emerges today as a prominent poetic voice for refugee experience in an understanding of the changing nature of the postcolonial:

> no one leaves home unless
> home is the mouth of a shark
> you only run for the border
> when you see the whole city running as well [...]
>
> you have to understand
> that no one puts children in a boat
> unless the water is safer than the land

Extract from 'Home' (2015)

Twenty-first-century versions of colonialism

Reading contemporary refugee experience as productive of new kinds of postcolonial literature asks us to situate power today not simply with any individual colonising nation-state, but also with a kind of roving colonialism. This form of colonialism polices borders and holds the power to name, to stop people and to move them on. Furthermore, as ecological questions move to the centre of the news agenda, questions of colonialism previously addressed mainly to nation-states are now being addressed to multinational corporations and to the joint responsibility for the planet that all peoples share and must collaborate upon.

Postcolonial literature shows that a dynamic of power exists in a wide range of relationships, and for that reason today it informs many questions linked to culture, politics, and the structures of capitalism. In practice, descriptions of the relationship between coloniser and colonised, in the context of literature, also encompasses commentary upon other relationships which are not strictly held within the coloniser/colonised relationship, but which are strongly intertwined with it. These might include relationships between a younger more modern postcolonial generation in a formerly colonised territory, and an older generation which is often more strongly rooted in the class, race, gender, sexuality and language dynamics of an earlier society. Today postcolonial literature is grappling with contemporary issues; Arundhati Roy's 2017 novel *The Ministry of Utmost Happiness*, a long-awaited follow-up to her much-loved *The God of Small Things* (1997), engages with queer, trans and sex-worker communities in India, continuing postcolonial literature's affirmed interest in using the power of discourse to enable the stories of those long marginalised within our societies to begin to be able to write back.

Questions to take your thinking further

- Why is the field of postcolonial literature important, and how does its importance shift over the decades since it was first named?
- How might an understanding of the key issues of postcolonial literature offer new ways of reading older texts, for instance William Shakespeare's *Othello*?
- How does postcolonial literature overlap with other kinds of literature?
- How has this chapter asked you to reflect upon questions of power and postcolonial literature?

Reading list

Boehmer, E. 1995. *Colonial and Postcolonial Literature*. Oxford: Oxford University Press.

McLeod, J. 2010. *Beginning Postcolonialism*. Manchester: Manchester University Press.

Nixon, R. 2011. *Slow Violence and the Environmentalism of the Poor*. Cambridge Mass.: Harvard University Press.

Said, E.W. 1993 [1978]. *Culture and Imperialism*. London: Chatto and Windus.

Williams, P. and L. Chrisman, eds. 2015. *Colonial Discourse and Post-Colonial Theory: A Reader*. London: Routledge.

THE GOTHIC AND THE SUPERNATURAL

Andrew Michael Hurley

Introduction

The first Gothic novel is generally considered to be Horace Walpole's *The Castle of Otranto* (1764) and while it reads like a five-part Shakespearean tragedy full of political intrigue, destructive lust, paranormal divination and bloody vengeance, it was an attempt to create a new mode of writing. Walpole's aim was to 'blend the two kinds of romance, the ancient and the modern', or in other words to fuse the fantastical medieval adventure that readers of the day would have expected from a 'Gothic' tale and the realist novel of the type being written by Henry Fielding and Samuel Richardson.

His literary experiment was subsequently taken up by Clara Reeve in *The Old English Baron* (1778), a work she considered to be the 'literary offspring' of *The Castle of Otranto*. However, she is critical of the success of Walpole's hybridisation. In her opinion he fails to contain his story within the 'verge of probability', making the events too outlandish to be wholly effective.

It may be a fair assessment. Any realism in Walpole's novel is quickly overrun by the supernatural and sensational. The story begins with Manfred, the Prince of Otranto, looking forward to the wedding of his son and heir, Conrad, to Isabella of Vincenza. Yet before the nuptials commence, Conrad is crushed to death by a giant helmet, awakening spirits in the castle and an ancient curse. Anxious to hold onto power, Manfred tries to persuade Isabella to wed him instead, even though he is already married. She refuses and, helped by the noble peasant, Theodore, makes her escape through the secret passageways and subterranean caverns of the castle. Thus, Walpole establishes some of the staples of Gothic horror: the mouldering aristocratic pile, fulfilled prophecies, restless spirits, uncanny doublings, the virginal damsel and her monstrous pursuer.

These images were repeated and developed in the Gothic novels which followed, notably Ann Radcliffe's *The Mysteries of Udolpho* (1794) and Matthew Lewis's *The Monk* (1796). But the Gothic was already being redefined and would develop again under Romantic poets such as William Wordsworth, John Keats and Samuel Taylor Coleridge into a framework for describing the relationships between the physical world and the inner landscapes of the emotions. In contrast to the often-theatrical romps of the eighteenth-century Gothic novel, Mary Shelley's *Frankenstein* (1818) develops the form into one that is fit for a serious philosophical debate about the meaning of 'humanity' and the moral responsibility that comes with scientific experimentation.

The Victorian era became a golden age for supernatural fiction, producing arguably the most well-known ghost story in the English language, Dickens's *A Christmas Carol* (1843), and the most enduring Gothic character, Dracula, in Bram Stoker's 1897 novel of the same name. In America, a different strain of 'Southern' Gothic emerged in the nineteenth century in the writing of Edgar Allen Poe and Ambrose Bierce, who often used the landscapes of the former slave states and the legacy of the Civil War to tell stories of decay, madness and murder. It's a strain developed by the modernist writer William Faulkner.

By the twentieth century, 'Gothic' had become a more fluid term with such a wide-ranging set of influences and traditions that it could encompass writers as diverse as Daphne Du Maurier and Stephen King. Added to literary Gothic was, of course, the Gothic of the screen, providing another layer of reference for writers working within the mode today. It's from this rich and complex history that my own novels come, both of which are discussed here.

The Loney (2015)

The Loney is narrated by an anonymous middle-aged Londoner who, after hearing the news about a child's body being washed up in Morecambe Bay on the remote Lancashire coast, recalls the Easter pilgrimage he made there with his family and fellow parishioners in 1976. That year is the first time the pilgrims have been led by Father Bernard, a young Northern-Irish priest brought in to replace the late Father Wilfred, a fervent, pious man much missed by everyone at the church. The aim of their pilgrimage is the same as it has been every year: to take the narrator's mute and mentally disabled brother, Hanny, to a Catholic shrine where, it is hoped, the holy water will 'cure' him. As the visit to the shrine approaches, the narrator notices that certain local people have been healed of their afflictions: a blind woman's sight has been restored and a man's cancer removed. Yet it appears that these miracles have not occurred through God's benevolence but through faith in a much older power.

It is a power that seems to be bound up in the landscape itself. These people have somehow harnessed the elemental energy that constantly alters the appearance of the bay, or 'the Loney', as the locals call it. It is a dangerous force to meddle with, however. As the narrator says, '…it was impossible to truly know the Loney. It changed with each influx and retreat of water and the neap tides would reveal the skeletons of those who thought they had read the place well enough to escape its insidious currents.'

The novel really began with a fascination of this capricious coastal geography, but I wanted the landscape to be much more a part of the story than in 'traditional'

Gothic fiction, where the dense forest, the storm-wracked mountain and the desolate heath often act as background scenery.

This set of aesthetics can be traced back to one of the most important works of the eighteenth century: Edmund Burke's *A Philosophical Enquiry into the Sublime and the Beautiful* (1757). The second section of his thesis was of particular interest to writers because it presented a list of phenomena which could be used to generate a sense of the 'sublime', or in other words a (not unpleasant) frisson of unease and astonishment in the reader's imagination. Burke selects, for example, obscurity, vastness, infinity, magnitude and loudness as the types of experiences likely to produce this psychological effect. And certainly, in the literature of the time, it *is* an effect. Readers then would have understood that employing sublime imagery was a dramatic artifice. Even as early as 1798/99, Jane Austen was able to satirise the cliché in *Northanger Abbey*. Henry Tilney excites the impressionable Catherine Morland, by sketching out the atmosphere she can expect during her stay: '…you will probably have a violent storm,' he says, '…peals of thunder so loud as to seem to shake the edifice to its foundation will roll around the neighbouring mountains.'

Although sublimity was rather hackneyed even then, the tropes persisted in the major works of the canon, for example Ann Radcliffe's *The Mysteries of Udolpho* (the novel which Austen parodies most in *Northanger Abbey*), *Frankenstein* and *Dracula*.

An illustration from all three gives a sense of the way in which these writers use landscape to heighten the thrill of adventure.

1. As Emily and her ailing father journey through the mountains in *The Mysteries of Udolpho*, they pause to regard the view: '…seated on some wild cliff, where only the ilex or the larch could flourish, [they] looked over dark forests of fir, and precipices where human foot had never wandered.'

2. In pursuing his monstrous creation through the Alps, Victor Frankenstein finds himself in a particularly dreary valley and describes how the 'vast mists were rising from the rivers which ran through it and curling in thick wreaths around the opposite mountains, whose summits were hid in the uniform clouds…'

3. En route to meet Dracula, Jonathan Harker remarks how the 'falling sunset threw into strange relief the ghost-like clouds which amongst the Carpathians seem to wind ceaselessly through the valleys.'

Used in this way, landscape is effective in foreshadowing terror, or instilling a sense of threat. But in *The Loney* I wanted to infuse the natural terrain with a genuine menace, not only in a physical sense – in that people could drown there or become stuck in the quicksand – but psychologically. I wanted there to be something about the landscape itself which forced the characters to confront their fears; for there to be no way a person could separate themselves from nature; that the Loney would be a place that flooded the psyche. This blurring of the border between the inner and the outer seemed to me to be mirrored in the topography of Morecambe Bay itself. Quite where the land ends and the sea begins is constantly changing and is perhaps unknowable, making this a place between worlds, a liminal space full of uncertainty – neither one thing nor another. In fact, 'uncertainty' is one of the primary mechanisms for creating 'horror' in Gothic fiction, and it was certainly the case in *The Loney*, not only because the supernatural is suggested rather than made explicit as it is in, say, *The Castle of Otranto* or *Dracula*, but also because doubt is the thing which destroys Father Wilfred.

Hitherto, Father Wilfred has always been able to account for (and so appease) the feral wilderness of the Loney by viewing it through a biblical lens: '…here on the beach,' he notes, 'even though it was bleak and deserted, God was still at work. Here was the wild God who made nature heave and bellow. The violent shadow that followed Jesus through his tender ministry […] there was nothing to be afraid of.' But when he is forced to experience first-hand the strength of the tide, he is so overwhelmed by the raw, natural power at work that he is brought to a state of metaphysical paralysis. He sees that the processes of life and death are entirely indifferent to him and all mankind and cannot be explained, especially in religious terms. His conception of the Loney is peeled back to reveal a place that is truly terrifying because it exists completely outside of human comprehension. In that moment, Wilfred's faith, and all that it has previously measured and simplified, becomes utterly redundant.

This dismantling of self-assurance and intellectual confidence recurs frequently in Gothic and supernatural fiction. One of the earliest examples of this is in Matthew Lewis's *The Monk*, a far more disquieting novel than those of Walpole, Reeve and Radcliffe which preceded it. Drawing on the lurid German *Schauerroman* ('shudder novel') as well as the work of his English contemporaries, Lewis describes the fall of Ambrosio – the virtuous Capuchin abbot of the title – in graphic detail. Once his self-righteousness has been undone by sexual temptation, Ambrosio descends inexorably into murder, rape, incest, black magic and a pact with the Devil himself. The subtext is that even the most virtuous can succumb to sin, or that it is folly to think that education is in itself an impenetrable armour. While we have to remember that Walpole, Reeve, Radcliffe and Lewis were predominantly producing works of (often rather camp) entertainment, they do ask an interesting question about the limits of reason and knowledge.

It's a question that is considered again and again in supernatural fiction and is often the source of the 'horror' in the story. In Bram Stoker's *The Judge's House* (1891) a student, Malcolm Malcolmson, rents the house of the title in order to study undisturbed for his exams, only to find that it has a reputation for being haunted. His assertion to his housekeeper that 'a man who is reading for the Mathematical Tripos has too much to think of to be disturbed by any of these mysterious 'somethings'' crumbles when in throwing his textbooks at the large rat which invades his room each night he discovers that they have no effect. It is his bible, actually, which frightens off the demonic creature, making superstition in this instance more powerful than science.

A similar pattern is seen in M.R. James's classic ghost story, 'Oh, Whistle and I'll Come To You, My Lad' (1904), which with its littoral setting and sense of the uncanny was a significant influence on *The Loney*. Just like Malcolmson in *The Judge's House*, the protagonist here is – at first – scholarly and level-headed. Prior to his excursion to the Suffolk coast, Professor Parkins rebuffs his colleagues who are teasing him about the supernatural: 'I hold that any semblance, any appearance of concession to the view that such things might exist,' he says, 'is equivalent to a renunciation of all that I hold most sacred.'

It's the same mind-set as Father Wilfred. And the same inflexible faith in the rigour of his own intellect that serves to intensify the terror in the moment of confrontation with the unknowable. After blowing an ancient whistle that he finds in a burial site, Parkins seems to draw some malevolent entity to him which only becomes manifest at the end of the story. In his hotel room, the professor's bedsheets gather themselves into a 'face of crumpled linen' and unable to reconcile what he is seeing with his conception of what is possible, Parkins is rooted to the spot, 'uttering cry upon cry at the upmost pitch of his voice.'

Devil's Day (2017)

My second novel is narrated by John Pentecost, a farmer's son from a hamlet called the Endlands on the edge of the Lancashire moors. At the start of the story, John has been living away from the farm for ten years or so, carving out his own life on the other side of the country as a teacher in a private school. When his grandfather – known as the Gaffer – dies suddenly, John and his pregnant wife, Kat, return to the Endlands for the funeral. It being the end of October, it is also the time at which the sheep are brought down off the moors for winter and so John and Kat are expected to help with this too. Back in the valley, John experiences a renewed sense of duty and he becomes determined to persuade Kat to stay and raise their child there. He sees himself as the Gaffer's heir, not only as a custodian of his farm but also of the supernatural stories that he used to tell.

The most important folk tale in the Endlands recalls an incident 'just over a century ago' in which the Devil disguises himself among the sheep as they are led from the moors. Once down in the valley, he wreaks havoc, killing animals and people before summoning a blizzard that buries the farms and the village. The following autumn, to ensure that the incident isn't repeated, the farmers decide to lure the Devil down from the moors before the sheep are gathered. They build bonfires, sing songs and ply the Devil with food and drink and put him to sleep in the fireplace, where he stays until the flock is safely in the pen. Every year since, the Endlanders have re-enacted this ritual, not because they necessarily believe that they are really inviting the 'Owd Feller' into their midst but because it is a means of bonding over the remembrance of a shared victory. The Devil is, for most of them, an embodiment of those natural forces, such as disease and the weather, over which they have little agency.

As it was in *The Loney*, my intention in *Devil's Day* was to create a landscape integral to the story. One of the most enduring influences in this respect was Emily Brontë's *Wuthering Heights* (1847), where the moorland setting is representative of and responsible for the psychological world of the characters.

'Ghosts' appear only fleetingly (if they actually appear at all) in Brontë's novel but there is an enduring sense of the supernatural nonetheless in the mysterious effect the moorland has on the mind. The cold, damp climate causes fevers and hallucinations both for Cathy and Heathcliff, removing them to a liminal place between reality and dreams. Like the bay in *The Loney*, the weather renders the moors in *Wuthering Heights* – and subsequently in *Devil's Day* – forbidding and mercurial. Heathcliff warns Lockwood that 'people familiar with these moors often miss their road…' – an idea that I explored further in my own novel, drawing a distinction between the well-mapped valley where the farmers live and the moorland above which is largely uncharted. To venture into a landscape scant with human history, is to pass through a portal into a very different terrain. For the Endlanders, the moors have become the breeding ground of folklore; a natural place for the Devil – as the personification of unpredictability – to dwell.

This conception of the wild as a home to evil is an ancient fairytale fear and one which Brontë gestures to in *Wuthering Heights*. From the moment the orphaned street child, Heathcliff, is presented to the Earnshaws he is associated with the diabolical, being '…as dark almost as if it came from the devil.' Throughout the rest of the novel he is referred to as 'fiend' and 'goblin', attaining an even more sinister appearance in the lead up to his death, prompting Nelly Dean to ask herself, 'Is he a ghoul, or a vampire?' There is no question that he can be human. Indeed, as a corpse, 'his sharp, white teeth sneered…'

In many ways, he is a quintessential Gothic villain – vindictive, violent, physically powerful and yet filled with a dangerously alluring eroticism; an amalgamation of, say, Manfred in *The Castle of Otranto*, Montoni in *The Mysteries of Udolpho*, or Lord Ruthven in John Polidori's *The Vampyre* (1819). However, Heathcliff is arguably a much more three-dimensional character. He loves, hates, laments and fights with equal energy. We are left with far more questions than answers about whether his motivations are born out of the bitter memories of his harsh upbringing or innate malice.

Exploring the provenance of 'evil' was something that preoccupied me more and more during the writing of *Devil's Day*. And in fact, the machinations of the Devil of local legend pale in comparison to the more insidious evil at work in the Endlands when the Gaffer commits a terrible crime and the other farmers conspire to keep it a secret in order to hold the community together.

Anxiety over the fragmentation of the family unit is a common theme in Gothic and supernatural fiction, with the cause of the breakdown often predicated on contested bloodlines and the drama played out in the turmoil prior to the restoration of order. The plots of both *The Castle of Otranto* and *The Old English Baron* deal with the violent consequences of corrupted lineages. The drama in *Wuthering Heights*, too, is largely founded on the tensions between the different factions of the Earnshaws and Lintons, and that Heathcliff is a true cuckoo in the nest and not the blood heir to anything that he comes to possess. In Gothic fiction, the dramatic tension stems partly from the inability of one generation to pass on power smoothly to the next.

This 'handing on' is of supreme importance in *Devil's Day*. The Endlands can only survive if the land – and the wisdom needed to work it – can be disseminated in perpetuity. When John realises that and knows that he *must* return, his priorities change. His wife's needs become secondary to the needs of the community. Yet, as Kat is an outsider her understanding of what these are is limited, making the valley a frightening place in which to be trapped.

In one sense, John and Kat echo the classic Gothic dynamic of the controlling patriarchal jailer and the powerless female prisoner, but in *Devil's Day* they have both been ensnared by an *idea* – predominantly the myth that the Endlanders, having established their own little fiefdom next to the moors, are somehow inured against the rest of the world and so exempt from its values and judgements. The greatest responsibility for the members of the community is to maintain this privilege, whatever the cost. And this was, for me, one of the main sources of horror in the novel – that this fundamentalism could warp myth into fact to such an extent that violence would become, to the characters, a necessary part of communal life. It's a thought that's pursued to a genuinely unsettling crescendo in Shirley Jackson's story of ritual sacrifice, *The Lottery* (1948), which was one of my ongoing reference points as I explored the normalisation of brutality.

Conclusion

To work in the Gothic mode offers a writer great freedom, not least because the term 'Gothic' has become so malleable. Today it is much less prescribed than it was in the eighteenth century and refers to ideas and patterns rather than a list of ingredients. Yet, it's the spirit of literary fusion in Walpole's pioneering novel that I still find exciting and inspiring. Stretching the edges of the recognisably real not only accommodates the unnatural and the uncanny but opens up a space in which characters have to confront what they don't understand, and that is the essence of true horror.

The future of Gothic

Almost certainly Gothic fiction will continue to reinvent itself as a form in which our fears are exhibited and explored. As a mode of writing it seems rather too important to fade away because unconstrained by realism it can, like science-fiction, often ask difficult existential questions in the most inventive way.

Debates about what it means to be human echo back and forth through time and it's often Gothic works that are revisited and reimagined as a way of articulating present and future concerns. *Frankenstein* is a case in point. The issue that Shelley raises about the extent to which we ought to interfere with natural processes has, for example, been applied to the argument against genetically modified or so-called 'Frankenstein' foods. Likewise, in the inevitable disputes to come about the development of artificial intelligence, Shelley's novel will no doubt be a touchstone in the discussion about the ethics and dangers of engineering sentient life.

As representations of the natural world are so integral to the Gothic, it would seem logical for it to respond to the effects of climate change, which will no doubt become the predominant concern in the coming decades. Ecogothic – or, the ways in which the Gothic relates to ecological issues – is a relatively new area of academic study but exploring the redefinition of our relationship with the wild will inevitably become more and more relevant. Already we're seeing this theme in some contemporary Gothic novels, many of which are rooted in the rural and regional. Jenn Ashworth's *Fell* (2016) is set, like *The Loney*, in Morecambe Bay, Benjamin Myers's *Beastings* (2014) in Cumbria, Fiona Mozley's *Elmet* (2016) in the Vale of York. In all of these examples horror is derived from landscape, whether it's in the stirring of some dormant preternatural power, or the brutality which is permitted by remoteness, or by taking the reader back into a community of a more barbarous age, just as the first Gothic novelists did. But beneath all that is a fear of loss.

Choosing to write about these places is an act of preserving their topographies and stories, real and imagined. However, this choice also suggests that these spaces are important in a psychological sense. We need contact with the wild because in doing so we experience a greater emotional breadth. This was the conclusion that I came to in *Devil's Day*. As John says: 'What we pass on in the Endlands isn't only the privilege of living here, but the privilege of living itself. Seeking out the struggle, I mean, rather than hiding from it. Inoculating ourselves with fear. Little doses and we find courage.'

In its first incarnation, Gothic literature emerged partly in opposition to Enlightenment rationalism. It was a fiction concerned about the potential stifling of creative, spiritual and emotive possibility. And maybe this is the fundamental fear which returns to haunt us, albeit in different shapes. For us in the twenty-first century it is bound up in the fate of our environment, in that if the natural world becomes depleted, we lose the opportunity to experience 'otherness'; and being thus confined to a purely human, materialistic world, we are diminished in imagination, which is perhaps our greatest fear of all.

Questions to take your thinking further

- How has the term 'Gothic' changed since the eighteenth century?
- To what extent is the Gothic or supernatural tale a moral story?
- How far would you agree that the 'horror' in Gothic stems from the clash of opposites: the modern and the ancient, the urban and the rural?
- What are the similarities and differences between Gothic and science-fiction?
- What relevance does Gothic fiction have in the twenty-first century?

Reading list

Botting, F. 2014. *Gothic*. London: Routledge.

Burke, E. 2015 [1757]. *A Philosophical Enquiry into the Sublime and the Beautiful*. Oxford: Oxford World's Classics.

Chaplin, S. 2011. *Gothic Literature*. London: York Press.

Macfarlane, R. 2015. 'The eeriness of the English countryside'. Article in the *Guardian* 10/4/2015

Owens, S. 2019. *The Ghost: A Cultural History*. London: Tate Publishing.

Scovell, A. 2017. *Folk Horror: Hours Dreadful and Things Strange*. New York: Columbia University Press.

DYSTOPIA

Nathan Waddell

The word 'dystopia' refers to an imagined place, society, or condition, usually located in the future, which in some unmissable way has gone desperately wrong. Some of the most famous dystopias in Anglo-American literature appear in George Orwell's *Nineteen Eighty-Four* (1949), Ray Bradbury's *Fahrenheit 451* (1953), and Margaret Atwood's *The Handmaid's Tale* (1985). In the dystopias depicted in such texts, hope is in short supply. They are, as their etymology suggests, bad (*dys*) places (*topias*). It's not merely the case that the imagined places we call dystopias have their problems. Fictional societies can be broken without being dystopias, although all the imagined worlds and societies we call dystopian are necessarily defective and damaged. The important point is that the magnitude of the wrongness in dystopias is off the scale. Very often they are places of oppression, bigotry, fanaticism, hatred, and xenophobia. When we write or talk about dystopias we usually have in mind a realm that is nasty, violent, brutish, and cruel, or a dream showing us the victories of the worst things in the world.

Generic origins

Usually when we refer to dystopias we put the emphasis on subject matter, on the *what* of the imagined society gone wrong; on what is feared and what is out of joint, the weight falling on the content of the imagined world, rather than on the process of imagining that world. A case in point is one of the earliest literary dystopias, E.M. Forster's short story 'The Machine Stops' (1909). Many discussions of 'The Machine Stops' focus on the unsettling characteristics of the omnipresent Machine mentioned in its title. This contraption has not only alienated human beings from each other, but also made them dependent on a telecommunications apparatus which further intensifies their disconnection: they live, insect-like, in hexagonal rooms, speaking via devices which anticipate the isolating tendencies of modern-day social media. But the way Forster's story is told is closely connected to its subject matter. Its placement of real concerns about the dehumanising effects of technology in an alternative reality is itself a strategy designed to encourage attention to the same effects in the real world. Forster's gambit is a time-honoured one. The fantastical mode of 'The Machine Stops' concentrates readers' minds on the problems of late nineteenth- and early twentieth-century faith in technology by rendering them in unfamiliar shapes. In this manner, their implications come more clearly into view. There is the tightest of connections between what Forster's story is about and how it is told, a point which can be generalised to the field of dystopian literature as a whole.

Alongside its evocation of a certain kind of subject matter, then, the word 'dystopia' also refers to ways of thinking and writing about, or otherwise representing, nightmarish places and societies. Dystopias amount to a generic form that includes some or all of the following: a technologically advanced, futuristic setting; an oppressive surveillance state; a tyrannical despot or domineering oligarchy; an underground resistance force; a rebellious protagonist; and the idea of hope against hope. In addition to their appearances in literary works, these same elements are familiar to us through films, television, commercials, and videogames, and in the language of journalists, politicians, and social commentators. Yet this proliferation of dystopian images and themes across so many media has consistently been connected to a tradition of formally innovative dystopian literary fiction, one that has grown in complexity over the last two centuries and been marked by anxieties about individual freedom, authoritarianism, and the future of civilisation on a planet whose ecosystems are increasingly threatened by industry, technology, greed, pollution, and waste.

As a specific tradition of modern literature, dystopias have an identifiable ancestry. Quite where we draw the line in searching for a 'first' dystopia, however, is a matter of debate. Aspects of Jonathan Swift's *Gulliver's Travels* (1726), for example, have a dystopian flavour, but many histories of dystopian literature point to late nineteenth-century precedents. Edward Bulwer-Lytton's *The Coming Race* (1871), Samuel Butler's *Erewhon* (1872), and Ignatius Donnelly's *Caesar's Column* (1890) are all important dystopian precursors which explore, respectively, the idea of a so-called 'master' race, the politics of mechanisation, and the oppressiveness with which capitalist societies so often treat people as resources to be used, rather than as entities to be valued in non-monetary terms. Similar concerns inform H.G. Wells's *The Time Machine* (1895), a novel very different from the mid-twentieth-century dystopias of Evgeny Zamyatin, Aldous Huxley, and George Orwell, but which nevertheless investigates many of the elements with which they engage, including the influence of technology upon human bodies, the fortunes of the working classes, the prejudices of elites and aristocracies, and the destiny of humankind.

Indeed, Wells matters not only as a writer who inspired later dystopian authors, but also as the author of several texts with clear dystopian elements. It's often thought that Forster was inspired to write 'The Machine Stops' in response to Wells's *A Modern Utopia* (1905), a book ostensibly concerned with an ideal, rather than nightmarish, society, but which shows how thin the dividing line between these two conditions can be. And although they are usually concerned with tales of adventure rather than with tales of societies gone awry, many of Wells's scientific romances are at least partially dystopic, or early expressions of later dystopian forms. *The Island of Dr Moreau* (1896) uses the microcosm of an island to investigate late-Victorian debates about the implications of vivisection and animal cruelty in relation to the concept of 'the human', while *The War of the*

Worlds (1898) exploits imperial fears of reverse colonisation to criticise the politics of imperialism; with England dominated by Martian invaders, one imperial culture sees its atrocious methods of subjugation uncannily reflected in those of a more powerful antagonist. Orwell deemed Wells's more obviously dystopian novel *The Sleeper Awakes* (1910) – which depicts the adventures of a man who wakes up in London after two centuries of sleep to find himself the richest person alive – to be an important account of an imaginary world 'in which the special problems of capitalism [have] been solved without bringing liberty, equality, or true happiness any nearer' (*The Collected Essays, Journalism, and Letters,* Volume 4). In the world that Wells's sleeper wakes up to, the living standards of the privileged have increased almost beyond recognition, resulting in a withering of much of the remaining populace.

Twentieth-century archetypes

Orwell saw *The Sleeper Awakes* as part of a group of texts – including Jack London's *The Iron Heel* (1907), Hilaire Belloc's *The Servile State* (1912), Zamyatin's *We* (1923), and Huxley's *Brave New World* (1932) – concerned with another staple element of the dystopian tradition: the tendency for planned societies to mutate into dictatorships. *We* is important here, partly because it seems to predict the brutality that marked the Soviet system throughout Stalin's rule. In a review of *We* published in 1946, Orwell praised the book for its grasp of the dynamics that underpin totalitarian thinking, noting that the novel is 'in effect a study of the Machine'; not Forster's Machine, but all machinic phenomena: 'the genie that man has thoughtlessly let out of its bottle and cannot put back again' (*The Collected Essays, Journalism, and Letters*, Volume 4). The book inspired Orwell to write *Nineteen Eighty-Four*, which explores similar questions.

A rather different dystopian future provides the focus for Huxley's *Brave New World*. In this novel, citizens are kept in line not because their desires are suppressed, but because they are indulged. Set six hundred years in the future, the World State of *Brave New World* achieves its goals by means of orgiastic gatherings and a range of technologies which satisfy psychological and physical cravings. The drug 'soma' pacifies the population by providing temporary release (so-called 'holidays') from day-to-day affairs. The 'Feelies', an interactive cinema technology, allow viewers vicariously to experience the physical sensations of the characters in the films they watch. These inventions subjugate the World State's population by prioritising bodily perceptions and pleasures. The world of the mind is controlled by more fundamental means. Biological engineering differentiates the citizenry according to strict genetic determinations. Inhabitants of the World State are grown artificially and conditioned into a hierarchy of castes, with Epsilon-Minus Semi-Morons at the bottom and Alpha-Pluses at the top. Hypnopaedia, a form of night-time instruction, tells children what to think, thereby ensuring a compliant population. The World State is an intellectual aristocracy that defines itself against the apparently primitive inhabitants of the 'savage reservations'. Those who do not conform, or whose genetic programming has somehow failed, are shipped away to remote islands where they have little chance of leading others astray.

Brave New World is not a novel about a system being overthrown so much as it is a story about how the World State's consumer society, in all its bouncing, promiscuous excess, makes a system all but irresistible. As long as the World State's citizens are playing Electro-magnetic Golf or Riemann-surface tennis, or seeking multiple sexual partners, or smelling the undulating fragrances produced by mechanical scent-organs, or addicting themselves to soma, they have little incentive to lead more meaningful lives. Why should they revolt when pleasure is so easily available? Why should discontentment, loneliness, and exile take the place of agreeable compliance? Such questions underpin the novel's evaluation of the acquisitive mindsets through which consumerism itself is maintained. *Brave New World* satirises what Huxley and many other conservative intellectuals of his time took to be the perceived ills of America's cultural and socio-economic influence upon the world, a process symbolically represented by the increasing ascendancy of the cinema – a technology many supposed turned its audiences into thoughtless machines. *Brave New World* imagines a society in which the consumerism associated with Americanisation has literally motored on and on, the age of the World State itself being measured in terms of years 'After Ford' – that is, in years since the Ford Model T motorcar went into production. To quote a character in Huxley's novel *Point Counter Point* (1928), the World State is ruled 'in the name of science, progress and human happiness! Amen and step on the gas'.

One of the most complicated aspects of *Brave New World* is that it mixes criticism of the supposedly liberal sides of Americanisation with admiration for some of the most oppressive means with which they might be held at bay. It can be reassuring to see dystopian authors as necessarily opposed to the social systems they invent. Yet Huxley is an atypical case, and *Brave New World* is a more internally contradictory literary dystopia than is often acknowledged. The fact that, at least in the late 1920s and early 1930s, Huxley shared many elitist and anti-democratic sympathies with the World State's rulers makes it hard to know where to place him in relation to the novel. The World State is unquestionably autocratic, yet *Brave New World* is probably best understood not as a literary dystopia per se, but as a conservative critique of mass culture, rather than of the kinds of totalitarianism associated with the work of Zamyatin and Orwell. The most difficult pill to swallow is the fact that for a time Huxley was a keen supporter of selective breeding. For Huxley, around the dates of the writing of *Brave New World*, 'eugenics was not a nightmare prospect but rather the best hope for designing a better world if used in the right ways by the right people'[1]. Contextual details of this kind should remind us that dystopias are not necessarily the 'timeless' anti-authoritarian critiques they are so often taken to be. Placing dystopias against their biographical and historical

---

[1] Joanne Woiak, 'Designing a Brave New World: Eugenics, Politics, and Fiction', *The Public Historian*, 29.3 (Summer 2007): 105-129

backgrounds allows us to see that the worlds they depict are, in some cases, the stuff of authors' dreams as well as their nightmares.

Orwell aligned Zamyatin's *We* and Huxley's *Brave New World* when he claimed that both novels 'deal with the rebellion of the primitive human spirit against a rationalised, mechanised, painless world' (*The Collected Essays, Journalism, and Letters*, Volume 4). His own dystopia, *Nineteen Eighty-Four*, shifts the action of rebellion into a future filled with pain. The novel is arguably the most famous of all literary dystopias, having established the template in response to which so many subsequent dystopian works are designed. The tired, middle-aged Winston Smith is adrift in Oceania, one of three political 'blocs', the other two being Eastasia and Eurasia, which are constantly at war with one another. This war has become normalised to the point of being a new kind of peace, one that has made the world a place of meagre supplies and dwindling hope. On this basis, *Nineteen Eighty-Four* satirises a socialism perverted to the worst extreme. As a member of the Outer Party, Winston works to make history fit whatever shapes are desired by Oceania's rulers – the Inner Party, and ultimately Big Brother. The past is constantly kept 'up to date'. Real history is destroyed by the perpetual adjustment of records and statistics. Those who remember the past most fully, the proletarians, are powerless to do anything with their knowledge. Telescreens, advanced surveillance devices, monitor and control daily life. Conformity to the will of the Party is paramount; all competing pleasures are being destroyed. Capture, interrogation, and finally Room 101, the ghastly chamber in which an individual's worst fears are used to torture them into final obedience, await those who fight back.

Feminist reimaginings

Orwell's imagined future inspired one of the most famous responses to *Nineteen Eighty-Four*, Margaret Atwood's *The Handmaid's Tale*. This novel has been celebrated for its scathing account of a patriarchal society in which women's dignity and humanity have not only been forgotten but are also constantly being eroded by the fascistic strategies with which the ruling men of Gilead and their accomplices conserve their power: mainly through acts of control over women's clothing, speech, and reproductive liberty. This places *The Handmaid's Tale* in the Orwellian tradition. Yet the novel is less frequently valued for how its story builds on that tradition by developing Offred's spur-of-the-moment, impressionistic recollections, a traumatic memory-sequence whose artificiality Atwood's protagonist ensures we notice. 'This is a reconstruction', Offred insists. 'All of it is a reconstruction. [...] It's impossible to say a thing exactly the way it was, because what you say can never be exact, you always have to leave something out'. And this constructedness is intensified by the fact that we are invited, in the 'Historical Notes' with which the novel concludes, to imagine that all of what we read in the novel is itself a fabrication. The 'Notes' gesture ahead to a yet-more-fictional time, long after Gilead has fallen, in which the handmaids' experiences have become a subject for academic study like any other, and in which Offred's story exists only as a transcription made by a team of scholars in homage to Chaucer's *Canterbury Tales*. Offred's memories reveal the details of her suffering. The textual condition of her story – its reconstruction of a reconstruction – reminds us that it is the reassembled testimony of a life put together long after the fact by academics (and by academic men, more importantly) with a superficial interest in the reality of her pain.

Here, the what and the how of dystopia are inextricably connected. The layers of Offred's tale evoke the ways her trauma has been over-written by the competing agendas of later generations. There is a sense in which Orwell's *Nineteen Eighty-Four*, to which *The Handmaid's Tale* is such a powerful response, can be thought about in similar terms. The jury is still out on whether the fact that the supplementary material which ends Orwell's text – an appendix exploring the principles of the novel's invented language, 'Newspeak' – is written in standard, past-tense English should make us question whether Oceania was ever quite so invulnerable as its leaders supposed. But what isn't in question is that the way Orwell's novel is told (broadly, third-person 'objective' realism) can itself be understood as a response to the dystopian scenario it depicts. Whereas the rulers of Oceania, the Inner Party, seek to eliminate all inventiveness, fantasy, compassion, doubt, and virtue from everyday life, the novel, *Nineteen Eighty-Four*, resists the Inner Party's degradations in its own inventive, fantastical, compassionate, doubt-laden, virtuous unfolding. This is why Douglas Kerr has argued that although *Nineteen Eighty-Four* 'tells a story that imagines the defeat of individual freedom, community, history, and conscience, it does so in a form of writing that continues to enact these very things every time it is read' (*George Orwell*, 2003). To invoke the dystopian scenario of *Nineteen Eighty-Four* without reference to the stylistic techniques through which it is articulated, or in the case of *The Handmaid's Tale* to concentrate on Offred's pain at the expense of how it is scrubbed over by the men who have inherited it, is to tell only half a story.

Dystopias today

Indeed, the telling of a fuller story is what characterises the most exciting work in dystopian studies today. And a particularly important dimension of such work is its renewed focus on dystopian novels written by women. Feminist scholarship has enabled a different and constantly expanding literary history to come into view, with the works by Zamyatin, Huxley, and Orwell so many readers have treasured being transplanted to new spots on a much more interestingly varied constellation of works, writers, and worldviews, with dystopian novels like Rose Macaulay's *What Not* (1918), Charlotte Haldane's *Man's World* (1926), Naomi Mitchison's *We Have Been Warned* (1935), Storm Jameson's *In the Second Year* (1936), and Katharine Burdekin's *Swastika Night* (1937) acquiring a new visibility. This modification of the literary-historical landscape is itself indebted to the utopian feminist and science-fiction novels of the late 1960s and 1970s, among them Ursula K. Le Guin's *The Left Hand of Darkness* (1969), Joanna Russ's *The Female*

Man (1975), and Marge Piercy's *Woman on the Edge of Time* (1976). Such texts openly challenge the domination by men of utopian and dystopian authorship throughout the preceding century, in being written by, and foregrounding the concerns of, women.

This new attentiveness to different kinds of dystopian fiction is inseparable from the power dynamics surrounding the problem of who gets to write literary histories and which authors and texts appear in them. And a questioning attitude of this sort is exactly what continues to inspire dystopian writers today, along with science-fiction writers inspired by the dystopias of the past, many of whom have moved away from the Huxleyan and Orwellian templates in favour of stories concerned with apocalyptic thinking, as in Samuel R. Delany's *Dhalgren* (1975), Cormac McCarthy's *The Road* (2006), and Lidia Yuknavitch's *The Book of Joan* (2017); climate change, as in George Turner's *The Sea and Summer* (1987), Maggie Gee's *The Ice People* (1998), and Atwood's *MaddAddam* trilogy (2003-2013); the intensification of state surveillance through social media and search engines, as in Dave Eggers's *The Circle* (2013); and, increasingly, the voices of individuals and communities from under-represented ethnic and racial backgrounds, as in Octavia E. Butler's Lilith's *Brood* sequence (1987-1989), Ambelin Kwaymullina's *Tribe* series (2012-2015), and Nana Kwame Adjei-Brenyah's *Friday Black* (2018). The category of 'dystopia' itself has been transformed by these developments, which have made the genre more inclusive and richer than ever before.

Filmic, televisual, and interactive dystopias are the forms which now tend to be consumed in the largest quantities, with the settings used in videogames like *Deus Ex* (2000), *Half-Life 2* (2004), *Bioshock* (2007), *Wolfenstein: The New Order* (2014), and, indeed, *Dystopia* (2007-present) revealing how the dystopian imagery sourced in older narrative modes inflects contemporary entertainment software. Another example of the exchange between dystopian forms is the fact that many filmic and televisual dystopias draw on literary devices and are usually adaptations of novels and short stories. Recent cinematic examples include the *Hunger Games* (2012-15), *Divergent* (2014-16), and *Maze Runner* (2014-18) film franchises, all of which are based on Young Adult (YA) dystopian novel sequences by Suzanne Collins, Veronica Roth, and James Dashner respectively. Fortune has smiled no less on television and streaming services, as is evident in the critical and commercial triumphs of the Amazon adaptation of *The Man in the High Castle* (2015-present), based on Philip K. Dick's 1962 dystopian novel of the same title, and the HBO adaptation of *The Handmaid's Tale* (2017-present), the latter being the reinforcing precursor to Atwood's forthcoming sequel novel, *The Testaments*. The Channel Four anthology series *Black Mirror* (2011-present) distinctively foregrounds the science-fictional emphases in dialogue with which dystopian narrative itself took shape throughout the twentieth century.

Atwood has suggested that part of what makes dystopias seem so real (and so terrifying) is not that they exist in some unilluminated space beyond the edge of the knowable world, and not only that they seem real, but also that they seem available to be mapped – that is, that they look and feel like places with which we are familiar, no matter how strange they might be. As Atwood puts it, unless readers can believe in dystopias as 'potentially mappable place[s]', they 'will not suspend [their] disbelief' (*In Other Worlds*, 2012) in a sufficiently willing fashion to accept them as credible, terrible nightmares. These nightmares are places, or societies, or cultures in which very little, if anything, is or can be good. This is one reason why Anthony Burgess – himself the author of the celebrated literary dystopia *A Clockwork Orange* (1962) – suggested in his book *1985* (1978) that dystopias might be characterised using the older word 'cacotopia', which evokes such related terms as 'cacophony', a word meaning a harsh sound (or a moral disharmony), and 'cacodemon', which means 'evil spirit'. And this sense of all-encompassing wickedness is precisely what motivates the literary critic Tom Moylan to describe dystopias, using a phrase borrowed from Kingsley Amis, as 'new maps of hell' (*Scraps of the Untainted Sky: Science Fiction, Utopia, Dystopia*, 2001). Dystopias are maps that help us to see how the paths on which we find ourselves lead to places we don't want to reach.

Questions to take your thinking further

- Why are dystopias one of our most important literary genres?
- Why is it important to read dystopian novels by a wide variety of authors?
- How does an understanding of historical context help us think differently about how literary dystopias work?
- To what extent do so-called 'young adult' dystopias reflect the concerns of the dystopias written in the 1920s, '30s, and '40s?
- How do modern televisual and filmic dystopias respond to and change their literary source materials?

Reading list

Atwood, M. 2012. *In Other Worlds: SF and the Human Imagination*. London: Virago.

Claeys, G. ed. 2010. *The Cambridge Companion to Utopian Literature*. Cambridge: Cambridge University Press.

Claeys, G. 2017. *Dystopia: A Natural History*. Oxford: Oxford University Press.

Huxley, A. 1994. *The Hidden Huxley*, ed. David Bradshaw. London: Faber and Faber.

Little, J.A. ed. 2007. *Feminist Philosophy and Science: Utopias and Dystopias*. New York: Prometheus Books.

Vieira, F. ed. 2013. *Dystopia(n) Matters: On the Page, on Screen, on Stage*. Newcastle: Cambridge Scholars.

CRIME

Christopher Pittard

Questions of origins: the pre-Victorians

It is always difficult to identify literary origins, but the history of crime and detective literature seems to present particular problems: confident assertions about the 'first' examples of the genre lay themselves open to the discovery of counterexamples. It is often claimed, for instance, that the first English detective story was Wilkie Collins's *The Moonstone* (1868), yet Charles Felix's *The Notting Hill Mystery* appeared in 1865. Charles Dickens's *Bleak House* (1852-3) is frequently described as the first fictional depiction of a police detective, but Dickens's novel was preceded by detective texts which, while purporting to be true crime narratives, were heavily fictionalised. Some critics move the origins of the genre back even further, reading Sophocles's *Oedipus Rex* as a prototypical detective story in which the detective realises he is himself the murderer (anticipating postmodern or metaphysical detective fiction). Another popular point of origin is William Godwin's *Caleb Williams* (1794), a novel concerned with the relationship between the individual and the state in terms of criminal justice.

The eighteenth century is most commonly seen as marking a clear starting point as the rise of crime and detective literature depends in part on modern forms of selfhood, governance, and property that emerge in the 1700s. Earlier crime narratives tend to focus more on crimes against property, and so are reliant on shifts in the ways in which property is conceived, and how the ownership of commodities becomes integral to identity. Daniel Defoe's *Moll Flanders* (1722) is an immediately more recognisable crime text than *Oedipus* because it represents criminality and its effects in specific economic and social circumstances.

Moll Flanders anticipated the rise of the literary criminal as cultural celebrity in the later eighteenth century, consolidated by the first publication of the *Newgate Calendar* in 1773. Named after the London prison, the *Calendar* was a collection of stories relating details of true crimes, and although these stories were usually accompanied by a preface emphasising the text's status as a moral warning, there was also a sense in which these early true crime narratives were also intended as entertainment. The continued success of the *Newgate Calendar* into the nineteenth century gave rise to the sub-genre of the 'Newgate novel', texts which heavily fictionalised the lives of historical criminals. If the *Calendar* had treated criminal biographies as a moral warning, however, the Newgate novels tended to view their subjects more sympathetically. Novels such as Edward Bulwer-Lytton's *Paul Clifford* (1830) treated criminality almost heroically, with individual transgressors standing against a corrupt law enforcement or decadent aristocracy. The most famous response to such fictions was Dickens's *Oliver Twist* (1837-9), an attempt to reinvent the Newgate novel on a more moral footing. Even then it was Fagin and his gang who caught readers' attention, in contrast to the angelic Oliver.

From criminals to detectives: the early Victorians

By the mid-nineteenth century, the literary criminal was usurped by a new figure. The establishment of the Metropolitan Police in 1829 inaugurated modern policing, replacing more local arrangements in law enforcement with a centralised force more closely aligned with the state. Earlier attempts had been made to establish such a force, but had met substantial opposition from those concerned that it would increase the power of the state over individuals and act as an invasion of privacy. These concerns were not entirely defeated by 1829, but sufficiently allayed to allow for the new force to be introduced. In 1842 the police force received what would become known as its first detective branch, consisting of two inspectors and six sergeants.

It is unsurprising that popular fiction quickly turned to representations of these new cultural figures, but more unexpected that the emergence of modern detective fiction actually predated the term 'detective' itself (first coined as an adjective in 1843, and not as a noun until 1850). The modern genre is usually traced back to its Gothic roots in Edgar Allan Poe's 'The Murders in the Rue Morgue' (1841), introducing the unofficial detective Auguste Dupin. Dupin assists the Paris police in solving a locked room mystery, a murder where it seems impossible that the criminal can have left the room where the crime took place. The critic Lawrence Frank persuasively reads the solution – that the killer is an escaped orangutan who is able to climb from the apartment's open window several storeys up – as a reflection on the evolutionary speculations of the 1840s, leading up to Darwin's *The Origin of Species* (1859). In this reading, which also highlights Dupin's references to astronomy, the close relationship between detective fiction and contemporary scientific discourses is demonstrated. It was a dialogue which only increased as the century passed. Dupin would appear in two more stories, 'The Mystery of Marie Roget' (1842) (blurring the boundaries between crime fiction and reportage of a real murder case) and 'The Purloined Letter' (1844), a story of particular interest to psychoanalytic and poststructuralist critics for its ironic solution of the missing letter being concealed in plain sight.

Dupin was, however, only an unofficial consultant. In the 1850s the official police detective became a new literary hero. One popular subgenre was that of fictionalised detective 'memoirs', including William Russell's *Recollections of a Police Officer* (1849). But the key figure was Dickens, whose series of articles on the police for his magazine *Household Words* (starting with 'On Duty with Inspector Field' (1851)) presented the police detective as the new hero of urban modernity. The date is significant: the census of 1851 showed that for the first time more of the population was living in urban spaces than in rural ones. The detective emerged at a period when communities, previously consisting of those who knew each other, were moving into living conditions in close proximity with unknown thousands. The significant expansion of London, and the establishment of modern industrial centres such as Manchester and Birmingham, called for a cultural hero who was adept at reading the signs of the city. Both Dupin and Field were urbanites; Dickens consolidated his depiction of the police with Inspector Bucket in *Bleak House* (1852-3), a panoptic (that is, all seeing) character who brings together the various threads of the novel, but whose powers fade the further he moves from the city.

The sensation novel

The next substantial shift in crime literature occurred with the emergence of the sensation novel in the 1860s, with novels such as Wilkie Collins's *The Woman in White* (1860) and Mary Elizabeth Braddon's *Lady Audley's Secret* (1862). These novels, dealing with themes of transgression, gender roles, madness, murder, bigamy, and conspiracy, moved crime narratives from the street into the home, challenging the popular conception of the family as the locus of mid-Victorian moral values.

The term 'sensation novel' came from three interconnected features of these texts. Firstly, their sensationalist content caused controversy with their sympathetic portrayals of (often female) criminality, as in Braddon's *Lady's Audley's Secret* and Collins's *Armadale* (1864-6). Secondly, these novels aimed at provoking bodily sensations in their readership, apparently causing physiological responses in readers excited by fast-moving plots or chilled by scenes derived from Gothic modes of literature. Finally, these novels were a commercial sensation, bestsellers widely read in ways that crossed social boundaries. As the reviewer W. Fraser Rae famously commented of Braddon, she had made 'the literature of the Kitchen the favourite reading of the Drawing room.'

One of the most famous sensation novels, and an important text in considering the move from sensation fiction to detective fiction, was Collins's *The Moonstone* (1868), focusing on the theft of the titular diamond from the bedroom of a middle-class girl, Rachel Verinder, after the jewel is presented as her eighteenth birthday gift. The crime is investigated by a police detective, Sergeant Cuff, but Cuff's enquiries are inconclusive and the mystery is eventually solved by the collaboration of a number of investigators, who divide the narration of the novel between them. *The Moonstone* crystallises a number of critical concerns surrounding Victorian crime fiction. Firstly, from a Freudian perspective, the Moonstone itself has been read as a metaphor for female sexual innocence, with the imagery of the lunar jewel being stolen from a young girl's room (with the only evidence being a suggestive mark on a nightdress). Psychoanalytic criticism has also made much of the fact that the thief acts unknowingly while sleepwalking, raising questions of the unconscious and the limits of selfhood. Secondly, psychoanalytic criticism has also seen the formal structure of the novel – constructed from the perspectives of several narrators and pieced together in an act of secondary revision – as paralleling the similarly fragmented structure of dreams proposed by Freud in *The Interpretation of Dreams* (1901). Finally, the colonial context of *The Moonstone* has attracted significant attention, with the opening chapter narrating the taking of the jewel from India at the 1799 siege of Seringapatam. As a result, the theft of the jewel from Rachel, the original crime from the perspective of the detective story, is seen as being preceded by a colonial theft. In making this point, Collins inaugurates an important theme in later Victorian detective fiction: that criminality is the result of the return of empire to the space of England. Dickens's unfinished *The Mystery of Edwin Drood* (1870) rewrites Collins's novel with its tale of Sri Lankan incursion into England and the influence of the exotic commodity of opium (also prominent in Collins's text). Likewise, the first two Sherlock Holmes novels *A Study in Scarlet* (1887) and *The Sign of Four* (1890) address the consequences of those returning from either ex- or current British colonies (America and India respectively).

Sherlock Holmes and *fin de siècle* detection

The 1890s saw a crowded field of authors publishing detective stories in new middle-class magazines including the *Strand Magazine*. The most famous of these writers was, of course, Arthur Conan Doyle, creator of Sherlock Holmes, but in the 1890s Doyle was only part of a much wider market for popular crime fiction.

In fact, Holmes was initially far from successful. Doyle's first two Holmes novels, *A Study in Scarlet* and *The Sign of Four*, were only modestly received. It was only with Doyle's move to the short story format in the new *Strand Magazine* in 1891 that Holmes's popularity took off. The character underwent some substantial changes with the move: his cocaine use largely disappeared, and the 'calculating machine' Watson describes in *The Sign of Four* becomes a slightly more intellectually rounded and less cold figure.

Though Holmes is fond of quoting Thomas Carlyle's definition of genius as 'an infinite capacity for taking pains', Holmes is nevertheless portrayed as closer to the Romantic idea of the inspired artist than the mid-century police detective who obtains results by putting in the footwork. Holmes does the work of examining evidence, but also occasionally solves mysteries at a distance, relying on ideals of abstract rationality. Holmes often makes use of the evidence of the senses, but he is also aware how the senses can be misled. He combines two forms of detection: the examiner of evidence who relies on various forms of the magnifying glass, and the abstract reasoner who works out a logical solution with his eyes closed so as not to be distracted by irrelevant sensory data. As befits Doyle's own medical background, the Holmes stories often refer to contemporary scientific and criminological debates: degeneration anxieties in 'The Creeping Man' and the new science of fingerprinting in 'The Norwood Builder'. Yet while Holmes is often read as the representative of scientific rationality, closer inspection reveals a more complex picture: Holmes's deductions are based more in social prejudices than objective principles. *The Hound of the Baskervilles* (1902) makes these tensions apparent: Holmes takes on the case of the spectral hound in order to use rationalism to dispel superstition. But Doyle subtly presents Holmes himself as a Gothic figure, a ghostly observer whose passages of sitting and thinking through the details of a case resemble out-of-body experiences.

Though closely connected with the 1890s and with late Victorian debates over science, degeneration, and rationality, the Holmes stories as written by Doyle appeared well into the twentieth century, with the last appearing in 1927. One of the few stories to have a recognisable historical setting was 'His Last Bow', detailing Holmes's engagement in World War One. The war would prove crucial in the development of crime literature.

The Golden Age

Following World War One, three trends became increasingly apparent in crime and detective fiction, moving into what is termed its 'golden age'. The first was a return to the novel form, following the late Victorian/Edwardian popularity of the short story. The second was a move from urban to more rural or enclosed locations. Victorian detective fiction had emphasised the complexity of London, with mysteries arising from the proximity of millions of strangers; interwar detective fiction, by contrast, tended to focus on a closed circle of suspects. The final move was the growing prominence of female authors and feminised detectives, particularly in the work of Agatha Christie, Dorothy L. Sayers, and Margery Allingham.

Gill Plain suggests that interwar detective fiction served as a kind of compensation for the traumas of war: thousands of senseless deaths could be replaced with a single totally knowable murder, where specific blame can be apportioned. Although death and violence were not entirely sanitised in such novels, they became secondary to the aim of providing a formal challenge whereby the reader would be invited to solve the mystery before the detective revealed the solution. While earlier detective fiction had revolved around mystery, the reader was rarely given all the necessary information to solve the case first; in the interwar period, the author was expected to 'play fair' with her readership. This 'whodunit?' format led to a double structure, as identified by the formalist critic Tzvetan Todorov: on one hand, the story of the crime is kept concealed from the reader, whereas the story of the investigation is told in a clear and accessible manner. The whodunit thus paradoxically moves backwards, attempting to reconstruct an event that has already happened, and it ends when the narrative of the crime replaces the narrative of the investigation.

There is another duality to the whodunit: the tension between presenting an abstract puzzle, and in engaging with the traumatic historical circumstances that led to the emergence of the golden age novel. The tension is particularly clear in the work of Agatha Christie, who introduced her detective Hercule Poirot in *The Mysterious Affair at Styles* (1920). Christie and Poirot came to wider prominence in *The Murder of Roger Ackroyd* (1926), a text which consolidates many golden age features. Firstly, while the novel takes place almost entirely in the English pastoral setting of King's Abbott (the name implying both monarchical and religious hierarchies), the effects of war are never far away. The young character Ralph Paton 'was in several air raids as a young boy. The results are apparent long after, sometimes, they say. People are not responsible for their actions in the least. They lose control, you know, without being able to help it... Like shell shock, you know,' and there are several references to the delayed reactions of trauma. Secondly, the twist ending of *Ackroyd* (which I will not reveal here) caused controversy for apparently not playing fair with the reader, emphasising the perceived status of Christie's works as games rather than social or psychological analyses of crime. Finally, the character of Poirot displays a conscious shift from the more masculine detectives of the 1890s. Poirot is fussy, effeminate, and obsessed with domestic order, all of which align him with the feminine. In this, he bears comparison with Allingham's Albert Campion and Sayers's Lord Peter Wimsey. Campion conceals his intellect behind a foolish persona, speaking in advertising clichés; Wimsey owes more to P.G. Wodehouse's Bertie Wooster than Sherlock Holmes. Their names are significant: Hercule Poirot ironically invokes Hercules, the masculine hero whom the diminutive Poirot in no way resembles; Campion, the flower; Wimsey, the whimsical. All three reject the Victorian and Edwardian models of heroic masculinity that led to war.

Hardboiled fiction

The British success of the whodunit was met with a competing form in the US: the hardboiled detective novel. Most closely associated with Dashiell Hammett and Raymond Chandler, hardboiled detective fiction moved away from the neat resolutions of the whodunit and towards more open-ended cases where the detective was not in a position of intellectual or moral superiority. Chandler's *The Big Sleep* (1939) distances itself from Christie both thematically and structurally: thematically, in its focus on motives and modes of transgression that did not appear explicitly in the British whodunit (including organised crime and pornography); structurally, in the novel's first-person narration from the perspective of the detective Philip Marlowe. British detective fiction was rarely narrated by the detective, since s/he was the intellectually superior figure who reserved the solution to the mystery until the end, making first-person narration difficult. In Chandler's novels, however, Marlowe has to find his way at the same pace as the reader. Likewise, rather than being outsiders who are brought in to resolve a closed circle's problems, hardboiled detectives are – by virtue of already being part of a wider corrupt urban society – as morally questionable as those they investigate. In the hardboiled world, nobody is wholly innocent.

Chandler's essay 'The Simple Art of Murder' (1944) presented a manifesto for hardboiled fiction, brutally (and unfairly) dismissing British whodunits as mere 'problems in logic and deduction' lacking artistic ambition. Yet there are two paradoxes arising from Chandler's characterisation of hardboiled crime writing. The first surrounds his claim that crime fiction should strive to a greater degree of realism, especially in its use of language: 'All language begins with speech, and the speech of common men at that.' But the everyday speech of Chandler's novels is often disorienting or unfamiliar. The heightened style of Chandler's novels, incorporating American criminal slang, wisecracks, and extensive use of simile and metaphor, appears in fact more self-consciously literary (and often more poetic) than the British fiction Chandler had dismissed as detached from the realist circumstances of crime. Marlowe's name likewise reveals Chandler's literary influences, recalling the Elizabethan tragedies of Christopher Marlowe.

The second paradox arises from the most famous sentence of Chandler's essay: 'Down these mean streets a man must go who is not himself mean, who is neither tarnished nor afraid.' Marlowe tries to be such a man (indeed, *The Big Sleep* is full of chivalric imagery), but fails. More contextually, however, the phrase 'mean streets', associated with a criminal American urban modernity, actually comes from British Victorian culture, echoing Arthur Morrison's slum fiction *Tales of Mean Streets* (1894). This connection challenges the normal opposition of the British whodunit to American hardboiled fiction, since both originate from 1890s crime literature. Christie and others had taken the mystery element from Doyle and turned it into a formal challenge between author and reader; Chandler and Hammett inherited the 1890s masculine detective, but made him flawed, a figure that still informs later representations of damaged male detectives, particularly in Scandinavian crime writing (the so-called 'Scandi-Noir' of Henning Mankell and Jo Nesbo) and in Ian Rankin's series of novels featuring John Rebus (starting with *Knots and Crosses* (1987)).

(Post)modern developments

The distinction between English and American forms of crime literature, never particularly tenable, became increasingly unstable following World War Two. Post-war detective novels on both sides of the Atlantic began to merge the more social and literary concerns of Chandler with the aspects of mystery associated with Christie (often with a return to the official police detective and with an emphasis on the procedures of police work), while the emergence of the modern psychological thriller reinvented late Romanticist Gothic.

There is a sense in which crime literature continues to be particularly aligned with female writers. In the US, the modern psychological thriller was pioneered by Patricia Highsmith, whose novels centre on themes of mental imprisonment and criminal paranoia (as in *The Talented Mr Ripley* (1955)); in the UK, a similar position was taken by Ruth Rendell, whose novels *A Demon in my View* (1976) and *A Judgement in Stone* (1977) explore themes of social and sexual alienation. Rendell is perhaps better known for her series of novels featuring Inspector Wexford (1964-2013), the success of this series in the later twentieth century indicating a return to the official police detective as the literary hero (also seen in Reginald Hill's Dalziel and Pascoe novels (1970-2009), and Colin Dexter's Inspector Morse series (1975-1999)). Rendell is often associated with P.D. James, author of a number of novels featuring Commander Adam Dalgleish (1962-2008). Both Rendell and James's work in these series owes something to the golden age format, but combine this with the more social approach of American fiction (informed by Rendell and James's own political careers, as peers for the Labour and Conservative parties respectively). If Victorian crime fiction had largely dismissed the official policeman as the representative of intrusive state surveillance (in favour of the brilliant but singular private detective), post-war British fiction returned to the official force as a means of exploring questions surrounding the effects of the newly established welfare state, the cultural and technological revolutions of the 1960s, 70s, and 80s, and rapid changes to Britain's social and racial demographics. In the same period in the US, however, the private eye still held sway, but updated to reflect shifts in gender politics. Sara Paretsky's V.I. Warshawski (introduced in *Indemnity Only* (1982)), presents a modernised female Marlowe figure; likewise, although Patricia Cornwell's Dr Kay Scarpetta (introduced in *Postmortem* (1990)) works for the police as a medical examiner, she is not herself a conventional detective, and the Scarpetta novels combine the independent detective with the focus on police procedures (especially in forensic science) that would become increasingly prominent in late twentieth-century crime literature.

Traces of Highsmith and Rendell can also be found in twenty-first century reinventions of crime literature. Kate Atkinson's *When Will There be Good News?* (2008) combines the mystery plot with a focus on familial and intimate relationships; the novel's dual temporality, moving from events thirty years ago to the present day, exemplifies a more recent trend for fictional crime to be understood both in terms of the influence of the past on the present, and also in terms of psychoanalytic trauma. Perhaps the most successful crime novel of the early twenty-first century is Gillian Flynn's *Gone Girl* (2012), a novel which plays with the postmodern fascination with crime reportage across both traditional and social media, but it is also possible to read this text as a postmodern sensation novel, in which the home is the focus of crime, female transgression is explored, and the narratorial voice is unreliable.

Questions to take your thinking further

- Does crime literature reinforce or challenge popular explanations of the reasons behind crime and transgression?
- As much of crime literature deals with the identification of an individual criminal, what assumptions about identity does it rely upon?
- In what ways do genres such as detective fiction reflect on the process of reading and interpretation themselves?
- In what ways have different forms of crime literature been associated with specific genders, both in terms of readership and authorship?
- Does crime writing endorse a rationalistic view of the world where everything is capable of logical explanation, or does it retain traces of its roots in more fantastical Gothic literature?

Reading list

Chandler, R. 1988 [1944]. *The Simple Art of Murder (and Other Essays)*. London: Vintage.

Frank, L. 2003. *Victorian Detective Fiction and the Nature of Evidence*. Basingstoke: Palgrave.

Horsley, L. and C. Rzepka eds. 2011. *A Companion to Crime Fiction*. Oxford: Blackwell.

Plain, G. 2001. *Twentieth-Century Crime Fiction: Gender, Sexuality and the Body*. Edinburgh: Edinburgh University Press.

Todorov, T. 1977. 'The Typology of Detective Fiction,' in *The Poetics of Prose*. New York: Cornell University Press.

Wiener, M. 1993. *Reconstructing the Criminal: Culture, Law and Policy in England 1830-1914*. Cambridge: Cambridge University Press.

THE SHORT STORY

Chris Power

Introduction

The short story is a literary genre with ancient roots, but it has only been a clearly definable form of prose fiction for about 200 years. In this chapter we will see how the short story, despite being defined primarily by its length (the 'short' story), and so seen as an apprentice form or lesser cousin to the novel, is in fact an entirely separate genre; one with its own effects, its own limitations and its own possibilities.

In 1911, in the foreword to his collection *The Country of the Blind*, H.G. Wells wrote, 'I refuse altogether to recognise any hard and fast type for the Short Story', and he was right: it is impossible to present one linear account of the short story because too many writers have taken it in too many different directions. This chapter will summarise the work of some of the writers whose stories have made major contributions to the development of the form, but many others who have produced significant work will be left out (there is no room for Tolstoy, Willa Cather, D.H. Lawrence, Franz Kafka, Isaac Babel, Samuel Beckett, Flannery O'Connor, Alice Munro, or many other writers of classic short stories). This is regrettable, but hopefully readers will see this chapter as a launch pad, rather than an end point.

Looking to the past

The first short story

The question of where the short story begins is a matter of debate. It can be argued that the linked tales in Giovanni Boccaccio's *The Decameron* (1349-1353), one of the great classics of Italian literature, are short stories. The English poet Geoffrey Chaucer was influenced by the structure and style of *The Decameron* when he wrote *The Canterbury Tales* (1347-1400), which can also be seen as a proto-story collection.

But the modern short story really took shape in several different places in the first half of the nineteenth century: in Germany in the 1810s with Heinrich von Kleist, in Scotland in the 1820s with Walter Scott, in 1830s Russia with Alexander Pushkin and Nikolai Gogol, and in the United States of America in the 1840s with Nathaniel Hawthorne and Edgar Allan Poe.

Poe had one of the most extraordinary imaginations of any nineteenth-century writer. In stories such as 'The Tell-Tale Heart' and 'The Fall of the House of Usher' he took the Gothic story that had been so popular in the 1820s and introduced a psychological dimension to it. In the figure of his brilliant analytical detective Auguste Dupin we have the blueprint for Sherlock Holmes and countless other crime-solvers. And in stories such as 'Hop-Frog', 'The Imp of the Perverse' and 'The Pit and the Pendulum', he exerted a lasting influence over horror fiction.

Poe influenced short story theory as well as practice. In 1842 he wrote a review of Nathaniel Hawthorne's *Twice-Told Tales* that has become one of the most famous essays ever written about the short story. Poe talked about the 'unity of effect' that a short story should possess if it is going to work successfully. This idea of how a short story works can be contrasted with the widely held idea of the novel as a looser form, which allows the writer the opportunity to digress from and return to their main theme or plot.

Maupassant and Chekhov

In her introduction to the 1937 *Faber Book of Modern Short Stories*, Elizabeth Bowen didn't trace the history of the short story further back than Guy de Maupassant and Anton Chekhov. The dominance of these two authors, she wrote, was so great that they could be considered the originators of the modern short story.

Maupassant was born in Normandy in 1850, and died at the age of 42. He produced an extraordinary amount of work despite his early death, including classic short stories such as 'Boule de Suif' (1880), 'Two Friends' (1882), and 'The Necklace' (1884). The latter is the most famous example of the 'twist-ending', a type of story where the final line throws an ironic or surprising light on what has come before. W. Somerset Maugham and Henry James both wrote versions of 'The Necklace', and the influence of Maupassant's twist endings is detectable in thousands of stories.

The short story was already a well-established genre in Russian literature when Chekhov began writing stories of his own: his influences included Gogol, Turgenev, Dostoevsky and Tolstoy. Unlike twist ending stories, which are like clever mechanisms designed to conclude in a single and obvious effect, Chekhov's stories (1880-1903) tend to be much more open-ended and mysterious. They can be returned to again and again, their details taking on different meanings each time. In stories such as 'The Lady With the Little Dog', 'Gooseberries' and 'In the Ravine' , Chekhov deals with illicit love, the nature of happiness and death, but he never tells us what conclusions we should draw from the situations he describes. In this regard, Chekhov, more than any other writer, defined a fundamental difference between the short story and the novel. In the novel, any question the book asks must be answered. In a short story, it is enough to ask the question and leave it to the reader to think about what the answer might be.

Perhaps it is Chekhov's acceptance of ambiguity, and his willingness to provide outlines that it is up to the reader to fill in, that makes his stories feel so much more modern than many others written at the same time.

Kipling, Conrad and Wells

Rudyard Kipling, Joseph Conrad and H.G. Wells all became household names in the 1890s and 1900s, renowned as much for their short stories as for their novels and journalism. All three are much less fashionable now but they were active at a time of extraordinary change for the short story in English.

Kipling found fame with *Plain Tales From the Hills* (1888), a collection of stories set in his birthplace of colonial India. Over the next forty years he published another twenty collections, including two volumes of the *Jungle Book*, stories about World War One, ghost stories, historical fantasies, comic stories, and some of the strangest and most innovative stories of the time. In work such as 'Mrs Bathurst' (1904), 'The Wish House' (1924) and 'Dayspring Mishandled' (1928), Kipling combines the qualities of the incident-packed late-Victorian style with the reticence and ambiguity of Modernism.

In his autobiography, *Something of Myself* (1937), Kipling describes his later, mystery-laden technique:

> A tale from which pieces have been raked out is like a fire that has been poked. One does not know the operation has been performed, but everyone feels the effect.

There are also mysteries at play in the stories of Joseph Conrad. Many of his stories are related to the reader by a third party or 'frame narrator', a method that introduces and highlights uncertainty: with each successive transmission of the story, Conrad suggests, the accuracy of what really happened becomes harder and harder to gauge. Conrad's stories (1886-1917) are fictions, of course, but they serve to communicate the idea that all truth is subjective.

In this regard, some of Conrad's stories take a more extreme position than Kipling's. Kipling's mysteries appear to be solvable, although some of the details are extremely difficult to work out. In some of Conrad's stories, such as 'Amy Foster' or 'Karain, A Memory', it is much less certain that there is any solution to find at all.

As a student of science, H.G. Wells was more interested in solving mysteries than enshrining them in his work. His high-concept stories, involving time travel, invisibility, inter-dimensional travel, utopia and the destruction of the world, have been particularly influential in the development of science-fiction and speculative fiction. In their willingness to explore the fantastical, or to posit what might result from current scientific discoveries, they are openly indebted to Edgar Allan Poe.

In turn, Wells influenced many writers in the following century, from Ray Bradbury and J.G. Ballard to Brian Aldiss and Ursula K. Le Guin. While many of his stories are entertainments to be read once and forgotten, he also developed and refined the idea of presenting extraordinary stories as factual accounts. 'The

Door in the Wall' (1911) is a good example of this, and underlines the central fact on which all storytelling depends: the audience has to believe what they are being told, even if only for the duration of the telling.

James Joyce

James Joyce claimed not to have read any of Chekhov's work when he wrote the stories that would eventually be collected as *Dubliners* (about ten years elapsed between most of the stories being written and the book being published in 1914). That may be true, but there is an undeniable similarity to the way both writers' stories imbue realistic details with symbolic meaning. Joyce's great formal contribution to the short story is the concept of the 'epiphany', a single moment when a protagonist experiences a life-changing realisation about themselves or their situation. It is a technique that has been employed in countless short stories for the past hundred years.

Dubliners is a story cycle, a term used to describe a collection of stories that can be read separately, but which create a particular effect when read together in sequence. The effect Joyce creates in *Dubliners* is not only to bring his native city to life, but also to show it in four particular aspects: childhood, adolescence, maturity, and public life. The most famous story in the book, 'The Dead', is considered one of the greatest short stories ever written. It ends with the following lines that, their beauty aside, seem to provide meaning to everything that has come before, but can also be interpreted in numerous different ways:

> Yes, the newspapers were right: snow was general all over Ireland. It was falling softly upon the Bog of Allen and, further westwards, softly falling into the dark mutinous Shannon waves. It was falling too upon every part of the lonely churchyard where Michael Furey lay buried. It lay thickly drifted on the crooked crosses and headstones, on the spears of the little gate, on the barren thorns. His soul swooned slowly as he heard the snow falling faintly through the universe and faintly falling, like the descent of their last end, upon all the living and the dead.

Mansfield and Hemingway

Katherine Mansfield had already published some short stories before she read Chekhov, but she described his work, and in particular its rejection of neat endings, as one of the most valuable things she ever encountered. All her masterpieces, including 'At the Bay' and the abandoned novel that became 'Prelude', were written after her encounter with his work, which seems to have happened in the late 1910s.

Hemingway, too, learned lessons from Chekhov, and from his fellow American Sherwood Anderson, whose 1919 story cycle *Winesburg, Ohio* represented a new direction for the American short story. Combining Anderson's spare approach to story with his friend Gertrude Stein's experimental use of language, Hemingway began producing prose of striking, even shocking, minimalism. Particularly in his early short stories, mostly written in Paris in the 1920s, his narrators do not comment on events, only report them. A man and a woman waiting at an out-of-the-way train station discuss an abortion, without that word ever being mentioned ('Hills Like White Elephants'); a man on a fishing trip is beset by the horrifying memories of war – again, without the war ever being mentioned ('Big Two-Hearted River'); two hitmen sit in a diner discussing the murder of a boxer, with the reason for the killing left unmentioned ('The Killers'). Hemingway describes scenes in short, simple sentences. There are no metaphors or flourishes.

Hemingway's ability to give a story depth, complexity and meaning without resorting to any of the usual methods of telling, or suggesting what conclusions they should draw, resulted in one of the most influential bodies of work in the history of the short story. After him, authorial interruption came to seem unattractive and old fashioned to many writers. Now other methods had to be found to imbue a story with meaning: the significant detail, the subtle exchange of dialogue, the notably unspoken fear or desire.

Short story classicism: the *New Yorker* story

The 1950s and 1960s saw the rise of a particular type of English language short story that is often called 'the *New Yorker* story'. The two most prominent exemplars of this style were John Cheever and John Updike, chroniclers of the tangled relationships and dissatisfactions of suburban life in affluent mid-century America. In fact, both writers' bodies of work are much more diverse, and often stranger, than their reputation suggests, and the *New Yorker* has always published a range of fiction too wide for the term '*New Yorker* story' to make complete sense, yet the generalisations still exist.

Even Cheever's Shady Hill stories, which form the centrepiece of his suburbs-set work, contain elements of fantasy and the surreal. In its final pages his most famous story, 'The Swimmer' (1964), takes a turn into the fabulous, and 'The Country Husband' (1954) consistently walks a line between realism and fantasy.

Updike's work (1959-2009) is similarly wide-ranging, although his stories can be roughly divided into those concerned with adolescence ('A & P', 'The Happiest I've Ever Been'), married life (in particular a story cycle focusing on the Maples family), and more lyrical pieces that he described as being written in an 'abstract-personal' style, which occupy a position between story and essay.

Another writer who became a *New Yorker* favourite at around the same time as Updike, and whose stories rank among the best of the last century, is Mavis Gallant. A Canadian who travelled to Europe aged 28 and remained in Paris for the rest of her life, her stories often concern travelling: north Americans on holiday, or living abroad, and the feelings of alienation that can result from these situations.

Postmodernism

At the same time that Cheever, Updike and Gallant were defining the mainstream with their versions of the Chekhovian short story, the experimental style of Postmodernism was growing in popularity. One of literary Postmodernism's fathers was the Argentinian story writer Jorge Luis Borges. He had been publishing short stories in Spanish since the 1930s, but it was in the 1960s that his fame spread through translations of his work. Borges's stories are short, essayistic, and extraordinarily imaginative. They largely dispense with character, reading like journal entries or reports, their subjects including infinite libraries, magical symbols, and fantastical variations on traditional detective stories. The most commonly recurring symbol in Borges's stories is the labyrinth, and reading his work can feel like travelling deeper and deeper into a mystery.

The Italian writer Italo Calvino began his career after World War Two as a Neorealist whose work bore the clear influence of Hemingway. In the 1950s and 1960s, however, his work grew more and more experimental. His *Cosmicomics* stories (1964-1984), almost all of which are narrated by the extraterrestrial being Qfwfq, describe the history of the universe, blending science and fiction in a way no writer had ever done before. His later works were influenced by Oulipo, the experimental French literary movement, and include narratives generated by tarot cards and computer processes, and Borgesian stories in which theory supplants character.

In America, two of the leading practitioners of postmodernist metafiction (fiction that calls attention to its own status as fiction, and therefore the opposite of Naturalism, which attempts to recreate real life on the page) were Donald Barthelme and John Barth. John Barth was primarily a novelist, but his story collection *Lost in the Funhouse* (1968) is a key text in the history of metafiction. All of the stories it contains find different methods of diverting the reader's attention away from the supposed subject of the story, and onto the process of producing fiction itself.

Donald Barthelme was the reverse of Barth in that the majority of his important work is in the short form. His stories are surreal, absurdist, and often very funny. He considered collage the primary method of making art in the twentieth century, writing in his 1964 essay, 'After Joyce', that in collage 'unlike things are stuck together to make, in the best case, a new reality'. This is why Barthelme's stories are so magpie-like in their references: popular culture, classical music, philosophy, advertising, fairy tale, high modernism and commercial fiction all get thrown into the mix.

Other important postmodern writers who worked in the short story genre include J.G. Ballard, who used science fiction and speculative fiction to explore his real field of interest: the psychology of the human mind; Angela Carter, who in *The Bloody Chamber* (1979) rewrote the fairy tales of the Grimms and Charles

Perrault from a feminist perspective; Danilo Kiš, whose short stories explored the methods of control and powers of storytelling at work in belief systems including totalitarianism and Christianity; and Grace Paley, whose fiction reflected her own life as a socialist, agitator and, in her own words, a 'combative pacifist', in the Bronx and Greenwich Village in the 1960s and 1970s.

Paley's 1972 story, 'A Conversation with My Father' displays both the witty self-consciousness of her style, but also how far the short story had travelled in the previous hundred years:

> 'I would like you to write a simple story just once more,' he says, 'the kind Maupassant wrote, or Chekhov, the kind you used to write. Just recognisable people and then write down what happened to them next.'

But while many writers did continue to write those kinds of stories, for the postmodernists it was impossible to go back.

Minimalism

If Postmodernism was a reaction to the dominance of the well-made realist story of the immediate post-war period, Minimalism was a back to basics movement that renounced the tricks, games and elaborations of Postmodernism. Its best-known practitioner is Raymond Carver, whose stories inhabit a familiar space – a more down-at-heel but similarly boozy suburban America as many of Cheever and Updike's stories – but use language so sparingly that a great deal is left for the reader to interpret. In 'Why Don't You Dance?' (1981) a man has put all of his furnishings outside and arranged them on his lawn: bed, couch, desk, turntable, lamp. Everything's for sale, and a young couple stop to browse. They get drunk with the man, but the reasons for his behaviour are never explained. Here Carver is even more Hemingway than Hemingway, cutting all exposition in a way that leaves the story hovering at the edge of solution.

It is worth noting that the work Carver produced when he was working with the editor Gordon Lish is significantly different to the work he produced alone. In 2009, Carver's widow published some of the stories from Carver's first two collections in their pre-Lish form. They were all longer, with much more backstory and exposition. Comparing the two versions to one another provides a fascinating look inside the editing process, and provides a stark example of just how much can be removed from a piece of fiction, and how that affects it.

Other writers who first came to prominence as minimalists (the term, it should be noted, is not always a popular one with those to whom it has been applied) include Jayne Anne Phillips, Tobias Wolff, Ann Beattie and Mary Robison. Although their subject matter is quite different, they share Carver's reticence and his willingness to leave the discernment of a story's meaning up to the reader. 'Errand' (1988), the last story Carver wrote, is an account of Chekhov's death in a hotel in Badenweiler, Germany. Aside from being a beautiful and memorable story, it is also an appropriate tribute that encapsulates the extent of the Russian writer's influence on the last century of short story writing.

The short story around the world

The short story is a global form. The account of its history given in this chapter suggests the centrality of the English-language story, and especially the American story, but there are writers from all across the world whom any student of the form would be advised to read. For reasons of space this is a whistle-stop tour, but it illustrates the universality of the short story.

In Africa, the Nigerian Chinua Achebe and Kenya's Ngũgĩ wa Thiong'o, South Africa's Nadine Gordimer, and Botswana's Bessie Head have all made striking contributions to the form. Gordimer in particular was devoted to the short story, producing more than 200 of them between 1937 and 2007.

The most revered Japanese writer of short stories is Ryūnosuke Akutagawa, whose work in the 1910s and 1920s was responsible for the short story coming to be regarded as an important form within Japanese literature. Yasunari Kawabata began publishing novels and stories just a year before Akutagawa committed suicide in 1927, and continued writing until his death in 1972. He specialised in what he called 'tanagokoro no shōsetsu' or 'palm-of-the-hand stories', poetic and richly symbolic pieces that are also very short (short enough, in fact, to be written on the palm of one's hand).

The South American short story is dominated by Borges, but other expert practitioners include his fellow Argentinians Julio Cortázar and Silvina Ocampo, Brazil's Machado de Assis – some of whose stories seem to prefigure Kafka – and Clarice Lispector, Columbia's Gabriel Garcia Márquez, whose early stories, including 'A Very Old Man With Enormous Wings' (1955), exhibit the magic realism he became famous for, and more recently Chile's Roberto Bolaño.

The present

The short story's present looks quite a bit like its past. The Chekhovian short story continues to be conformed to and adapted by skilled writers with stories to tell: Alice Munro, Tessa Hadley, Yiyun Li, Jhumpa Lahiri, Viet Thanh Nguyen, Ottessa Moshfegh, Akhil Sharma and many more. At the same time, experimental approaches continue to develop. Carmen Maria Machado's work marries a genuine love of genre styles (the police procedural, body horror, erotica) to a literary sensibility; Eley Williams takes the stream of consciousness to surprising new places in her collection *Attrib.* (2017); Jennifer Egan and David Szalay have both written books – *A Visit from the Goon Squad* (2011) and *All That Man Is* (2016), respectively – that straddle the border between the linked story collection and the novel, and prompt the question, just what is a short story, anyway?

Renaissance or decline?

The short story has always been on the verge of collapse or revival. In 1911 H.G. Wells complained that the 1890s were a much better time to be a short story writer. In 1941 H.E. Bates, a better critic of short stories than he was a writer of them, predicted that short fiction would be the 'essential medium' of World War Two and its aftermath. In 1962 he admitted his mistake, and a decade after that predicted that the short story was on the verge of dying out altogether. That same year, however, the editor of *The Second Penguin Book of English Short Stories* claimed that the form was undergoing a revival to be celebrated, and in the decades between then and now these contradictory views have persisted.

Why? Well, in part because 'the renaissance of the short story' is an easy hook to hang a news story on. Whether it's a short story specialist like Alice Munro winning the Nobel Prize in 2013, or Kristen Roupenian's story 'Cat Person' becoming a viral sensation in December 2017, or the short story being identified as the ideal form for our modern short attention spans, there are frequent opportunities for someone to claim that the short story is 'back', when in fact it never went away in the first place.

The future

Where is the short story headed? It is difficult to say with any certainty, and to an extent the boring answer is the most accurate one: it will continue muddling along as it has done since its inception, sometimes more in fashion, sometimes less so. One interesting thing to note, however, is that due to the rise in popularity of creative writing courses, more people than ever are critically studying the short story, and producing short stories as part of their coursework. That fact might have an impact on the amount of stories being written, and also the type of stories being written. The assumption that is generally made is that there will be an increase in stories of a particular type: the 'workshop' or 'MFA story' (postgrad creative writing courses in the United States confer a 'Master of Fine Arts' degree). But that seems overly pessimistic: a more optimistic reading of the situation is that the most interesting writers will want to strain against any perceived dogma regarding what a story should or shouldn't be, and instead show readers all the things it can be.

Questions to take your thinking further

- From a narrative perspective, what are the strengths of the short story form? And what are its shortcomings?
- What challenges do short story writers face in finding an audience for their work?
- Is reading a short story a less satisfying experience than reading a novel?
- Why should a short story be more suited to a reader with a short attention span than a novel?
- Aside from being published in books, how else might short stories find their way to readers?

Reading list

Allen, W. 1981. *The Short Story in English*. Oxford: Clarendon Press.

Halpern, D. ed. 1987. *The Art of the Tale: An International Anthology of Short Stories, 1945-1985*. New York: Penguin.

Head, D. ed. 2016. *The Cambridge History of the English Short Story*. Cambridge: Cambridge University Press.

Jarrell, R. ed. 1958. *The Anchor Book of Stories*. New York: Doubleday.

May, C. ed. 1976. *Short Story Theories*. Athens: Ohio University Press.

O'Connor, F. 1963. *The Lonely Voice: A Study of the Short Story*. London: Macmillan.

ISMS AND THE CRITICAL READER

Nicolas Tredell

Introduction

'I don't like *isms*.' You sometimes hear this response to nouns that incorporate *ism* as a suffix – Postmodernism or Structuralism, for example. Such a response expresses an aversion to the application of apparently abstract labels to rich and complex sets of ideas and/or artistic practices that seems to reduce them to monotonous monoliths.

Isms may seem especially inappropriate in the study of literary texts, which produce vivid and specific effects on the imagination, emotions and nervous system of the reader. The fear is that the attempt to generalise about them with *isms* could dissipate these effects.

Literary criticism, however, is itself an *ism* and a student who reads even a little of it soon enters a forest of other *isms*. These are of four main kinds.

- First, they can designate particular approaches within literary criticism as an academic and cultural field: for instance, Leavisism and New Criticism.

- Second, they can indicate styles and movements that are important in the production of literature itself, such as Realism and Naturalism, as when we say that Elizabeth Gaskell's *North and South* (1855) is a realist novel and Theodore Dreiser's *An American Tragedy* (1925) a naturalist novel.

- Third, they can indicate styles and movements that spread across the arts and include painting, sculpture and music, like Neo-classicism, Romanticism, Aestheticism, and Modernism (this last also includes other forms of cultural production such as architecture and cinema).

- Fourth, they can refer to broad movements of thought and culture that usually have some philosophical basis, that do not necessarily engage much with the arts, but can fruitfully inform the interpretation of literary texts – for example, Feminism, Marxism, Structuralism, Poststructuralism, Postmodernism and Postcolonialism.

Isms did not develop out of a desire to bewilder, though it may sometimes seem that way. In literary studies as in other fields, they result from a felt human need to organise and classify experience in order to make more sense of it and ultimately to enrich it. But *isms* cannot do these jobs alone. It is perfectly legitimate, for instance, to take three poems – let us say, Blake's 'The Sick Rose' (1794), Wordsworth's 'A slumber did my spirit seal' (1800) and Coleridge's 'Kubla Khan' (1816) – and declare that these are all examples of Romanticism; but this is only a starting point and any interpretation would need to attend closely to the verbal detail and significance of each poem in terms of vocabulary, imagery, rhythm and meaning and to relate these elements to the overall idea of Romanticism, allowing them to modify that overall idea, if appropriate.

In literary criticism as elsewhere, *isms* are fertile as long as they are grounded in specific aspects of any given literary text through the practice of close reading – a practice itself closely associated with two *isms* that we consider further below: Leavisism and New Criticism.

This essay first looks to the past, offering a history of key *isms* in literary criticism from the late eighteenth century to the twenty-first century; it then looks at the present state of criticism; and lastly it looks to the future. Given the proliferation of *isms*, it has been necessary to be selective, so the focus will be on the most influential of them – though this selection, like any other, can be contested.

Looking to the past

Romanticism

Romanticism emerged towards the end of the eighteenth century, alongside the historical tumults of the French and industrial revolutions. It was a movement, or convergence of movements, whose philosophical basis lay in German thought and it spread across the arts, impacting upon literature, music and painting; it also fuelled, and drew energy from, political attitudes and action.

Romanticism stressed passion over propriety, daring over decorum, boldness over balance, outrage over order. It rejected the prescribed polite poetic diction of eighteenth-century Neoclassicism and promoted a rougher, more robust language closer to common speech, even to the speech of the poor and deprived, as in some of Wordsworth's poems about the hardships of rural life. It contended that poetry should come from what Wordsworth called, in the Preface to *Lyrical Ballads* (1800), 'the spontaneous overflow of powerful feelings'. It also pitched into regions of vision, dream, hallucination, fantasy and myth, as in Coleridge's ballad *The Rime of the Ancient Mariner* (1798).

Coleridge was also the chief theorist of English Romanticism. In his *Biographia Literaria* (1817), he developed a distinction between 'fancy' and 'imagination', in which the former was a relatively mechanical association of ideas, as in the philosophy of David Hume, and the latter an organic, holistic process akin to the divine work of creation itself. This Romantic perspective gave the imaginative writer, especially the poet, an exalted role: Blake began his 'Songs of Experience' (1794) with a commanding appeal to the reader's attention because of the importance of what the poet had to say and his direct line to God: 'Hear the voice of the Bard! / Who Present, Past, & Future sees / Whose ears have heard, / The Holy Word, / That walk'd among the ancient trees.' In his prose work *A Defence of Poetry* (written 1821; published 1840), Percy Bysshe Shelley called poets 'the unacknowledged legislators of the world', the unrecognised people who nonetheless draft, through their poetry, the laws by which human beings can best live.

Romanticism generated a critical approach that sought, in a literary text, those points of intensity that seemed to transcend the increasingly regulated world created by Napoleon's new form of warfare, which involved mass conscription, and by the industrial revolution, with its stress on timekeeping and quantifiable, repeatable, machine-driven productivity. This stress on points of intensity continued, with variations, into Aestheticism and Modernism.

Aestheticism

Aestheticism, a movement summed up in the phrase 'art for art's sake', gathered strength in England near the end of the nineteenth century. It was a reaction against the Victorian moral earnestness Oscar Wilde satirised in his play *The Importance of Being Earnest* (1895). While Romantic attitudes, vocabulary and imagery had continued to inform Victorian literature, especially poetry, Romanticism seemed to have become, by this time, tamed and domesticated, subdued to the starched proprieties of Victorian middle-class life.

Aestheticism sought to revive Romantic intensity but in a specialised artistic sphere, counselling inner withdrawal from the industrial world: 'Forget the snorting steam and piston stroke', as William Morris put it in his poem *The Earthly Paradise* (1868). Walter Pater, whose writings, especially *The Renaissance* (1873), profoundly influenced a younger generation that included Oscar Wilde, defined success in life not by material or moral criteria but by the capacity to 'burn always with [a] hard, gemlike flame'. Art could help to ignite you in this way but only if it eschewed the rising damp of conventional morality. In a kind of preface to his novel *The Picture of Dorian Gray* (1890), Wilde summed up the credo of Aestheticism in maxims like these:

> There is no such thing as a moral or an immoral book.
> Books are well written, or badly written. That is all.

The credo concludes: 'All art is quite useless'. The implication is that a critic should not evaluate a literary text in terms of its supposed moral or social effects but offer an appreciation of it that attempted to convey its artistic qualities. This could lead, however, to vague critical writing that rhapsodised about works of art the critic liked without specifying the qualities in those works that justified their response.

Aestheticism bloomed just as English Literature was starting to emerge as a suitable subject for university study, but it could not supply the focused criticism this new subject needed to establish itself as an academic discipline. As the nineteenth century turned into the twentieth, a much more rigorous and challenging set of artistic practices and critical attitudes developed that made Aestheticism seem insipid: the attitudes and practices of Modernism – or, given the plural and sometimes contradictory proliferation of modernist movements, Modernisms.

Modernism

Modernism was an early twentieth-century movement or medley of movements that transformed art and culture in the fields of literature, painting, sculpture, architecture, music and dance, and grew in tandem with the new medium of cinema, hardly accepted yet as an art form.

Romanticism had exploded the Neoclassicism of eighteenth-century culture, but Modernism demolished artistic structures and practices that had seemed solid since the early modern era, such as painting in perspective to give an illusion of three-dimensional space. The political and social upheavals of the epoch – World War One, the Russian Revolution, the rise of the USA – accelerated and amplified this cultural earthquake.

The two most emphatically modernist literary works appeared in 1922: T.S. Eliot's poem *The Waste Land* and James Joyce's novel *Ulysses*. Eliot created a montage of his own electric lines and of words drawn from classical, early modern, and seventeenth, eighteenth, nineteenth and twentieth-century high-cultural and popular sources. Joyce portrayed one day in Dublin on 16 June 1904, structuring it around one of the founding texts of Western culture, Homer's *Odyssey*, and employing a range of rhetorical techniques and styles from early English to modern stream-of-consciousness. Each text, in a sense, offered a compendium of the key elements of the literature that had preceded it and implied that the forms of such literature were no longer adequate to explore and express a complex, contradictory and fragmented modern reality.

Modernism, especially as exemplified in texts as powerful as *The Waste Land* and *Ulysses*, had two major consequences for literary criticism. Unless you simply dismissed such texts, you had to find ways to understand and interpret them; if you approached *The Waste Land* expecting it to be like Tennyson's *In Memoriam* (1850), or *Ulysses* expecting it to be like George Eliot's *Middlemarch* (1871), you might well be baffled and disappointed; you had to change your expectations and reading strategies.

The other consequence of Modernism was that it made it necessary to interpret the literature of the past differently, reconfiguring and revaluing the whole literary field. T.S. Eliot, a major critic as well as a major poet, played a key role in this critical revolution.

Leavisism

Eliot's criticism fed into the development of English literature as an academic subject in England. At Cambridge University, I.A. Richards aimed to bring greater rigour and accuracy into the interpretation of literary texts and to exclude extraneous associations and information (for example, about the author's life). His student William Empson brilliantly explored the ways in which language in literary texts could mean more than one thing in his seminal book *Seven Types of Ambiguity* (1930).

It was, however, the Cambridge-based critic F.R. Leavis, his wife Q.D. Leavis, and the group of students and young lecturers, such as L.C. Knights, associated with the magazine *Scrutiny*, who combined their own insights with elements of Eliot, Richards and Empson to produce a powerful *ism* named after their leader: Leavisism (his followers were often called Leavisites).

Leavis mounted a wholesale critique of modern society, which he saw as dominated by a combination of unthinking technological development and the utilitarian philosophy associated with the early nineteenth-century thinker Jeremy Bentham. Utilitarianism proposed that the criterion of social and ethical action should be the greatest good of the greatest number, a perspective which could seem to dissolve individuals into a mass of statistics. Reading the right literature was crucial in the fight to rescue a full humanity from this reductive society.

Leavis constructed an influential canon of the 'right' literature: a great tradition of the English novel that consisted of Jane Austen, George Eliot, Henry James, Joseph Conrad and D.H. Lawrence; and a lineage of English poetry, adumbrated in T.S. Eliot's criticism, which included Shakespeare, Donne, Pope and Keats but excluded Milton, Byron, Shelley and Swinburne because their poetic language failed to unite the senses, emotions and intellect.

Leavisism would dominate English literary criticism from the 1930s until the 1980s. The dominant force in the USA in the same period was New Criticism.

New Criticism

Like Leavisism, New Criticism focused on close reading; but it did not share the same sense of social mission and set aside the historical and contemporary contexts of literature. New Criticism particularly valued the kind of literary text that explored contradictions and oppositions but finally contained them in an organic whole that was both existentially penetrating and artistically pleasing. It was a critical approach especially suited to the analysis of the short lyric poem.

New Criticism largely eschewed theory, but it did generate one important concept: the intentional fallacy: the alleged error in the interpretation of a literary text of taking account of any statement by its author of what they intended the work to mean. Once published, the work was a public object, complete unto itself, and should be judged as such. This ran counter to an approach that both took account of an author's statements of their intentions and granted them extra authority because they came from the work's creator. To some extent, the attack on the intentional fallacy anticipated the key structuralist and poststructuralist idea of the 'death of the author'.

By the end of the 1970s, however, both Leavisism and New Criticism seemed repetitive, negative and shut off from both contemporary literature and fresh critical approaches – and from the political and social challenges reverberating from the 1960s. Critics and readers in Britain and the USA sought alternatives and opened the floodgates to a torrent of *isms*.

Structuralism

Structuralism searched for the underlying structures of societies, myths and literary texts. It saw all these phenomena as like language: the behaviour and rituals of a tribe, for instance, had an implicit grammar, a set of rules, that gave meaning and significance to particular actions and symbols, as the set of rules of a language give meaning and significance to its spoken and written utterances. You could infer this grammar from what people actually did and the meanings that their actions had within their society, just as you could infer the grammar of a particular language from what people actually said and the meanings that their words had within their language group.

In literary criticism, Structuralism was important in prompting a move away from the concepts of author and character. The idea of the 'death of the author', given classic expression in a 1967 essay of that title by Roland Barthes, does not mean that the biological author had not existed or did not exist, but that the author should not be a guiding concept in the interpretation of literary texts; we can link this with the idea, in New Criticism, of the intentional fallacy. Neither the author's life, nor their stated or inferred intentions, should be used to explain the works attributed to them.

Instead of character, Structuralism inclined towards the notion of 'actants' that performed functions necessary to the narrative, such as helping or hindering. Actants could be humans, animals, supernatural creatures such as fairies or goblins, or inanimate objects; they did not have to be psychologically motivated and their functions did not have to be consistently performed by the same figure – for example, several figures might perform the helping function in a narrative and this was due to their position in the system of the narrative rather than to their benevolent temperaments.

A crucial component of structuralist analysis was the identification of binary oppositions such as light/dark, good/bad, right/wrong, and male/female. In these oppositions, the second term was inferior to the first. For instance, in John Milton's epic poem *Paradise Lost* (1667), male and female, as incarnated in Adam and Eve in the Garden of Eden, have different relationships to God: 'He for God only, she for God in him' (Book 4, line 299). In a structuralist perspective, such oppositions occur everywhere; they are universal, even if they appear in different forms in different cultures.

Structuralism fell out of favour because of this universalising tendency, its reduction of all social and cultural phenomena to the same underlying patterns, its implication that apparent difference and development were really repetitions, its acquiescence in existing hierarchies such as male/female. The work of structuralist literary critics, such as Tzvetan Todorov's 1970 book on fantastic literature, is still well worth reading; and key techniques of structuralist analysis – bracketing out the idea of the author, looking for actants rather than characters, and identifying binary oppositions – can still prove fruitful; but as a movement it seemed to stall and gave way to Poststructuralism.

Poststructuralism

Poststructuralism broke away from the idea of rigid, repetitive underlying structures to stress that meaning was always mobile, that it could never be finally fixed. Applied to literary criticism, this helped to account for the endless proliferation of critical interpretations that literary texts, especially major ones, had generated over time. Frank Kermode, in his book *The Classic* (1975), drew on poststructuralist approaches to redefine the literary classic not as a work that conveyed universal and unchangeable truths, but as a text that was so vibrant and complex that it constantly generated new interpretations.

This contributed to a revised concept of literary criticism; instead of being a progressive process of working through incorrect interpretations of a text towards the one true reading that everyone could or should accept – the definitive interpretation of *Hamlet* (c 1600), say – it was a field in which a range of different interpretations could and did co-exist. This did not mean a critic could interpret a text in any way that they liked; close reading and careful argument were still essential, perhaps more so than ever before; but it did permit a greater tolerance of multiple interpretations and allowed critics to venture new readings without asserting their absolute validity.

Deconstruction(ism)

Although the term Deconstructionism is sometimes used, Deconstruction, without the *ism*, is more common – but it still counts, in effect, as an *ism*. Deconstruction, primarily associated with the philosopher Jacques Derrida, is close to Poststructuralism but not quite the same: rather than allowing interpretative freedom, it offers a technique of interpretation that is, in principle, applicable to all texts, literary and non-literary.

The key technique of Deconstruction is to show that a text will always, if closely scrutinised, undermine its ostensible argument and always defer delivering a final meaning (and in fiction and drama and poetry, this argument is likely to take an implicit form, conducted through evoked characters and situations and through imagery much more than through explicit assertion).

Like Structuralism, Deconstruction(ism) is interested in binary oppositions in which one term is held to be superior to the other: but rather than simply identifying them it deconstructs them by a two-stage operation: the supposedly superior term is shown to be dependent on the supposedly inferior one and each term is then held in suspension, without restoring any hierarchy. If we take, for example, one of the oldest binary oppositions, male/female, a deconstructionist approach would aim to show that the idea of the male depends upon the contrasting idea of the female, that this dependency means that female can become the superior term, and that, ultimately, there is no need for either term to surmount the other.

In the case of Milton's assertion of Adam's superiority over Eve in *Paradise Lost*, for instance, a deconstructionist approach would tease out all the ways in which the text reveals Eve's superiority over Adam (she is the one, for example, brave enough to eat the forbidden fruit), and then keep both male and female elements in play, free of attachments to a specific biological gender or hierarchy.

Deconstruction was, and remains, a remarkably effective technique for demonstrating that literary and other texts, and binary oppositions, are self-subverting, but, like Structuralism itself, perhaps even more so, it can become predictable and mechanical. Despite its emphasis on difference, it tends to yield, in general terms, the same result, even though its findings for any particular text may be intriguing and innovative. Feminism offers much more variety.

Feminism

Feminism, like Romanticism and Modernism, should perhaps more accurately be a plural noun, Feminisms, to indicate the multiplicity of feminist perspectives, some of which clash with one another; a feminism informed by psychoanalysis, for instance, sits uneasily with a feminism informed by empirical historical research.

Feminism is one of those broad movements of thought and culture that does not focus primarily on literature – it is perfectly possible to pursue feminist philosophy, social action and advocacy without reference to literary texts – but that has nonetheless had great influence upon literary criticism and the writing of literature itself.

Early feminist criticism tended to focus on the representations of women characters in literary and dramatic texts, exploring strong but often conflicted figures such as Beatrice in Shakespeare's *Much Ado About Nothing* (1598), Jane Eyre in Charlotte Brontë's novel of that title (1847), and Anna Wulf in Doris Lessing's *The Golden Notebook* (1962).

Later feminist criticism, particularly if drawing on Poststructuralism, moved away from a character-based approach to tease out the contradictions in literary texts, not necessarily centred in characters, which subverted any fixed notions of feminine – and masculine – identity.

Subsequent feminist criticism has been more eclectic, combining a sense of the fluidities of identity, structural and stylistic analysis, historically informed perspectives drawn from areas like medicine and psychology, and burgeoning contemporary fields such as trauma theory. One key critical focus has been on neo-Victorian novels such as Sarah Waters' *Fingersmith* (2002) or Jane Harris's *The Observations* (2006), which articulate and dramatise issues relating to gender and sexual orientation that were implicit but largely unspoken in nineteenth-century fiction.

Looking at the present

Feminist criticism continues to flourish in alliance with an array of feminist social movements. A recent development has been the reinterpretation of literary texts in the context of the increased contemporary awareness of rape, sexual harassment and other forms of physical and psychological violence against women.

Ecocriticism, linked like Feminism to various forms of social activism, is also flourishing and continuing to expand beyond its initial focus on writing about 'the natural world' – in 'nature poetry', for instance – to explore the literary representations of ecosystems created by the combination of artificial and natural elements in the environments in which human beings and animals live.

Cognitive literary criticism explores the continuity between how we know the world in our everyday lives and how we know the world in literary texts – for example, by making mental maps, inferring other people's mental processes, deciphering images and intimations, reconfiguring the past and predicting the future.

Looking to the future

Feminist criticism, Ecocriticism and Cognitive criticism will continue to develop in the future and are likely to cross-fertilise one another. There are two further fields, among many others, of possible development.

Trauma and narratology

Narratives of trauma – as a result, for instance, of abuse, accident, illness, oppression, war – have become pervasive in global culture and circulate in a wide variety of forms including blogs, films, videos, social media postings, legal testimonies, print articles and books. They often evoke strong emotions and provoke action. A crucial area of future exploration is the relationship between trauma and narratology: how should literary critics, specialists in narratological analysis, understand such narratives and link them to literature in ways that are both sensitive to the experiences narrated, and intellectually and ethically responsible?

Economo-criticism

We live in an age of unprecedented financial volatility and fragility, with economic processes increasingly eluding our control and understanding, and with money becoming more and more pervasive at the same time as its material presence, in the form of coins and notes, becomes less and less visible, like the Cheshire Cat. Economo-criticism would focus on money not only as a major theme in literary texts but also as a symbolic system of distribution and exchange, with material markers and consequences, which resembles literature itself in key respects. Rather than applying a specific economic theory – Marxism or Neo-liberalism, for example – to literary texts, it would seek ways in which economic and literary texts might mirror, interrogate and illuminate each other.

Conclusion

We live in a golden age of access, as the author Sir Philip Pullman has said. The digital world makes literary and critical resources more widely and freely available than ever before, creating a global library without walls. Seeking wisdom on its virtual shelves, we need not fear *isms*; they can help rather than hinder our quest; we should see them not as enervating, draining the life from literature, but as energising, offering ways in which to marshal and maximise the varieties of literary experience.

Questions to take your reading further
- Why should we study the history of literary criticism?
- Can past critical approaches still be useful to critics today?
- Should literary criticism focus only on literary texts or have a social mission as well?
- Does the concept of the author have a place in literary criticism?
- Has digital technology fundamentally changed the ways we read and analyse literature?

Reading list

Barry, P. 2007. *Beginning Theory: An Introduction to Literary and Cultural Theory*. Manchester: Manchester University Press.

Culler, J. 2011. *Literary Theory: A Very Short Introduction*. Oxford: Oxford University Press.

Eagleton, T. 2008. *Literary Theory: An Introduction*. Oxford: Wiley-Blackwell.

Plain, G. and S. Sellers, eds. 2007. *A History of Feminist Literary Criticism*. Cambridge: Cambridge University Press.

Upstone, S. 2017. *Literary Theory: A Complete Introduction*. London: Teach Yourself.

EXPERIMENTAL LITERATURE PAST, PRESENT AND FUTURE

Andrew McCallum

Introduction

This chapter offers an overview of significant movements in experimental literature over the past hundred years or so. It considers experimental literature to be work that pushes at the boundaries of literary forms, breaking with conventions, or using conventions in radically new ways. As such, it often prioritises *how* something is written over *what* is written.

As part of this process, the chapter explores what happens when the experimental is absorbed over time into the mainstream. It asks whether or not this makes the term 'experimental' increasingly redundant, or whether it transforms experimental literature into a form in its own right, with its own distinctive set of conventions, as well as the ongoing potential to shape itself anew.

Looking to the past

Literary Modernism

Laurence Sterne's *The Life and Opinions of Tristram Shandy, Gentleman* (1759) is often cited as the first work of experimental literature. Filled with digressions and graphic devices, such as the use of an entirely black page to mark a character's death, it self-consciously draws attention to its form. However, not until the modernist period, beginning almost 150 years later, did experimental forms begin to flourish. Modernism, as explored more fully by Stephen Donovan (see pages 71-82), was an artistic movement that developed as a response to far-reaching changes in Western society at the end of the nineteenth and start of the twentieth centuries, and which evolved further in response to social and technological changes brought about by World War One.

Early experimental work by modernist writers mirrored and borrowed from the visual arts, in which radical non-realist forms of representation were developed to express the increasing complexity of the modern world. Gertrude Stein's poetry collection, *Tender Buttons* (1914), for example, took its cue from Cubism, an early twentieth-century art form practised by Pablo Picasso, which was characterised by the use of interlocking planes and shapes that allowed the artist to represent different views of the same subject at the same time. The most famous poem in Stein's collection is 'A Carafe that is a Blind Glass', reproduced in full here:

A kind in glass and a cousin, a spectacle and nothing strange a single hurt color and an arrangement in a system to pointing. All this and not ordinary, not unordered in not resembling. The difference is spreading.

The poem draws attention to the words from which it is created as the reader puzzles to work out their relationship to one another; and to the grammar, which slices through the piece at odd angles, much like the lines in a Cubist painting. While it resists clear interpretation, close study opens up possible meanings, each lying on top of the other.

After World War One, modernist writing developed experimental responses to the inability of traditional literature to capture the horrors of mass conflict. T.S. Eliot's *The Waste Land* (1922) is a disjointed collage of citations and references from high and low culture, sometimes in languages other than English. It is an attempt to represent the shattered nature of society after the war, with Eliot seeking to piece it back together, as shown in the famous line, 'These fragments I have shored against my ruins'.

Modernist writing also experimented with new ways to represent everyday experience. James Joyce's *Ulysses* (1922) and Virginia Woolf's *Mrs Dalloway* (1925), for example, both employ a range of narrative techniques to recount a single day in the life of their central characters. Perhaps the most innovative of these techniques was 'stream-of-consciousness', used to depict a character's flow of thought unimpeded by conventional description or dialogue. Stream-of-consciousness is used memorably by Molly Bloom in the final chapter of *Ulysses*. Her closing words give a flavour of the whole:

> [...] I was a Flower of the mountain yes when I put the rose in my hair like the Andalusian girls used or shall I wear a red yes and how he kissed me under the Moorish Wall and I thought well as well him as another and then I asked him with my eyes to ask again yes and then he asked me would I yes to say yes my mountain flower and first I put my arms around him yes and drew him down to me so he could feel my breasts all perfume yes and his heart was going like mad and yes I said yes I will Yes.

From Surrealism to Oulipo

In 1924 Paris, André Breton published the *Manifesto of Surrealism*. Surrealism seeks to bring together conscious and unconscious thought, the imagined and the real. Applied most notably to art, with Salvador Dali its best-known practitioner, surrealist literature juxtaposes incongruous elements of narrative to create bizarre stories that blend dream and reality. Surrealism's founding principles were revolutionary in tone. It sought to free people from the false rationality, restrictive customs and traditional structures that it felt lay behind the barbarity of World War One.

Surrealism bears similarities to other well-known examples of experimental literature. Franz Kafka's work, which predated the artistic movement, fuses fantasy and the real. For example, in *Metamorphosis* (1915), the central protagonist, Gregor Samsa, wakes up one morning to discover he has turned into a giant insect:

> One morning, when Gregor Samsa woke from troubled dreams, he found himself transformed in his bed into a horrible vermin. He lay on his armour-like back, and if he lifted his head a little he could see his brown belly, slightly domed and divided by arches into stiff sections. The bedding was hardly able to cover it and seemed ready to slide off any moment. His many legs, pitifully thin compared with the size of the rest of him, waved about helplessly as he looked.

Magical realism, which developed in the latter half of the twentieth century among South American writers such as Gabriel Garcia Marquez, Jorge Luis Borges and Isabel Allende, uses similar techniques, though tends to offer a more realistic view of the world, adding in magical elements, often drawn from folklore. It is favoured by writers in geographically, socially and economically marginalised countries, allowing them to create alternative perspectives that reposition those of established, dominant narratives. Consequently, it has also been drawn on in postcolonial English-language novels (see pages 111-119), such as Salman Rushdie's *Midnight's Children* (1981) and Arundhati Roy's *The God of Small Things* (1997) and in American novels exploring black American identity, such as Ishmael Reed's *Mumbo Jumbo* (1972) and Toni Morrison's *Beloved* (1987).

Magical realism is perhaps more widely read than many experimental forms because it does not stray too far from realist representations of the world. Surrealism itself often offers readers less opportunity to develop a confident reading because of its focus on the unconscious. For some, this diminishes its value. This was the view of writers who, in 1960, formed Oulipo, the *Ouvroir de Litterature Potentielle*, French for *Workshop of Potential Literature*. Oulipo writers sought to counter the excessive freedoms of Surrealism with experiments in writing to rigid constraints. They were influenced by mathematics as well as literature. Raymond Queneau's *One Hundred Thousand Billion Poems* (1961), for example, consists of 10 sonnets, arranged one on top of the other. A serrated line separates each line of poetry which readers must cut along so that the line can be lifted away to reveal another underneath. This allows for combinations of lines with the potential to produce one hundred thousand million different poems (100,000,000,000,000 in numerals). The resulting poems are, arguably, not particularly good, but they do demonstrate the astonishing versatility of language and literature.

Queneau also exploited this versatility in *Exercises in Style* (1947). Its first page offers a simple description of an incident on a bus. Called 'Notation', it is just over 100 words long. He then retells this simple account in another 98 ways. He writes it, for example, as back slang, as a sonnet, in comic form, using passive speech, as free verse and as a mathematical formula. These lines from a version called 'Zoological' give a flavour of the playfulness involved:

> In the dog days, while I was in a bird cage at feeding time, I noticed a young puppy with a neck like a giraffe who, ugly and venomous as a toad, wore yet a precious beaver upon his head.

Sometimes the constraints require writers to use astonishing linguistic dexterity. For example, Georges Perec's *La Disparation* (1969) is a novel written without using the letter -e. This form of writing is called a lipogram. Perhaps just as remarkably, Gilbert Adair translated the novel into English, also without using an -e, using the title *A Void* (1995). The translation is about fifty pages longer than the original.

In one sense lipograms are an elaborate form of wordplay. In another, though, they offer a window into how language is drawn on to create meaning. When certain words are unavailable, much can be revealed in the choice of alternatives. For example, look what happens to a line from Shakespeare's *Hamlet* when different letters cannot be used.

Original:	To be, or not to be, that is the question
Lipogram in -a:	To be, or not to be, this is the question
Lipogram in -e:	Survival or oblivion, such is our quandary
Lipogram in -t:	Being or non-being, such is my dilemma

Postmodernism

Postmodernism is a difficult to define concept, the name of which clearly indicates that it comes after Modernism. Indeed, postmodernist writing shares many of the experimental characteristics of its predecessor, for example rejecting realist forms of representation and often relying on fragmented narrative techniques. It differs from Modernism, though, in its aspirations for what literature can achieve. Eliot's previously cited line, for example, 'These fragments I have shored against my ruins', recognises the broken nature of society, but offers the prospect of literature pulling the fragments together. Postmodernism, on the other hand, rejects such a possibility. Instead, it foregrounds playfulness and often uses metafiction (fiction about fiction) to reflect on the process of writing, rather than making any bold claims for what it can do.

One well-known example was written by a member of Oulipo. Drawing inspiration from a mathematical model, Italo Calvino's *If on a Winter's Night a Traveller* (1979) combines Oulipo's interest in form-based constraints with Postmodernism's interest in writing that draws attention to writing. Eleven numbered chapters are interwoven with ten first chapters to imaginary novels, each written in a radically different style (including detective story, magical realism and Japanese erotica). The protagonist is the actual reader, cast into a bewildering world in which they can begin novels but never get beyond the first chapter.

Paradoxically, the reader simultaneously reads a complete novel in getting to the end of the book.

Calvino's experimentation with genre is a common trope of Postmodernism. Angela Carter's short story collection, *The Bloody Chamber* (1979), for example, recasts traditional fairy stories in a process that defamiliarises well-known narratives. J.G. Ballard, who began his career as a science-fiction author, writes short stories in the most unlikely of forms. 'The Index' (1977) begins with an editor's note explaining that only the index remains of 'the unpublished and perhaps suppressed autobiography of a man who may well have been one of the most remarkable figures of the twentieth century'. The story is then presented in the form of this index, which lists the unknown figure's involvement with numerous significant events and characters from the twentieth century.

Like magical realism, postmodernist writing can be a very readable, with several of its tropes now absorbed into the mainstream. For example, David Mitchell's hugely popular *Cloud Atlas* (2004) is a novel that experiments with form in similar ways to Calvino. Five interlinked stories, each set in a different time and place, end half way through, to be resumed later on, with a sixth story in the middle, set in the distant future, told in its entirety straight away. Margaret Atwood's work often draws attention to the conceit by which it is written. *The Handmaid's Tale* (1985) ends with some 'Historical Notes'. Located far in the future, they explain to the reader that what they have read was a reconstruction made up from a series of tapes, unnumbered and 'arranged in no particular order'. They might even be forged. They challenge the reader to consider the nature of what they have just read, something emphasised by the final words of the whole novel: 'Are there any questions?'

The present

Uncreative writing

Jonathan Lethem's 'The Ecstasy of Influence' (2007) is a brilliant essay, several thousand words long, about plagiarism. The reader is presented with a ground-shifting twist in the final few paragraphs – the entire piece is itself a plagiarism. An example of patchwriting, a text that stitches together writing copied from multiple different sources into a coherent whole, the essay is more than an elaborate piece of trickery. It sheds light on a range of issues central to literary production. Who, for example, is the author of this work? Is it Lethem, or does its provenance lie with the dozens of writers he credits at the end of the essay? Is it a work of genius, or mere trickery? And do the words, copied exactly from their original sources, mean the same as when first used, or have they come to mean something different?

'The Ecstasy of Influence' is nowhere near the first example of patchwriting. As explored above, Eliot's *The Waste Land* draws significantly on other works through both allusion and citation; and Joyce's *Ulysses* contains several passages made up of texts 'borrowed' from elsewhere. One lengthy passage about the properties of water is an amalgamation of phrases from encyclopaedia entries. There is a key difference between earlier and later patchwriting, though. While Eliot and Joyce relied on extensive reading, laborious work practices and prodigious memories, Lethem was able to cut and paste his essay from material found online. It's an example of what one critic, Kenneth Goldsmith, calls 'uncreative writing' and another, Marjorie Perloff, 'unoriginal genius'. Goldsmith has written a whole book on the way that the internet is changing the way that we write: *Uncreative Writing: Managing Language in the Digital Age* (2011). In it, he argues that the state of 'textual abundance' created by the internet renders unnecessary any attempts to write something new. He comments:

> Faced with an unprecedented amount of available text, the problem is not needing to write more of it; instead, we must learn to negotiate the vast quantity that exists. How I make my way through the thicket of information – how I manage it, how I parse it, how I organise and distribute it – is what distinguishes my writing from yours.

Goldsmith is not arguing for the replacement of traditional literary forms by his examples of 'conceptual writing', but he is drawing attention to how language can now be treated as a material resource that can be moved from one place to another simply by cutting and pasting text from one document to another. He does this himself in *Seven American Deaths and Disasters* (2013) by transcribing the live radio commentaries of seven seminal moments in American history and putting them inside a book. The effect can be startling and, arguably, every bit as powerful as carefully crafted poetry or prose, as in this example from 'World Trade Center':

Can you believe it?

I ... I can't. I just see dust. This is insane. I'm shaking. I'm covered in dust and stone. My clothes are all ripped.

The World Trade Center has been virtually eliminated to nothing by virtue of these terrorist attacks this morning. Two buildings are not in evidence as I sit and look at what is the outline of half a moon just over, uh, midtown Manhattan.

La ... Ladies and gentlemen, the World Trade Center buildings are gone. The World Trade Center buildings are gone. They are ashes. And, um, it's ... it's ... it is a situation beyond description.

If Goldsmith's work seems too removed from mainstream literature to be widely read, it's worth noting that 'found' writing like this has already had commercial success. Claudia Rankine's best-selling collection of prose poems, *Citizen: An American Lyric* (2015), features whole passages 'borrowed' from other sources. One poem about Hurricane Katrina, which destroyed much of New Orleans in 2005, is comprised of quotes collected from the CNN news channel.

Dramatic productions using similar techniques have also been well-received. 'Verbatim theatre' constructs plays from the precise words used in real-life events and testimony. For example, Richard Norton-Taylor and Nicolas Kent wrote *The Colour of Justice* (1999), using words from the Macpherson Inquiry into the murder of black teenager, Stephen Lawrence. Gillian Slovo's *The Riots* (2011), about the 2011 riots that started in Tottenham, London, and spread across the United Kingdom, is crafted from testimony from rioters, victims, police, politicians and even Twitter feeds. While verbatim theatre is not an entirely new phenomenon, the increasing number of plays written in this way has been made possible by the ease with which writers can find and manipulate text digitally.

Experimentalism that draws on web and computer technology has also entered the mainstream in more direct ways. One chapter in Zadie Smith's *NW* (2012), for example, transcribes a set of walking directions in the style of Google Maps; a chapter in Jennifer Egan's *A Visit from the Goon Squad* (2011) is written as a PowerPoint presentation.

The past in the present

It is possible to recognise experimental literature as a genre in itself now that it is over a century since modernist writers brought experimentalism into the mainstream. Thus today's experimental writers are often not so much breaking new ground as deliberately exploiting anew conventions developed over the past hundred years or so. Several recent winners of the Man Booker Prize, the most prestigious UK award for literary fiction, can be placed in this category. Marlon James's *A Brief History of Seven Killings* (2014) is a multi-voiced novel that takes the form of an imagined oral biography, told by ghosts, witnesses, killers, members of parliament, drug dealers, conmen, beauty queens, FBI and CIA agents, reporters and journalists. Its playful fragmentation and use of genre make it identifiably postmodern. Anna Burns's *Milkman* (2018) is set in an unnamed location (easily recognisable as Belfast during the Troubles) and narrated by the unnamed 'middle sister', as she is harassed by a paramilitary figure called Milkman. Its weighty subject matter and difficult 'stream-of-consciousness' prose place it in a modernist tradition.

There is even a literary prize for experimental writing. The Goldsmiths Prize is awarded annually to a novel 'that breaks the mould or extends the possibilities of the novel form'. The annual shortlists showcase a range of fascinating novels, but these are as likely to draw on what are now the established conventions of experimentalism as to genuinely break the mould. For example, Eimar McBride's *A Girl is a Half-formed Thing* (2013), with its fragmented, difficult narrative, reads like a modernist novel, as does Mike McCormack's *Solar Bones* (2016), which is entirely without punctuation. One novel identifiably different in its experimentation is the 2017 winner, *H(A)PPY*, by Nicola Barker, which uses multiple fonts and graphic designs in a range of colours. The story and form of the novel itself, though, borrow extensively from early experiments in dystopian fiction, most obviously Aldous Huxley's *Brave New World* (1932) and Yevgeny Zamyatin's *We* (1924).

The future

It would seem remiss not to include a nod to the future in a chapter about experimental writing, given its own commitment to moving literature into new territories. In terms of form, it is difficult to see what might emerge in the next few years or decades. Perhaps, as shown by recent prize-winning novels above, experimental writing will flourish as a literary genre in its own right, reworking and adapting now established conventions. It is, however, possible to make some tentative suggestions about how experimental writing might be produced in future years.

Computers themselves are now capable of writing short newspaper reports. Details of financial transactions and other basic events are fed into a programme and a short, coherent piece of text emerges. A similar process is already being used to produce some poems. So rapid is the development of 'the linguistic web' – the ability of web-based technologies to understand and produce human language – that many computer scientists are confident that a computer will soon be able to write a novel. Regardless of its literary worth, this would offer profound challenges to ideas about authorship and writer's intent. And what would be the experience of reading a novel not written by human hand?

Conclusion

In offering a survey of experimental literature over the past one hundred years or so, it has become apparent that experimental writing responds to different times in different ways. The new certainties that modernists sought after the collapse of Western society during World War One, were inadequate to cope with a worldview that began to accept and embrace fragmentation towards the latter half of the twentieth century (hence Postmodernism).

Experimental forms do not simply emerge and then disappear from existence, though. Once they have come into being, they remain as a possible resource for writers to draw upon. All of the strategies mentioned in this chapter are currently used to write literature in one way or another, and this is likely to remain the case.

We are left, then, with a situation in which experimental writing has become a genre in its own right. This does not mean that the term itself is becoming redundant. Even where experimental literature draws on what has gone before and long been established, it is work that seeks, self-consciously, to explore form and literature itself. It is questioning and drawing attention to the processes and functions of writing rather than trying to hide and naturalise them.

Questions to take your reading further

- What is the point of writing and reading experimental literature?
- What is the relationship between experimental literature and literature as a whole?
- What is the relationship between experimental literature and social and technological change?
- To what extent is experimental literature a genre in its own right?
- Is it still possible to create literature that pushes at and extends the boundaries of what has gone before?

Reading list

Armstrong, J. 2014. *Experimental Fiction: An Introduction for Readers and Writers*. London & New York: Bloomsbury.

Caws, M.A. 2018. *The Milk Bowl of Feathers: Essential Surrealist Writings*. New York: Norton and Company.

Chivers, T. 2012. *Adventures in Form: A Compendium of Poetic Forms, Rules and Constraints*. London: Penned in the Margins.

Goldsmith, K. 2011. *Uncreative Writing: Managing Language in the Digital Age*. New York: Columbia University Press.

Matthews, H. and A. Blotchie eds. 2005. *Oulipo Compendium*. London: Atlas Press.

CONTRIBUTORS

Peter Barry, FEA, FLSW, Emeritus Professor of English, Aberystwyth University, is author of *Beginning Theory* (1995, 4th edition, 2017), *New British Poetry* (co-edited with Robert Hampson, 1995), *Contemporary British Poetry and the City* (2000), *English in Practice* (2000, 2nd edition, 2013). *Poetry Wars* (2006), *Literature in Contexts* (2007), *Reading Poetry* (2013), and *Extending Ecocriticism* (co-edited with William Welstead, 2017). He co-edited *English*, 1989-2007, and headed the 2012-15 Leverhulme 'Devolved Voices' project on poetry in Wales.

Pamela Bickley taught in the English department at Royal Holloway, University of London, and at the Godolphin and Latymer School, and is a Fellow and Trustee of the English Association. She is the author of *Contemporary Fiction* (CUP, 2008) and the co-author, with Jenny Stevens, of *Essential Shakespeare: The Arden Guide to Text and Interpretation* (2013) and *Shakespeare and Early Modern Drama: Text and Performance* (2016), as well as articles on modern fiction, poetry, and Shakespeare for *emagazine*.

Stephen Donovan teaches English literature at Uppsala University, Sweden. His research interests include Joseph Conrad, empire writing, and British periodicals history, and his publications include *Conrad and Popular Culture* (2005) and (with Matthew Rubery) *Secret Commissions: An Anthology of Victorian Investigative Journalism* (2012). He is also the creator of *Conrad First: The Joseph Conrad Periodical Archive* (www.conradfirst.net), which he shamelessly recommends to all students of Modernism.

Robert Eaglestone is Professor of Contemporary Literature and Thought at Royal Holloway, University of London. He works on contemporary literature and literary theory and contemporary philosophy. His books include *Ethical Criticism* (1997), *The Very Short Introduction to Contemporary Fiction* (2013) and *The Broken Voice: Reading Post-Holocaust Literature* (2017).

Malcolm Hebron teaches at Winchester College. His publications include *Key Concepts in Renaissance Literature* (Palgrave) and *How to Read a Poem* (Connell Guides). He is a regular contributor to *emagazine* and edits the English Association journal *The Use of English*.

Andrew Michael Hurley is the author of two short story collections, *Cages* and *The Unusual Death of Julie Christie*. His first novel, *The Loney* won the 2015 Costa 'First Novel' award and the 2016 British Book Industry awards for 'Debut Novel' and 'Book of the Year.' His second book, *Devil's Day* (2017) was joint winner of the 2018 Royal Society of Literature Encore Award. His short fiction has appeared widely, including in *Granta* and *The Best British Short Stories 2017*. He teaches Creative Writing at Manchester Metropolitan University's Writing School.

Leila Kamali specialises in African American and Black British literature and questions of diaspora, race, aesthetics, and transnationalism. She has held academic posts at the University of Liverpool, at King's College London and at Goldsmiths University. She is the author of *The Cultural Memory of Africa in African American and Black British Fiction, 1970-2000* (Palgrave Macmillan, 2016). She is currently working on her next book, entitled *Narrative and Black Political Activism, 1965-2020*.

Andrew McCallum is Director of the English and Media Centre. He developed an interest in experimental literature while researching *Creativity and Learning in Secondary English* (Routledge, 2012). One section of the book explores what constraint-based experimental writing can teach us about how language works. In his work with schools, he specialises in contemporary literature for young adults. He is a regular contributor to *emagazine*.

Sean McEvoy teaches mostly at Murray Edwards College, University of Cambridge. His most recent books are *Tragedy: The Basics* (2016) and *Theatrical Unrest: Ten Riots in the History of the Stage, 1601-2004* (2015), both published by Routledge. A study of Jez Butterworth's plays is forthcoming. He is a frequent contributor to *emagazine*.

Christopher Pittard is senior lecturer in Victorian Literature at the University of Portsmouth, and course leader for the MA in Victorian Gothic. His books include *The Cambridge Companion to Sherlock Holmes* (2019), *Purity and Contamination in Late Victorian Detective Fiction* (2011) and *Literary Illusions: Performance Magic and Victorian Literature* (forthcoming from Edinburgh University Press). He has published widely on Victorian literature, including in *Studies in the Novel*, *Victorian Periodicals Review, 19*, *Victoriographies*, and *Clues: A Journal of Detection*.

Chris Power's short story collection *Mothers* was published in 2018. He has written for the BBC, the *Guardian*, *The New York Times*, the *Wall Street Journal* and the *New Statesman*. His fiction has appeared in *Granta* and *The White Review*, and been broadcast on BBC Radio 4. He lives in London.

Michael Rosen is a writer, performance poet and broadcaster. He presents BBC Radio 4's *Word of Mouth*, as well as regularly presenting documentary programmes for BBC Radio 4 and BBC Radio 3, including the Sony Gold Award-winning *On Saying Goodbye*. He has published in the region of 200 books for children and adults, including *The Sad Book* with Quentin Blake, *We're Going on a Bear Hunt* with Helen Oxenbury and *What is Poetry?* on writing poetry. He was Children's Laureate 2007-2009 and is currently Professor of Children's Literature at Goldsmiths, University of London.

Judy Simons is a Research Fellow at the School of Advanced Studies, University of London, and Emeritus Professor at De Montfort University, Leicester. She is a former Chair of the Council for College and University English and Chair of the Council of Deans of Arts & Humanities. Her books include *Diaries & Journals of Literary Women*, *What Katy Read* and *Rosamond Lehmann*. She is a regular contributor to *emagazine* and is a Fellow of The English Association.

Emma Smith is Professor of Shakespeare Studies at Hertford College, Oxford, where she teaches early modern literature. Her most recent books are *This Is Shakespeare* (Penguin 2019) and *Shakespeare's First Folio: Four Centuries of an Iconic Book* (paperback, Oxford University Press 2018), and her podcasts are available at Apple Podcasts and podcasts.ox.ac.uk. She has lectured widely at universities, schools, theatres, libraries and literary festivals, presented literary documentaries for Radio 3 and 4, and served as script consultant on the 2018 film *Mary Queen of Scots*.

Jenny Stevens has taught English at both undergraduate and secondary level. She currently combines part-time teaching with academic writing and editing. Her publications include *Faith, Fiction and the Historical Jesus* (2010), a study of the mid-to-late Victorian novel; she is co-author of *Essential Shakespeare* (2013) and *Shakespeare and Early Modern Drama* (2016) and is currently working on Shakespeare adaptation for a forthcoming Arden publication.

Nicolas Tredell is a writer and lecturer who has published 20 books and around 400 essays and articles in the UK and USA on authors from Shakespeare and Milton to Zora Neale Hurston and Zadie Smith, and on key issues in literary and film theory. He has made a range of contributions to *emagazine* and to emagclips, and has given talks at a variety of schools and other venues. He is Consultant Editor of Macmillan International's Essential Criticism series, which now runs to 88 volumes. He formerly taught literature, drama, film and cultural studies at Sussex University.

Nathan Waddell is a Senior Lecturer in the Department of English Literature at the University of Birmingham, where he teaches and researches twentieth-century culture. He is the author of three books – *Modern John Buchan* (2009), *Modernist Nowheres* (2012), and *Moonlighting: Beethoven and Literary Modernism* (2019) – and has edited an essay collection on Aldous Huxley's *Brave New World*. He's currently editing *The Cambridge Companion to 'Nineteen Eighty-Four'*.